Village Ties

Village Ties

Women, NGOs, and Informal Institutions
in Rural Bangladesh

N AYMA Q AYUM

RUTGERS UNIVERSITY PRESS

NEW BRUNSWICK, CAMDEN, AND NEWARK,

NEW JERSEY, AND LONDON

Library of Congress Cataloging-in-Publication Data
Names: Qayum, Nayma, author.
Title: Village ties: women, NGOs, and informal institutions in rural
    Bangladesh / Nayma Qayum.
Description: New Brunswick: Rutgers University Press, [2022] |
    Includes bibliographical references and index.
Identifiers: LCCN 2021003344 | ISBN 9781978816442 (paperback) |
    ISBN 9781978816459 (hardcover) | ISBN 9781978816466 (epub) |
    ISBN 9781978816473 (mobi) | ISBN 9781978816480 (pdf)
Subjects: LCSH: Rural women—Bangladesh—Social conditions. |
    Bangladesh—Rural conditions. | Non-governmental
    Organizations—Bangladesh.
Classification: LCC HQ1745.6 .Q29 2022 | DDC 305.42095492—dc23
LC record available at https://lccn.loc.gov/2021003344

A British Cataloging-in-Publication record for this book is available from the British Library.

⊖ The paper used in this publication meets the requirements of the American National Standard for Information Sciences—Permanence of Paper for Printed Library Materials, ANSI Z39.48-1992.

www.rutgersuniversitypress.org

Manufactured in the United States of America

For my parents, M. A. Qayum and Salma Qayum

Contents

Figures

Tables

Abbreviations

ADP	Adolescent Development Programme
AL	Awami League
BNP	Bangladesh Nationalist Party
CEDAW	Convention on the Elimination of All Forms of Discrimination against Women
CEP	Community Empowerment Program
CTG	caretaker government
EC	Executive Committee
FYP	Five-Year Plan
JI	Jama'at-e-Islami
MFI	microfinance institution
MHD	Medium Human Development
NGO	nongovernmental organization
PESP	Primary Education Stipend Programme
PO	program organizer
PRSP	Poverty Reduction Strategy Paper
PS	Polli Shomaj
RA	research assistant
RED	Research and Evaluation Division
Tk.	taka
UN	United Nations
UP	Union Parishad

Prologue

Everybody in Ghorpara knew Ayesha Begum.[1] At least this was the case according to one of her ward's elected officials, Md. Aslam Hossain. Ayesha Begum had never attended school. Well into her sixties, she had long been a widow. She lived in a large extended household. Between her children, their spouses, and their children, ten people lived under her roof; there were several mouths to feed. Like many poor women from the rural global South, we would expect her to live on society's periphery. But Ayesha Begum played a leading role in various nongovernmental organization (NGO) programs over the years. She was a longtime community health worker for the BRAC health program. Locally known as *shasthyo apas* (health workers), these women went door to door providing services, advice, and contact with health care providers.[2] For the last decade, Ayesha Begum had served as president of Polli Shomaj (PS), a local organization created by the Community Empowerment Programme (CEP) of the development agency BRAC (previously Bangladesh Rural Advancement Committee).

I met Ayesha Begum in early 2010 as nine months of fieldwork came to an end. But I knew of her even before my trip to her home in Manikganj Sadar—a bustling urban center adjacent to Dhaka city. My Polli Shomaj study out of BRAC's Research and Evaluation Division (RED) was coming to a close. The research assistants (RAs) had just wrapped up their work across the country. They were now on the last leg, a monthlong data collection effort in four locations. In the meantime, I moved between the sites and watched over data entry back at the Dhaka headquarters. During a regular phone check-in, the team leader for Manikganj RAs mentioned Ayesha's work. He told me, "Nayma *apa* [sister], you must meet her." The trip was, perhaps, an indulgence. The study had been in the field for far too long. But Manikganj was right outside of Dhaka city. I could do this in a day.

We reached Ghorpara by midmorning. I was traveling with one of my co-researchers for the PS study and our BRAC driver, our regular companion. As our small SUV pulled up by the side of the traffic-clogged main road, it dawned on me that we would not be going any further. This particular PS—a name that translates to "rural society"—convened at the center of a busy urban metropolis. Many PS groups were located in villages, some so remote that one could access them only by foot, bicycle, tractor, or boat. Others began in rural areas, but rapidly expanding towns engulfed them over time. But Manikganj Sadar was a city. Our RAs waited by the roadside. As we got out of the car and exchanged pleasantries, they said that Ayesha Begum would be free in a few hours.

The delay was good. I wanted to check in with the research team first. The RAs led us through a winding path surrounded by concrete and tin-roofed houses, sometimes through wide openings between homes and at other times through narrow alleys between gray cement walls. We walked further and further from the ruckus of town, and after what felt like forever, came upon a vast open space. A wide, partially paved road spread out in front of us. Paddy fields bordered it on each side. Somewhere far away, trees and faint outlines of houses marked the horizon. The shrill noise of trucks on a distant highway pierced the air. And there, in a wide-open space, under a massive tree and adjacent to the wooden benches of an outdoor tea stall, a group of RAs huddled over a map. Locals sat around the stall, sipping tea, chewing *paan* (betel leaves), and smoking cigarettes. As RAs discussed the next stage of fieldwork, these men and women chimed in.

Ghorapara residents seemed unfazed by this massive undertaking—city researchers walking around their village, knocking on doors, and talking to people at local spots. Bangladeshi villagers are no strangers to development NGOs. Since the 1970s, development organizations have flooded villages with resources, such as credit, income generation training, immunization, birth control, food aid, and productive assets, alongside the government. PS is one of the countless development programs that saturate rural Bangladesh. But its work differs from that of the typical NGO program. The women who ran Manikganj Sadar's PS group received no services. Instead, they challenged oppressive norms and practices that made poor people's lives difficult. In the past year, these PS members negotiated with the local government—the Union Parishad (UP)—to secure thirty safety net cards for poor families. They also stopped a child marriage. When Ayesha Begum discovered that her neighbors had arranged their thirteen-year-old daughter's wedding, she gathered three other PS members and confronted the family. The women were not welcome. "The [girl's] mother said, you are breaking off a wedding, this is not a good thing" they recalled. The women returned to the house three times. Dismayed, they approached the groom's parents next. Eventually, the families gave in and canceled the wedding.

Later that afternoon, I met Ayesha Begum back in town. She greeted me like we were friends, as if being associated with BRAC made us allies in the battle against injustice. Her community saw her as an advocate for the poor. Other PS members said that she always helped the underprivileged. Aslam Hossain, a local UP member, did not know what PS was. But he knew Ayesha Begum as the community health worker. "Ayesha helps villagers on behalf of BRAC," he said. He even felt that she had personal qualities to run for elections. "That is because most people in the village know her. She comes to the aid of people when they are in trouble." Shaila, the ward's woman UP member, echoed this sentiment. Ayesha had come to her often, recommending villagers for government safety nets. Shaila added, "She can draw people close to her." The two women were distant relatives. In fact, Ayesha Begum had helped Shaila with her election campaign. In her parting words to me, Ayesha Begum shared that she had devoted a large chunk of her own life to BRAC. She hoped to visit Dhaka, and perhaps BRAC would honor her as a leader.

BRAC has made headlines as one of the world's largest and most influential international NGOs.[3] The organization began as a relief project in 1972 as Bangladesh recovered from a double tragedy—a brutal war of secession from Pakistan and a devastating cyclone. At the time, BRAC worked in remote Sulla, in the northeastern district of Sylhet, providing clothing and shelter, and implementing livelihood projects. Inspired by thinkers such as Franz Fanon, Paulo Freire, and Ivan Illich, founder Fazle Hasan Abed made education the primary focus of the organization's work.[4] Now, BRAC runs programs on a massive scale. It works across multiple sectors, including children's education, adult literacy, legal aid, health care, and community organization. Critics have even claimed that the organization—like many other NGOs—operates as a shadow state.[5] But BRAC staff insist that they could never replace the government. Rather, they work in partnership with the government, especially in hard-to-reach areas. Indeed, BRAC operates in all of Bangladesh's sixty-four districts. While in the field, local staff would say that BRAC staff dared to visit places that others avoided. In 2018, the NGO reached 3.3 million people through its education and training programs, delivered health services to 15.9 million people, helped 43,682 households come out of ultra-poverty, and provided safe water to 158,836 people.[6] Those traveling in Bangladesh could not miss the white and magenta signboards marking BRAC offices. They were everywhere.

When CEP—then the Social Development Programme—started PS in 1998, the program drew on BRAC's microfinance clients as its first members. BRAC's microfinance program disburses loans and collects repayments through Village Organizations (VOs), composed of women from the same community. The earliest PS groups began as a federation of VO members at the ward level.[7] Soon, they expanded their membership to encompass the entire ward. Eventually, any poor woman—and sometimes man—could join a PS group. By the time I started the Polli Shomaj study in 2009, over 12,000 PS groups were in place. Ten years later, 12,800 groups were operating across the country.

PS groups take on four types of activities. They assist community members in accessing government and nongovernment services and resources; participate in the local power structure; undertake local developmental activities; and prevent and respond to violence, particularly against women—for example, in addressing child marriage, dowry, domestic violence, and sexual assault.[8] BRAC field staff called program organizers (POs) supervise PS. Each PO is in charge of a designated number of PS groups. In the interest of creating sustainable organizations, POs encourage PS members to pursue these goals with minimal intervention; eventually, the groups are expected to function on their own. Indeed, this book captures PS activities from 2009 to 2010, and the program has changed substantially since then. Now, POs supervise PS groups with the lightest of footprints.

The name Polli Shomaj—which translates to rural society—references a famous 1916 novel by the Bengali writer Sarat Chandra Chattopadhyay. The story takes up the plight of the marginalized in a colonial Bengali village, where poverty and caste inequalities run rampant. PS echoes this theme. It fulfills its mission through grassroots mobilization efforts. CEP describes the program as "a platform which enables the rural poor to raise their voice, gain better access to locally available GO-NGO resources, address systemic inequities, take collective action against exploitation and social injustice, and play a more active civic role."[9] It takes on a radical purpose. Defying stereotypical images of women from the rural global South—backward, isolated, and helpless—PS members challenge the very power structures that cast them out. Their story demonstrates that poor women can change politics, even in the direst of circumstances. How they achieve this goal lies at the heart of this book.

PART I

Setting the Stage

Institutions

When poor women from the global South make headlines, it is often as oppressed victims rather than inspiring leaders. Popular media valorizes elite actors who "do good"—development organizations, nonprofits, philanthropists, UN goodwill ambassadors, and young leaders who uplift the marginalized in impoverished parts of the world. Their faces grace glossy magazine covers. They win big awards. Newsrooms chase them to line up expert panels. In contrast, the narrative casts poor women as needing liberation—from their oppressive societies, controlling husbands, and pitifully destitute lives. Indeed, the words development aid stir up imaginations of impoverished women and children, starving, partially naked, and living in squalor and ill health. We see them as helpless. Our hearts long to rescue them. As for those doing the saving—we celebrate them as heroes.

Development organizations are at the forefront of human development work. Indeed, it would be erroneous to challenge the development industry's enormous successes. According to the World Bank, poverty is declining in many parts of the world.[1] Women are making tremendous strides. According to the 2019 Human Development Report, they have achieved better health, education, engagement in markets, and political participation than ever before.[2] But development organizations have also faced scathing critiques for their neoliberal development approach, especially toward poor women of the global South. At the policy level, this includes privatization, austerity, trade liberalization, reduced government involvement, and a uniform World Bank–imposed development strategy. It upholds the Western development path as the modern ideal to be replicated in the allegedly backward global South. In the field, neoliberal development manifests in individualized service delivery programs—for example, loans, grants, health care, and education stipends. These programs measure women's empowerment through financial well-being over more encompassing indicators that incorporate power, leadership, and dismantling oppressive structures.

Neoliberal development hinges on the idea of the rational individual. It assumes that people are free to make informed, independent decisions as they use services that development programs provide. But human beings do not live isolated lives. We are social creatures, deeply embedded in our relationships, communities, and social fabric. In rural Bangladesh, poor women cannot make decisions freely. Their actions are bound by institutions—rules, norms, and practices that dictate their everyday lives. For example, most development NGOs provide poor women with microfinance services, small loans without collateral. But studies have documented that many women borrowers do not control loan use, as men make financial decisions in the household.[3] Young mothers may have access to birth control methods, but cannot use them as their husbands and in-laws determine when they will bear children. Government welfare cards may exist in plenty, but service providers often distribute them through clientelist networks that poor women cannot infiltrate.[4] These examples illustrate that despite the availability of services, institutional barriers often thwart individual action.

Can development programs bring about institutional change in the rural global South? Can they shift relationships between women on the one hand, and state and society on the other? Studying BRAC's PS initiative in rural Bangladesh, this book argues that in contrast to neoliberal development that hinges on the individual, programs centered on the collective can lead to institutional change if they embrace anti-oppression as their goal, embody deliberate decision-making processes, and are embedded in their communities. The women of PS negotiate with state and society to shift the rules of the game—the institutions that disenfranchise them. In the process, they change poor people's relationships with the state, with NGOs, and with each other.

In rural Bangladesh, social relationships are governed by multiple and overlapping institutions. Some are formal; they exist on paper. Others are informal—invisible and unwritten. Many of these institutions marginalize the rural poor. When local politicians hand out welfare goods through clientelist networks, they shift resources away from the poorest recipients. Village courts draw on gendered family laws and traditional norms when adjudicating cases—for example, related to inheritance, domestic violence, dowry, and child marriage. Women reporting domestic abuse may be forced to cohabit with violent spouses, as they cannot initiate divorce. All of these outcomes demonstrate bias against the disenfranchised—the poor, and especially poor women. They result from both formal and informal institutions.

PS groups challenge these oppressive practices; they contest the "rules of the game." They negotiate with state and society to change expectations about what is right and good. They craft knowledge and create shared understandings around poor peoples' problems through deliberative decision making. As they operate in Bangladesh's NGO-rich terrain, their embeddedness in local communities opens up crucial access to information and channels for negotiation. They impose sanctions on the local elite and hold them accountable to the rural poor. Their work creates a complex and rapidly transforming world where multiple and overlapping practices exist—some old and some new, some desirable and some less so. As PS groups challenge prevailing institutions, sometimes formal rules are exercised. Elsewhere, new informal institutions replace the old ways. These new institutions—unintentional consequences of negotiations—also violate formal institutions. But people accept them and see them as the "next best" set of rules. The coexistence of multiple institutions, both formal and informal, begs for questioning the idea of inequality as unidimensional, of informal institutions as monolithic, and of progress as linear.

Since the 1970s, Bangladesh's governments have pursued an aid-based neoliberal development model that has shifted the rural landscape. They increased development spending, embraced World Bank–prescribed national development plans, and partnered with national and local organizations to provide services for the rural poor. Development organizations emerged as influential actors in the villages, giving rural citizens new resources under their own development programs. They worked hand in hand with the government. These organizations—collectively known as NGOs—include United Nations (UN) agencies, bilateral development organizations, multilateral lending agencies, large national organizations, religious and faith-based organizations, and smaller organizations that often serve as contractors.

Most NGOs serve rural women. They provide physical services, such as microcredit loans, cash or in-kind grants, health care, and legal support. They run information-sharing workshops on health care, civic awareness, and human rights. Many deliver services through a group-based service delivery model, organizing village women into community groups. Some bring services to people's doorsteps through field organizers. Together, these new actors—NGOs, their staff, their members, and the groups that they organize—have created an infrastructure for service delivery that parallels that of the state. They have also crafted new relationships between actors. Typically, rural women belong to several NGOs. Their many engagements embed them in an intricate web of connections.

NGOs have played a complicated role in Bangladesh's development. Elora Halim Chowdhury writes of three approaches to this debate—NGOs as providing critical services in the absence of the state, NGOs as "agents of neoliberal development implementing new forms of imperialism," and a position in between, which "emphasizes the complex and often contradictory roles that NGOs play, and the multifaceted relations they foster with states, donors, and clients." I situate this book—alongside that of Chowdhury—in the third group, which is more "useful and honest" in navigating the postcolonial world given the multiple challenges of "globalization, neoliberalism, and patriarchy."[5] To this end, I identify a new role for development NGOs. In addition to advocacy or filling in gaps left by the state—both roles that they play in Bangladesh—NGOs can link marginalized citizens to state and society.

This book contributes to a significant body of literature exploring the political lives of women in Muslim societies. Much of this scholarship comes from the Middle East and North Africa. To this, I add the story of Bangladesh—a majority Muslim country in South Asia that appears far from oppressive at first glance. It not only oscillates between the religious and the secular, but also prioritizes women's development. Thus, this book challenges the myth of oppressed Muslim women in need of saving, sometimes from the alleged violence of their faith, elsewhere from their own men. This is not to claim that Muslim women cannot be oppressed. But the nature of this oppression is complex, layered, and diverse. As Lila Abu-Lughod writes, one must evaluate the nature and cause of women's suffering; these are instrumental to charting pathways to women's empowerment.[6] In Bangladesh, NGOs operate in a rapidly transforming rural society. Elite organizations—both religious and secular—compete with each other and the state to define how poor women should live their lives.[7] However, Bangladesh also has a strong history of women's activism. Women may be expected to conduct themselves with modesty, but they do not necessarily live their political lives behind closed doors. Their actions are simultaneously private and public. Indeed, women like Ayesha Begum do not rely on outside saviors. They save others around them.

This book falls within two rapidly growing research areas in political science, informal institutions and feminist institutionalism. It presents new ways of measuring informal institutions, especially around gender and logics of appropriateness. It takes the informal institutions literature beyond the study of organizations into the larger society; it shows how institutions dictate people's everyday lives. Finally, this book is about how marginalized people solve political problems. I contribute to the growing number of political science works that study ordinary people's lives through their lived experiences.[8]

Institutions: Old and New
Rules

We live our lives by rules. From traffic laws that compel safe driving to the ways that we greet friends, acquaintances, and colleagues, our actions are prescribed by social standards, norms, and practices that our communities honor. Some—like traffic laws—are formal or parchment rules. They are obvious, established, and typically written on paper. They exist on unambiguous terrain and command little debate. Others are informal institutions; outsiders may not know or readily recognize them. But they are no less important than formal rules. Community members acknowledge, accept, and abide by them.

People do not follow rules just because they exist. Consider those who throw their garbage in the streets. Cities and towns may pass laws against littering, but in order for such laws to be effective, governments must enforce them. Nor are rules universally liked. Speed limits may cause the utmost annoyance for the traveler who has somewhere to be. But whether one finds speed limits inhibiting or values them for making streets safe, people generally expect others to abide by them. Violators would face the penalty of traffic tickets; they are held accountable by the police, enforcers of the rules.

This is a book about the institutions—formal and informal rules, norms, and practices—that shape behaviors. It is concerned with the ties between citizens, the state, and nonstate actors, and the rules that depict how they interact with each other. At one time, institutions dominated political science; they were the "historic heart" of the discipline.[9] The old institutionalists conducted formal-legal analysis; for them, the political realm was limited to formal structures of the government where policies were made and implemented. Their scholarship—empirical and fact-based—described government as it operated.[10] In the 1980s, new institutionalism emerged in response to the behavioral and structural-functionalist revolutions. New institutionalists come from diverse disciplines and disagree on many things.[11] But they agree that institutions play an important and autonomous role in politics. Robert Putnam writes that new institutionalists come together on two points: that institutions shape political outcomes, and that they are themselves shaped by history.[12] Institutions are not just structures of government; they are autonomous and have a life of their own.[13] They are simultaneously stabilizing—thus robust—and dynamic.[14]

Three Institutionalisms

In its broadest iteration, new institutionalism falls into three categories—rational choice, historical, and sociological. Rational choice institutionalists view the world as a consequence of strategic actions and interactions.[15] They see people as utility-maximizers who devise institutions to reduce uncertainties. Once in play, institutions shape behavior by structuring incentives. They shape costs and benefits, enabling or restricting action.[16] However, historical and sociological institutionalists view the world as far more complicated than rational choice models depict. For them, rational choice places far too much emphasis on action and overlooks social structures and cultural practices.

Historical institutionalists examine how the institutional design of government systems influence individual decision-making.[17] Along these lines, Peter Hall defines institutions as "the formal rules, compliance procedures, and standard operating practice" that shape relationships between people on the one hand, and the polity or economy on the other.[18] Hall depicts institutions as

relational; they influence and are influenced by interactions, and consequently, impact policy decisions. Historical institutionalists are most often
concerned with formal organizations or administrative units. I draw on their
work, but acknowledge that this approach is far too limiting for a study that
addresses larger society, and one set in a context like Bangladeshi villages,
where the formal and the informal, state and nonstate, and traditional and new
organizations blend into each other. The rules that I explore exist across multiple spaces—within government institutions, NGOs, traditional organizations,
households, and extended families.

Sociological institutionalists cast a wider net; they ask whether choices "can
be properly understood outside of the cultural and historical frameworks within
which they are embedded."[19] Mark Granovetter argues that human beings are
embedded in structures of social relations that will always be present, making it
impossible to imagine a world without them. These structures make the very
concept of rationality dependent on one's environment.[20] What we acknowledge
as our self-interest can never be an independent choice; it is defined by our very
roles and identities. March and Olsen argue that institutions shape behaviors,
not by structuring choices, but rather by shaping "values, norms, interests, identities, beliefs."[21] Actors do not behave strategically in a vacuum, based on
rational calculations. Rather, their actions are bound by appropriate standards
of behavior.[22] They do what is expected of them.

This book takes a position between the historical and sociological institutionalists.[23] It often finds itself in the terrain of feminist institutionalism, which
takes the position that institutions both "profoundly shape political life" and are
"inescapably gendered."[24] Straddling disciplinary divides becomes particularly
important for gaining a comprehensive understanding of institutions in Bangladesh, which we know little about beyond the structures of government. Robert
Goodin writes of institutionalism's disciplinary diversity as a strength, acknowl-
edging that understanding the larger truth can only come from the realization
that institutions are not "one thing but many."[25] I take a fairly broad definition
of institutions, adopting Kathleen Thelen and James Mahoney's definition of
institutions as "relatively enduring features of political life (rules, norms, and
procedures) that structure behavior and cannot be changed easily or instanta-
neously."[26] I depict institutions as rules and use the two terms interchangeably.
Institutions have the following additional characteristics.

Institutions are not organizations. While organizations are actors, institutions
are rules. In his Nobel Prize lecture, Douglass C. North writes of economic institutions, "If institutions are the rules of the game, organizations and their entre-
preneurs are the players. Organizations are made up of groups of individuals
bound together by some common purpose to achieve certain objectives."[27]
Organizations are one of the many actors who play by the rules. In the PS story,
these players involve both individuals (PS members, NGO staff, elected officials,

and various service providers, like doctors, nurses, and schoolteachers) and organizations (PS, UP, BRAC field offices, and other NGOs). Organizations like the UP and PS are also arenas for politics; rules are negotiated here. In both of these roles, organizations are distinguishable from the rules shaped by and enacted within them.

Institutions can be formal or informal. Unlike formal parchment rules, informal institutions are often invisible. We do not always abide by formal rules. Sometimes we shun them in favor of practices that we may vaguely recognize but cannot quite put a finger on. We may not speak of these informal practices as rules, but we certainly follow them as if they were. Including informality in the conceptualization of institutions can illuminate behaviors that formal laws cannot explain. It allows scholars to "build a more fine-grained, and realistic, picture of what *really* constrains political behavior and decision-making."[28]

Institutions vary between settings. This is especially true for informal institutions. What seems obvious in one community can be less so in another. Accordingly, our actions differ from place to place, based on the rules that dictate appropriate behavior in each setting. Guillermo O'Donnell explains how one is supposed to drive a car in South Bend, Indiana, versus Rio de Janeiro or Buenos Aires, highlighting that in certain Latin American cities, "you have to be nuts (or a very naïve foreigner)" to follow formal driving rules. Stopping at a red light or stop sign after dark would run drivers the risk of being hit by the car behind them—whose driver does not expect them to stop—or being robbed.[29] What makes this an institution—the rule of the game—would be the fact that all involved actors know and expect this. Daniel Brinks explores the impunity with which police officers kill perceived violent criminals in Buenos Aires and São Paolo; the police, prosecutors, judges, and so on fail to punish cases even when it is clear that the officer was in violation of the law. The rule that governs is "impunity for police officers who kill, at least so long as they are seen to be carrying out their social cleaning function."[30] In both cases, written rules differ from the norm. And what is acceptable in one place is not acceptable in another.

Formal and informal institutions can coexist. Much of the scholarship on informal institutions examines how they interact with—or at least exist relative to—formal institutions. Louise Chappell and Fiona Mackay write that some scholars write of formal and informal institutions as a continuum, where the informal crystallizes, freezes, or morphs into the formal.[31] Others find this relationship to be dichotomous, where informal institutions interact with formal ones; they can reinforce or override one another.[32] Gretchen Helmke and Steven Levitsky write that in weak institutional settings, formal and informal institutional outcomes converge to form substitutive informal institutions and diverge to form competing informal institutions. Substitutive informal institutions "achieve what formal institutions were designed, but failed, to achieve."[33] They strengthen overall institutional outcomes. Alternatively, competing informal institutions have divergent outcomes from formal institutions; they structure incentives such that "to follow one rule, actors must violate another."[34] They crowd out formal ones and result in the various forms of patronage such as clientelism, patrimonialism, clan politics, and corruption.[35]

Whether this relationship is scalar or categorical, competing or substitutive, there is an implicit assumption that the two are inherently different and that informal institutions hold the corresponding formal institution as a standard. This can be misleading. While informal institutions cannot be studied independent of the formal institutions they coexist with, one should be wary of holding formal institutions as the ideal. Formal institutions are not sacrosanct. They may themselves be inequitable or enacted in ways that encapsulate positions of power. Nor are they always the best fit for a given society; sometimes they camouflage enduring and successfully functioning informal institutions. Indeed, a strict distinction between the formal and the informal may be messy, sometimes impossible in the real world. Lowndes et al. borrow Ostrom's concept of "rules-in-use"—the specific combination of formal and informal rules, or the dos and don'ts on the ground, which I adopt.[36] This helps shed any preconceived notion of what is right and good, and helps avoid over-specification, especially in the real world where multiple rules-in-use are often deeply enmeshed.

Institutions are gendered. By gendered, I refer to the socially accepted and shared meanings of masculinity and femininity that guide human interactions. Gender not only operates through individual action or interpersonal exchanges; it is "also a feature of institutions and social structures, and a part of the symbolic realm of meaning-making, within which individuals and actors are 'nested.'"[37] In Bangladesh, gender relationships are an intrinsic part of how institutions operate. Women are locked into particular behaviors because their roles as daughters, wives, mothers, laborers, and employees dictate that they have to behave a certain way. This is how they are expected to behave.

Measuring Informal Institutions

Measuring the informal can be tricky. Formal institutions can be traced through written rules—laws, procedures, and established practices. Informal institutions do not leave a paper trail.[38] But they manifest in everyday exchanges between actors. Thus, they are best measured, not just through the rules themselves, but also through outcomes—that is, what one would expect to see if indeed practices deviate from formal rules.

I propose a three-step approach to confront this dilemma, adapting the three strategies used by scholars in Helmke and Levitsky's edited volume.[39] First, I seek evidence of informal institutions by asking whether actors' behaviors deviate from formal rules.[40] Brinks proposes this as the first step to determining whether informal institutions exist. If there is no deviation—that is, if actions match up to formal rules—then we can determine that no informal institution exists.[41]

These deviations must be repeated behaviors and not singular, isolated events. Indeed, as Chappell and Mackay write, informal institutions are *"enduring* rules, norms and practices that shape *collective behavior* that *may or may not be recognized by institutional actors."*[42] Those abiding by the institutions may not identify them as such, but their longevity and collective scope become important markers in locating them.

Once patterns of behavior become clear, one still has to determine that they are rules and not random irregularities. The first step toward this to ask if there are either shared expectations or clear "logics of appropriateness" regarding the activities or outcomes in question. One may measure shared expectations by exploring actors' mutual understanding of rules and constraints placed on their behaviors.[43] Or one may ask what kinds of behaviors are seen as right or good, particularly through the lens of actors' roles and identities. James March and Johan Olsen write that people follow rules of appropriate behavior even when it is not in their best interest to do so, because they see such behaviors as "natural, rightful, expected, and legitimate."[44] They act based on their roles in society, reflecting the "ethos, practices, and expectations of its institutions."[45] While March and Olsen write about formally organized political institutions, their conceptualization can be applied to a broader understanding of politics as decision making and of what constitutes appropriate behavior in one's larger social world. For the purpose of this book, it is important to pay attention to whether expectations or logics of appropriateness are gendered—that is, do rules subscribe different behavioral standards to men and women? Are "good" women expected to behave a certain way?

Finally, I look for the sanctions that violators face. If informal institutions are enduring, accepted, and expected, then failing to abide by them must come with penalties. Actors will enforce rules through sanctions or rewards.[46] These sanctions can be visible or invisible, legal or illegal, ranging from "social disapproval (hostile remarks, gossip, ostracism), to the loss of employment, to the use of hired thugs and other forms of extrajudicial violence."[47]

DATA AND METHODS

From August 2009 to March 2010, I spent ten months in the field studying PS as part of a BRAC research team. The project, "An Evaluation of Polli Shomaj," was to be a comprehensive study of the program.[48] At the time, I was a researcher at RED, BRAC's independent research wing and one of Bangladesh's oldest research units within an NGO.[49] The PS research team included two staff researchers, a field manager, forty-five research assistants (RAs), and myself, the principal investigator. Together, we conducted over 6,000 interviews in 671 wards across Bangladesh. These included group interviews with PS leaders, individual interviews with PS members and a control group, household-level interviews with every household in four selected wards, and individual interviews with BRAC staff, local government officials, and other stakeholders.[50] What I discovered lies at the heart of *Village Ties.*

When I first started working at BRAC in summer 2009, I had not lived in Bangladesh for fifteen years. Having left at fourteen for boarding school in India and subsequently college in the United States, I fell into the strange category of third-culture kid, someone who had lived part of their life in a country that was not of their origin. My intellectual curiosity is tied to a longing for home that has been a constant in my life. I had been a mesmerized BRAC intern at twenty-one. But in 2009, I was a PhD student and former researcher at the United Nations Development Programme headquarters in New York. The rose-tinted glasses had come off. I approached the study with a healthy dose of skepticism for development programming. Based on explicit instructions from my unit coordinator, I had limited interactions with CEP staff. This, he insisted, was integral to maintaining neutrality. But having spent months in the field with PS groups, I developed a closeness with the program and admiration for the women who run it. This will undoubtedly appear in my work.

Field visits were a novel experience. I was, for the first time, traveling entirely on my own. I was accompanied by my co-researchers, RAs, and our driver. But it was all new people and unfamiliar places. I grew to love many things about field visits. There were the sparkles of light marking roadside markets where shopkeepers sold wares by tiny lamps or single lightbulbs. They grew few and far between as one traveled deeper into the villages at night. There was my chargeable nightlight, which I had balked at when my dad first suggested I take it. It became invaluable in the villages where power cuts were so frequent that people did not say we "lost power" but rather "power came" because you had electricity for a few meager hours in the day. I had learned to charge my phone aggressively during those treasured moments. I woke up in astonishingly beautiful villages with misty, dew-laden fields, humble homes clustered into small *paras* (neighborhoods). I journeyed down muddy brown rivers, monstrous in the monsoons and serene in the winters. And very importantly, I knew which of the traffic-clogged routes in and out of Dhaka would be the fastest on any given day.

This book draws on mixed methods with quasi-experimental research as the primary quantitative method. I employ the latter in part II of the book when I explore whether PS members do things differently from the control group. Unlike a randomized experiment, where a researcher assigns subjects to groups randomly prior to the allocation of a treatment, the PS team chose a control group from PS-adjacent wards. Qualitative data was gathered through semi-structured interviews and analyzed thematically. I draw on primarily two sets of questionnaires. Part II mostly examines outcomes at the individual level, drawing on 2,684 semi-structured interviews with PS members and the control group. Part III studies PS at the organization -level, drawing on 671 group-level interviews with PS members, primarily PS leadership. I also draw on interviews with BRAC staff and UP officials as well as extensive field notes.

The outstanding performance of NGOs makes Bangladesh an extreme case. This allows exploratory analysis on how NGO involvement influences women's political behaviors in rural societies undergoing rapid socioeconomic transformations.[51] Studying Bangladesh at a singular point of time also provides a natural laboratory. One can hold national-level factors constant, such as ideology (the influence of religious groups), policy (aid-based neoliberal development), regime type (hybrid regime), and macro-level institutional design (decentralized service delivery) and performance.[52] Within Bangladesh, I chose to study PS due to its geographic scope and focus on poor women. Both PS and BRAC have extensive national-level coverage. BRAC operates in all districts, and in 2009, PS covered 30 percent of all rural wards in Bangladesh.

Overview

This book is divided into three parts. Part I, "Setting the Stage," creates the backdrop for this book. Chapter 2, "A Gendered Story," addresses the historical context within which the PS story unfolds. When Bangladesh became independent in 1971, it had survived a brutal war of secession, a devastating cyclone, and years of resource drain under united Pakistan. Five decades later, it has become the poster child for human development. But this narrative is incomplete when one fails to center women, the focus of the earliest—and to this day most—development programs. In seeking to tell a more gendered story, this chapter argues that Bangladesh's development trajectory encompasses multiple components that—despite making remarkable improvements in women's lives—have fallen short on enhancing women's agency. The story has four intersecting strands. Bangladesh's governments embraced an aid-based development strategy that addressed women's needs primarily through welfare. This allowed NGOs to enter the villages with an assortment of development programs and change the rural landscape. Women's movements—once tied to nationalist movements—have NGO-ized over time. And finally, the religious and secular elite compete with each other to dictate how women should run their lives. Together, these elements have made women's issues the subject of externally imposed mandates, shifting them away from grassroots mobilization efforts that could enhance women's agency.

Chapter 3, "Poor Women's Politics," explores PS as an alternative to the neoliberal development model. It argues that PS centers on the collective—but in addition to being anti-oppressive in its goal, it embraces deliberative decision making and is embedded in the community. PS groups challenges injustice. As with other programs of its kind—for example, those run by Nijera Kori and Nagorik Uddyog in Bangladesh and Mahila Samakhya in India—its members push back against oppression and the structural inequities that manifest in poor people's lives. Deliberative decision making allows collective learning and the realization of goals, grounding decision making in the community. Finally, PS groups are vertically and horizontally embedded in their communities, partly due to NGO density in Bangladeshi villages and partly by design. Providing a closer look at what PS groups do and how they do it creates the foundation for subsequent chapters.

Part II, "Formal and Informal Institutions," teases out the rules-in-use in two major areas of PS activity. It takes the first steps toward establishing whether informal institutions exist and if PS presence influences this outcome. As informal institutions are invisible, these chapters ask whether a deviation from formal rules can be observed.[53] Subsequently, they compare the behaviors of PS members with the control group to identify whether something different is occurring in PS areas. This part focuses on the individual level. I draw on 2,684 semi-structured interviews with PS members and a control group, and use descriptive statistics, multilevel logistic regression, and qualitative analysis.

Chapter 4, "Clients, Rules, and Transactions," uncovers the rules-in-use around distributive politics—who gets services and how. It argues that in Bangladesh, the rural poor acquire services through multiple overlapping institutions, both formal and informal; these rules are different in PS areas. This chapter demonstrates that older clientelistic power structures are rapidly becoming dismantled. Big men no longer use services to retain their political power. While clientelism still exists, it is not the dominant mode of exchange. This chapter also illustrates that service delivery looks different in PS areas. Exchanges involving PS members are more likely to embody the informal institution of transactionalism—short-term monetary exchange—over clientelism. Transactionalism defies formal rules; it is a form of corruption. But it also allows the rural poor to acquire services that clientelism—with its closed net of beneficiaries—has deprived them of in the past. Exchanges involving PS members also embody a wider set of relationships, suggesting that service networks in PS areas extend beyond the traditional elite and their clients.

Chapter 5, "Rule of Law," examines the rules-in-use for the judicial system. Rural Bangladeshis lack access to legal services. Many conflicts are negotiated and resolved in the household or village courts (*shalish*). Decision-making processes embody the power relationships prevalent in society. They can be disproportionately biased against women, minorities, and the poor. This chapter argues that in rural Bangladesh, legal disputes are resolved through a mix of formal and informal rules. These rules are different in PS areas, where more reported legal issues are resolved, women's voices are better represented in legal processes, and embeddedness opens up access support networks. This chapter illustrates that conflict resolutions can embody formal and informal institutions, but can still provide justice in the absence of the state.

Part III, "Negotiating with State and Society," investigates how PS groups change informal institutions. These chapters examine negotiations between PS and various actors—their communities, the state, and NGOs. They ask whether the deviations observed actually represent institutions and not mere irregularities, and illustrate how PS groups challenge—and even overturn—unjust informal institutions. This section focuses mostly on the organization level. It draws on 671 group-level interviews with PS members and uses qualitative analysis and descriptive statistics.

Chapter 6, "Changing Distributive Politics," brings the story back to service delivery. It argues that PS groups shift distributive practices by negotiating with both state and society. They negotiate with the community to change expectations regarding who gets what; these negotiations take place within deliberative decision-making processes that are central to the functioning of PS groups. They bargain with elected local government officials applying democratic accountability based on morality, where morality is equated with serving the poor. Embeddedness plays a crucial role in this process by providing access to information and opening up spaces for negotiation.

Chapter 7, "Negotiating Justice," argues that PS groups create an informal justice to address poor people's legal needs when the state fails to administer rule of law. PS groups make rule of law accessible, representative, and equitable toward the rural poor. They negotiate with society for adherence to legal codes over traditional norms, and advocate for the disenfranchised in their negotiations with the community. They challenge the logic of appropriateness around young women's prescribed behaviors, and threaten social and legal sanctions. In doing so, they create the space for a different kind of justice—one that involves both formal and informal institutions—in spaces where the state does not deliver.

Chapter 8, "Governing Locally," argues that PS groups change the nature of women's representation in local governance. They campaign for elected seats within the UP. They undertake independent community initiatives that should ideally fall under the purview of local government. And finally, they participate in local committees within alternative governing infrastructure created by NGOs. PS groups negotiate with the community to shift expectations around women's leadership and whom elected politician serve. Their work illustrates that women's representation can occur in multiple spaces of governance, both within and outside of the local government.

CHAPTER 2

A Gendered Story

Bangladesh showed little promise for economic and political development in the aftermath of independence. Its first Awami League (AL) government inherited a land that was devastated by war, disaster, and years of resource drain under West Pakistan. In 1971, United States ambassador Ural Alexis Johnson famously called it an international basket case in a National Security Council Special Actions Group meeting.[1] But despite adverse beginnings, ineffective governing institutions, and frequent wobbling between democracy and authoritarianism, Bangladesh has surpassed many of its peers on human development.[2] How the country became a development miracle—its signature label—despite such odds has befuddled social scientists. Bangladesh now falls into the Medium Human Development (MHD) category.[3] The UN recognized it as one of thirty-eight countries that reached Millennium Development Goal 1 of eradicating extreme poverty and hunger ahead of schedule.[4] It has made strides in improving the lives of rural women. And NGOs get much of the credit for this success.

The narrative is compelling, but incomplete. In seeking to tell a more gendered story, this chapter argues that Bangladesh's development trajectory encompasses multiple components that—despite making remarkable improvements in women's lives—have fallen short on enhancing women's agency. This is particularly relevant for a society where women play subservient roles, both at home and in their communities. First, in their efforts to climb out of the postwar crisis and ensure rural people's survival needs, Bangladesh's governments have embraced an aid-based development strategy that addressed poor women's needs primarily through welfare. Second, the influx of foreign aid allowed development NGOs to enter the villages with new resources. Reliant on the World Bank's neoliberal development model, they shifted their focus from mobilization to service delivery. Third, the women's movement—once tied to nationalist movements—has NGO-ized and deradicalized over time. And finally, religious organizations compete with NGOs to dictate women's roles in society.

The first section of this chapter presents a very brief political history of Bangladesh, with a focus on development and decentralization efforts. The second section addresses the development strategies of various governments. The third section examines the role of NGOs. The fourth section traces the women's movement over time. The last section addresses the influence of Islamic organizations on poor women's lives.

A Brief Political History
The Road to 1971

Bangladesh's history is marred by crises that put people's survival needs center stage. The country became independent in 1971 after a brutal war of secession from West Pakistan. Naomi Hossain describes the war as "the second in a two-part struggle against colonial exploitation and neo-colonial underdevelopment."[5] Under British colonial rule, Bangladesh was part of the Bengal Presidency, Bengal Province, and later, split from its western counterpart into East Bengal. During the 1947 partition of the subcontinent, East Bengal merged with Pakistan to become East Pakistan. India bordered the new province on three sides, placing thousands of miles between its capital, Dhaka, and the national government in the west. The Pakistan central government directed all development efforts to the west; this included investments, foreign aid, and profits from the east's flourishing industries. Mahmud Ali writes that West Pakistan saw significant benefits from state investments, such as those in education. For example, after decolonization, West Pakistan had 8,413 primary schools, and East Pakistan had 29,663. Twenty years later, West Pakistan had 39,418, while East Pakistan had only 28,308.[6] East Pakistan faced a massive resource drain as most investors in the region belonged to West Pakistani families. Most modern industries were controlled by the state or non-Bengalis, with six families owning "more than 40 percent of the province's total manufacturing assets, 32 percent of industrial production, and 81.5 percent of the national jute industry."[7] The region also suffered from periodic natural disasters, while the government directed most international aid to the west. Bengalis were largely underrepresented in the civil services. The selection process favored Punjabis, and students from Pakistani public schools and other Westernized institutions.

After partition, a movement emerged in East Pakistan following the central government's decision to adopt Urdu as the state language.[8] A five-year resistance culminated in a mass student protest and five deaths on February 21, 1952. The AL, formed in 1949 to counter West Pakistan's Muslim League, led its five-party coalition, the United Front, to victory in the 1954 provincial elections to the East Bengal Legislative Assembly. Sixteen years later, the AL won Pakistan's general election under Sheikh Mujibur Rahman (Sheikh Mujib). As West Pakistan's leadership opposed the forming of an AL government, Sheikh Mujib sought autonomy for Bangladesh. On March 7, 1971, he delivered a speech at Dhaka's Race Course Maidan declaring the beginning of Bengali resistance. Soon, the Pakistan army began a gradual occupation of East Pakistan, and the region became embroiled in a brutal nine-month war of secession. The Pakistan government imprisoned Sheikh Mujib in West Pakistan. A number of AL leaders crossed the border into India and formed a government in exile.

The Mujib Regime (1972–1975)

Bangladesh became independent on December 16, 1971, after a devastating war marked by genocide, war crimes, and crimes against humanity. Sheikh Mujib returned from Pakistan's custody the following year. In 1973, he was elected prime minister under the AL. He inherited a country destroyed by war and disaster. A UN Mission report states that the events of 1971 had "imposed an almost total hiatus on the economy" with backsliding development and significant population movements.[9] Sheikh Mujib confronted this crisis with a socialist development strategy. Bangladesh's 1972 constitution established a country upon the values of socialism, democracy, nationalism, and secularism.[10] Sheikh Mujib nationalized all industries and stressed the importance of labor-intensive sectors. Although Bangladesh did not become a member of the UN until 1974, he engaged with the international community while staying nonaligned in his foreign policy. He visited numerous countries, attended the conference of the nonaligned nations in Algiers, and received aid from both bilateral donors and multilateral agencies.[11]

In 1974, a devastating famine spread through the country.[12] The new AL government—just getting its administrative bearings—fell short in its distributive efforts. Sheikh Mujib had centralized power under the AL and restructured local government. He replaced Pakistan-era union councils with Union Panchayats (later Union Parishads), and government-appointed Union Relief Committees controlled aid operations.[13] The state established rural cooperatives in villages, each with an elected managing committee. However, cooperatives could not operate freely due to local-level corruption.[14] By 1974, the regime faced massive opposition from various groups that mobilized the common people around subsistence issues.[15] In 1975, Sheikh Mujib and many of his family members were brutally assassinated in an army coup.

The Zia Regime (1977–1981)

After a series of coups and countercoups, Ziaur Rahman was elected president in 1977 through a yes/no referendum. He established the Bangladesh Nationalist Party (BNP) and reinstated multiparty politics formally, while curbing dissent at the same time. The Zia regime's focus on rural development led to increased donor reliance for Bangladesh—including stronger relationships with Muslim states—gradual Islamicization of state and society, and decentralized local governance. In an effort to appease donors, Ziaur Rahman shifted the economy toward World Bank–favored market-based policies. He denationalized many large industries, removed the word socialism from the constitution, and embraced an economic program that combined privatization with rural development. He moved away from India and Moscow, and strengthened alliances with the West, Muslim countries, and China. During the Zia years, Bangladesh received $808.63 million in aid from Muslim states, while China offered financial and technical assistance as well as security.[16] Table 2.1 shows selected development indicators measuring the availability of resources. It illustrates that official development assistance increased dramatically during this time. Most assistance came from the Organization for Economic Co-operation and Development donors, primarily the United States, other Western states, and Japan.[17]

The Zia regime also saw the beginning of a gradual Islamicization of the Bangladeshi state and society. Ziaur Rahman shifted the state ideology from the secular Bengali nationalism to what is now seen as the more Islamic Bangladeshi nationalism; he claimed that this respected and honored the rights of the country's many non-Bengali tribal and linguistic groups.[18] However, this moved the country away from the Bengali cultural identity, which had driven the independence movement, toward a religious one. The 1972 constitution declared secularism as one of the country's founding principles. But in 1977, Ziaur Rahman amended the constitution, removed secularism, and added a reference to the almighty Allah in the Preamble. He created a new Ministry of Religion and transformed the Islamic Academy, a small research institution, into the Islamic Foundation, a large umbrella organization.[19] He restored Bangladesh's civil service by bringing back senior officials who had been removed on allegations of collaboration with West Pakistan in 1971. This included leaders of the Jama'at-e-Islami (JI)—many of whose members were charged with war crimes—and other religious parties that the Mujib government had banned after the war.[20] By 1979, the JI had re-emerged as a political party. On decentralization, Ziaur Rahman delegated all development responsibilities to the village level. He created Village Defense Forces to reinstitute order and elected village governments (*gram sarkar*) to address development issues, such as increasing food production, mass literacy, family planning, and rule of law issues, including dispute resolution.[21] However, Ziaur Rahman was assassinated in 1981 and *gram sarkar* eliminated the following year.[22]

The Ershad Regime (1982–1990)

Less than a year after Ziaur Rahman's assassination, Lieutenant General H. M. Ershad forced the sitting president, Abdus Sattar, to resign and established martial law with himself as chief martial law administrator. Ershad organized

TABLE 2.1

BANGLADESH: SELECTED DEVELOPMENT INDICATORS BY YEAR

Year	GDP growth (%)	Net ODA (millions of US$)	FDI (millions of US$)	World Bank loans (millions of US$)	Remittances (millions of US$)	Energy production index	Food production index
1972	−13.97	223.76	0.09	3.04	–	1030	40.35
1973	3.33	421.47	2.34	91.22	–	1404	44.68
1974	9.59	531.39	2.20	258.88	–	1549	43.22
1975	−4.09	1071.62	1.54	349.67	–	1627	47.81
1976	5.66	497.89	5.42	471.32	18.76	1769	45.66
1977	2.67	784.36	6.98	559.53	78.88	1934	48.76
1978	7.07	995.01	7.70	662.62	115.44	2219	50.53
1979	4.80	1162.66	−8.01	825.19	171.14	2402	50.12
1980	0.82	1286.72	8.51	980.90	338.67	2353	51.05
1981	3.80	1099.04	5.36	1139.71	381.05	2662	50.75
1982	2.38	1337.40	6.96	1324.91	526.46	3036	52.77
1983	4.02	1042.43	0.40	1513.65	642.41	3433	53.99
1984	5.18	1186.82	−0.55	1727.02	500.75	3966	54.30
1985	3.22	1126.53	−6.66	2075.75	502.47	4528	56.17

1986	4.25	1428.05	2.44	2510.83	576.28	4800	56.85
1987	3.73	1792.60	3.21	3055.43	747.81	5587	56.95
1988	2.16	1614.36	1.84	3253.66	763.62	6541	57.86
1989	2.61	1799.49	0.25	3503.49	757.98	7115	63.56
1990	5.94	2092.76	3.24	4158.63	778.87	7732	64.29
1991	3.34	1880.24	1.39	4424.37	769.37	8270	65.71
1992	5.04	1818.39	3.72	4594.17	911.76	8894	66.60
1993	4.57	1383.26	14.05	4881.22	1007.38	9206	66.53
1994	4.08	1742.89	11.15	5435.77	1150.88	9784	63.99
1995	4.93	1281.74	1.90	5692.37	1201.66	10806	66.85
1996	4.62	1228.07	13.53	5759.33	1344.66	11474	70.56
1997	5.39	1012.30	139.38	5739.38	1526.50	11858	71.50
1998	5.23	1162.86	190.06	6203.72	1606.08	12882	74.11
1999	4.87	1219.43	179.66	6458.72	1806.79	14450	84.29
2000	5.94	1172.84	280.38	6454.98	1967.53	15771	89.51
2001	5.27	1043.74	78.53	6456.05	2104.55	17392	87.56
2002	4.42	906.25	52.34	7075.58	2858.06	18665	90.16
2003	5.26	1394.89	268.29	8069.10	3191.66	19712	92.79

(continued)

TABLE 2.1

BANGLADESH: SELECTED DEVELOPMENT INDICATORS BY YEAR (continued)

Year	GDP growth (%)	Net ODA (millions of US$)	FDI (millions of US$)	World Bank loans (millions of US$)	Remittances (millions of US$)	Energy production index	Food production index
2004	6.27	1443.85	448.91	8894.55	3583.82	24684	91.01
2005	5.96	1318.85	813.32	8687.88	4314.50	26506	102.85
2006	6.63	1221.18	697.21	9297.24	5427.52	29879	106.15
2007	6.43	1515.24	652.82	10077.30	6553.13	31286	112.06
2008	6.19	2070.63	1009.62	10612.97	8925.33	34957	120.40
2009	5.74	1225.82	732.81	10746.04	10520.65	37862	121.63
2010	6.07	1414.95	918.17	10653.18	10850.21	42347	129.65
2011	6.71	1497.76	1137.92	10712.23	12067.83	-	132.11

Source: World Bank, "World Development Indicators."

Note: Official development assistance (ODA) includes disbursement of loans made on concessional terms and grants by official agencies of the members of the Development Assistance Committee (DAC), multilateral institutions, and non-DAC countries. It includes a grant element of at least 25 percent, calculated at a discount rate of 10 percent. Foreign Direct Investment (FDI) refers to direct investment equity flows. World Bank loans refer to all loans and credit from the World Bank group. All numbers reflect value in current US$ as of April 20, 2011. World Bank, "World Development Indicators."

parliamentary elections in 1986 and 1988, and presidential elections in 1986. He established the Jatiya Party and ran for president as its head. However, he kept the army dominant in governance, justifying a strong military as a necessary precursor to democracy.[23] Ershad took drastic measures to liberalize the economy, lifting limits on investment, privatizing hundreds of industries, expanding Export Processing Zones, and encouraging investors to legalize black income by paying taxes on it. In the process, he created a national bourgeoisie, many of whom would later join his administration.[24]

Ershad continued the earlier governments' strategies of decentralization and rural development through donor engagement. Funds for poverty programming increased (table 2.1). He took the country further down the path of Islamicization. He strengthened alliances with the Muslim world and claimed that Bangladesh would not survive unless it embraced Islamic rule, the country's only means of emancipation.[25] He introduced Arabic and English as compulsory languages in Bangladesh's education curriculum, which sparked the first student protest against his regime in 1983. Ershad also implemented a massive decentralization program, centered on 460 police stations (*thana*) or sub-districts governed by elected representatives who had substantial freedom over their operations.[26] These councils were connected to the union councils, the lower tier of local government. Sub-District councils received substantial financing for development; budget allocation increased from Tk. 400,000 under the previous system to Tk. 5 million.[27] They were "more powerful than any such elected authorities in the history of Bangladesh."[28] The Ershad regime faced an organized opposition spearheaded by the BNP under Begum Khaleda Zia, the widow of Ziaur Rahman, and by the AL under Sheikh Hasina, the daughter of Sheikh Mujib. Following ongoing demonstrations demanding his removal, Ershad stepped down in 1990 and called for elections under a neutral caretaker government (CTG).

Post-Transition (1991–2010)

Bangladesh transitioned to multiparty government in 1991. Both the BNP and the AL held alternate governments until 2006, forming alliances with Ershad's Jatiya Party and the now-banned JI. However, the country has moved from an electoral authoritarian regime to virtually a single-party system. In 2006, the BNP government was forcefully removed amid agitation by the opposition. An army-backed CTG ruled until elections in 2008. But in 2013, Bangladesh slipped into another crisis. Two years earlier, the AL had passed the Fifteenth Amendment to the Constitution, which removed the CTG system that had provided independent electoral oversight since 1996. The BNP opposition called numerous strikes in an effort to bring back the CGT provision, and on January 5, 2014, the country went into elections that the opposition boycotted. The AL won a landslide victory in two subsequent elections, held in 2014 and 2018, amid allegations of massive electoral irregularities.

DEVELOPMENT

Neoliberal Development

As an ideology, neoliberalism imagines a world where the market reigns. John Campbell and Ove Pedersen situate its rise in the last two decades of the twentieth century, with the election of new conservative governments in North America and Europe, austerity in Latin America, and the fall of communism in Europe and the Soviet Union.[29] George Monbiot writes in the *Guardian*, "Through the IMF, the World Bank, the Maastricht treaty and the World Trade Organization, neoliberal policies were imposed—often without democratic consent—on much of the world."[30] Soon neoliberalism became synonymous with the phrase "Washington Consensus," a term coined by John Williamson referring to a ten-point set of policy reforms that institutions in Washington—the World Bank, the International Monetary Fund, and the U.S. Treasury—had prescribed for Latin America.[31]

Neoliberalism dominates the international development discourse. Development itself refers to progress of a certain kind, movement along a prescribed path and toward a predetermined goal. According to James Ferguson, it signifies a process of modernization, a shift from a traditional to an industrial economy with capitalist development at its center.[32] Modernization theories assume that developing economies—mostly the postcolonial third world nations—drag their feet behind advanced industrial economies as they lack certain technological, institutional, and ideological innovations. Thus, the very idea of development assumes that with the right kind of push, the struggling postcolonial world could catch up with their industrialized counterparts.[33] Others approached development as global poverty reduction. Today, this ideal is enshrined in global development standards, such as the Sustainable Development Goals. As the development project established its roots across the global South, the two concepts behind development converged, and poverty reduction started to go hand in hand with the ideas espoused by modernization—industrialization, privatization, and capitalist accumulation.[34] Arturo Escobar writes that development was everywhere, with "governments designing and implementing ambitious development plans, institutions carrying out development programs in city and countryside alike, experts of all kinds studying underdevelopment and producing theories ad nauseam."[35] Many postcolonial states jumped on the development bandwagon, with the industrialized economies at the helm. Along the way, development embraced a moral component. It became the right—and possibly only—way to emancipate the global South.

Neoliberalism has multiple components. Peter Evans and William Sewell identify its four facets as theory, ideology, policy, and social imaginary.[36] In Bangladesh, neoliberalism manifests most visibly in national policies—in particular, World Bank–directed national development strategies that highlight economic growth and rural development. The country was founded upon socialist principles, and neoliberal policies came much later, as a pragmatic endeavor, hand in hand with foreign aid. For women, neoliberal policies emphasized welfare over structural inequalities. But women's marginalization predates the influx of donor aid—it begins with the 1971 war.

Women and War

During the Liberation War, the Pakistan army, aided by their paramilitary units Al-Badr and Al-Shams and local collaborators—including JI members who opposed the war—committed massive war crimes and crimes against humanity. Estimates for loss of life stand between 300,000 and 3 million. War and genocide displaced several million people, and between 200,000 and 400,000 women were raped.[37] During the war, women participated in multiple capacities, from social workers to combatants. Some fought in battle. Most worked in clinics and cared for the wounded.[38] Yasmin Saikia writes that women desired to fight for their state and the nation, but could not penetrate this patriarchal space.[39] And now, despite their extensive contribution to the war from the clinics to the battlefields, women are most often honored in collective memory as gendered victims—the brave survivors of brutal sexual violence.

Following the war, Sheikh Mujib honored rape survivors with the publicly designated title of *birangona*. The term translates literally to brave or courageous woman; the government gives it the meaning of war heroine.[40] Sheikh Mujib hoped that the move would allow survivors to claim a space in the war and in public discourse, where their sacrifices could be seen as equivalent to those made by *muktijoddhas* (freedom fighters), mostly men.[41] The government set up a multipronged program to rehabilitate *birangonas* and prevent society from ostracizing them. Sara Hossain and Bina D'Costa write that the government placed urgent emphasis on supporting women survivors with "ground-breaking" services.[42] Rescue and rehabilitation programs provided medical assistance and abortions for pregnant survivors. Income generation schemes trained women in areas "such as sewing and garments, or jute and tapestry production; spice grinding, and separate economic assistance to widows to enable them to use their entrepreneur skills."[43] Men received incentives for marrying *birangonas*. Communities participated in social awareness programs. Efforts to rehabilitate war babies—children born of war rapes—and orphans centered on arranging adoptions and constructing orphanages.[44]

This effort—progressive and placing Bangladesh far ahead of other postcolonial nations—uplifted women in many domains while limiting their agency in others. The eulogization and rehabilitation of raped women painted the shiny new nation as modern and dynamic, leaving behind the trappings of traditional Muslim society.[45] On the one hand, it removed women from what Naomi Hossain identifies as the patriarchal bargain—a social contract that ties women's economic lives to gender relations.[46] The devastation of war meant that women could no longer rely on men for livelihoods, prompting the government to integrate women's issues into policymaking. Women took charge of their economic lives; they participated in skills training workshops and labored in public work schemes.[47]

On the other hand, the public narrative around *birangonas* depicted women's violations and trauma as a loss of honor for the nation.[48] It sought to restore women's respectability by painting them as mothers, both to past and future citizens and to the nation as a whole.[49] Public discourse spoke to "kinship norms" of purity and honor, not just of the women, but also their families, communities, and the nation.[50] Survivors themselves played no role in shaping the narrative—rather, powerful actors in the government engineered their accounts of suffering and survival.[51] Rehabilitation policies did not prevent social ostracizing. Instead, when *birangonas* emerged to claim their story, society viewed them as fallen women and pushed them to its margins. Men who married *birangonas* often left their marriages after receiving compensation.[52] Yasmin Saikia writes that *birangonas* received little of people's love, respect, and understanding, and hid their experiences for fear of social stigma.[53] In her study of three *birangonas* in Enayetpur, Nayanika Mookherjee finds that the women received social sanctions (*khotas*, or censorious remarks) once they had traveled to Dhaka with local village leaders to testify in *gono adalot*, a citizen-initiated mock trial for war criminals held in 1992. As their stories appeared across the media, villagers punished them for defying their gender roles—limited by notions of purity and silencing the impurity of rape—and going public with their status as war heroines.[54]

Famine

Scholars commemorate the 1971 war as the definitive point in Bangladesh's history. Hossain writes that it is not the war, but the 1974 famine that forms a critical juncture for the country. As Bangladesh struggled to recover from the rubble of war and famine, Western donors essentially "held the country hostage" till they adopted World Bank policies.[55] Mujib's government—initially determined to develop Bangladesh on a strategy of self-reliance—gave in and shed its socialist principles under donor pressures. Talukder Maniruzzaman writes that as the economy "virtually collapsed by the middle of 1974," the government modified its socialist program, raising the ceiling on domestic private investment and allowing uncapped foreign investment.[56] Aid poured in and the government signed contracts with foreign oil companies for offshore oil explorations.[57]

Hossain attributes these failures to the prioritization of urban over rural aid.[58] Before 1971, the Public Food Distribution System was limited to cities. Though the program later reached the villages, it required that the government prioritize six urban centers (only 6 percent of the population) and designated populations.[59] These restrictions took rations away from rural areas that desperately needed them. The government set up 5,792 relief camps, which fed 4.35 million people.[60] But camps did not distribute enough grains and protect against diseases.[61] Hossain identifies this period as the major turning point in Bangladesh's history, when a number of social contracts emerged between key actors—within the ruling class, recognizing that human development and provision of social protections are essential to their survival, between the ruling class and the people for providing these protections, and between elites and the international community to pursue a kind of development that was both pro-market and pro-poor.[62] As the government prioritized feeding the nation, the first Five-Year Plan (FYP) and the subsequent Two-Year Plan focused mostly on agricultural growth. The two plans addressed women's needs through welfare, recognizing them primarily as mothers instead of addressing their rights and agency.[63]

Military Regimes

During the Zia regime, most foreign funds went into rural development. The second FYP (1980–1985) placed a major thrust on poverty reduction; its main purpose was to improve the life of the common man through increased income and employment. The government adopted a nineteen-point development program focused on rural development, self-reliance, decentralization, and population control. It built family planning centers where health staff provided birth control information and services, and created massive public works programs around building embankments, irrigation canals, and roads.[64] Rural Bangladeshis did some of this work voluntarily, some for money, and the rest under the government's safety net programs, such as Food-for-Work.[65] Women participated in many of these programs, which included both service delivery and labor. The Vulnerable Group Feeding (VGF) program, possibly the largest and most significant food aid program in Bangladesh, was created in response to the famine of 1974. It shifted attention from urban to rural areas.[66]

The government's focus on rural development continued under Ershad's third FYP (1985–1990). VGF was transformed into an initiative with longer-term development goals; by the 1990s, the new Vulnerable Group Development (VGD) program was implemented through partnerships between the national government, the UP, and NGOs.[67] The government also made remarkable progress on health care. At the time, Bangladesh had started implementing the Extended Program for Immunization—initiated in 1974—with the help of various partner agencies and NGOs.[68] With the support of UNICEF and various NGOs, the Department of Public Health launched a massive campaign to promote sanitary latrine use.[69] Bangladesh underwent massive infrastructural development. Roads and bridges were built. Many isolated rural areas received access to electricity. These programs benefited rural women, but structural gender inequities remained unaddressed.

Post-Transition

Bangladesh's post-transition governments expanded the reach of safety nets under subsequent FYPs.[70] They also embraced an increasingly market-oriented approach, providing skills and education through mainstream programs. In 1999, the World Bank and the IMF declared that the Poverty Reduction Strategy Papers (PRSPs) would form the basis for all their lending. Inspired by the Washington Consensus, they emphasized rapid growth paired with safety nets for the most vulnerable.[71] Bangladesh adopted an interim PRSP in 2002 and the first PRSP in 2005. Though the PRSPs were expected to embody national ownership, the process of developing them was messy, with little coordination and insufficient research on the country's diverse needs.[72] The 2005 PRSP addresses women's issues primarily in terms of health and promoting their integration into the market. However, it recognizes the importance of women's rights and advancements through increased mobility, improvement of women's status in society, and addressing gender gaps in health and education.[73] Subsequent development strategies take a more comprehensive approach to gender. The government adopted the sixth FYP in 2011 and the seventh FYP in 2016. The newer FYPs promote enhancing women's status at home and in the community and equitable decision making in political institutions. The government has also adopted additional policies, such as the National Women's Development Policy of 2011, the Domestic Violence (Prevention and Protection Rules) of 2013, and the Prevention and Suppression of Human Trafficking Act of 2012.[74] On mainstream programs, the government made a massive commitment to education after embracing the global Education for All agenda. It has built schools, hired teachers, reformed the education sector, and introduced stipends and school feeding programs.[75] Introduced in 2002, the Primary Education Stipend Programme (PESP) provides cash incentives for school attendance. These initiatives have helped bring rural girls into school. Indeed, Bangladeshi women have made significant strides on education; women have 5 years of schooling compared to men at 5.6 years, and they surpass women in other MHD countries on secondary education.[76]

NGOs

Bangladeshis' familiarity with NGOs predates the current donor influx.[77] They have worked with voluntary organizations, for example, through village public works programs, religious initiatives, self-help groups, and infrastructure projects, such as building schools and hospitals, taken on by Christian missionaries.[78] In the 1960s, Bangladesh became the "aid lab" for the rest of the world as the Pakistan Academy for Rural Advancement—with funding from the Ford Foundation and researchers from Michigan State University—set up the Comilla Academy to conduct experiments in rural development.[79] The Comilla Academy sprouted with the Cold War as its backdrop. As the Soviet state strengthened its global influence, the United States sought to expand its development influence along liberal capitalist lines.[80] Contrary to modernization theory's assumed relationship between democracy and capitalism, the United States found the third world's autocratic leaders to be an ideal conduit to shepherd their societies out of tradition and into modernity.[81] East Pakistan—given its backwardness—was the perfect lab. If poverty could be solved here, it could be solved anywhere.[82]

In line with modernization ideals, the Comilla model attacked the poverty problem with new technology. For women, these advances involved contraceptives—condoms, foaming tablets, and eventually intrauterine devices. FYPs included disseminating these technologies—for women, for example, including "the proportion of citizens to be brought under birth control regimes."[83] Proponents of modernization viewed tradition as backward. In East Pakistan, these new progressive ideals were viewed as a contrast to the "defeatism as despair" of religious fatalism.[84] The Comilla model was not completely divorced from the principles of collectivization; agricultural technologies were implemented along with cooperatives.[85]

In the 1970s, new NGOs emerged amid postwar devastation and widespread disillusionment with the government.[86] Founded by progressive young Bangladeshis during a time of immense crisis, organizations like BRAC, Grameen Bank, Proshika, and ASA (formerly the Association for Social Advancement) provided relief, built infrastructure, gave loans without collateral, and undertook a range of poverty alleviation efforts.[87] In 1972, BRAC began its work in remote Sulla, first providing relief and then long-term development through the creation of schools and cooperatives for fishermen and farmers.[88] In 1976, Dr. Muhammad Yunus began Grameen Bank as a project that provided micro loans to poor women who lacked collateral. Centered on a group-based lending model that is now implemented by many other NGOs, Grameen's programs served 8.81 million borrowers by 2015.[89] ASA—the organization that pioneered the highly standardized and cost-efficient "Ford" model of microfinance—was formed in 1978 and started loan operations in 1981.[90] Most of these programs targeted rural women. Created in 1976, Proshika took a participatory development approach, organizing women around the sentiments of the Liberation War.[91] Lamia Karim writes that the NGOs of the period embodied patriotism and communitarianism, inspired both by "a missionary sense of altruism for the poor" and "patriotism for the newly independent country."[92] Many of their founders were inspired by Paulo Freire's conscientization approach; they built their programs on the foundations of consciousness-raising and social mobilization.[93] Initially providing immediate relief, these NGOs went on to implement programs in health and sanitation, legal aid, livelihood support, and eventually microfinance. At the time, foreign NGOs stepped in to provide humanitarian assistance. They also rehabilitated the "unwanted" children of 1971, protected the non-Bengali community during and after the war, and organized relief and rehabilitation after the 1974 famine.[94]

NGOs have grown in size, scope, and numbers. Over time, they have shifted their focus from civic awareness, conscientization, and women's mobilization to service delivery, with a massive focus on microfinance.[95] A 2005 study that surveyed 6,559 NGOs and their branch offices in Bangladesh found that 92 percent of the NGOs provided microfinance as a service. The authors attribute this popularity to the fact that microfinance is an important revenue generator and enables NGOs to move away from donor funding to financial self-sufficiency.[96] This shift reflects the realities of neoliberal development, which promoted increased private initiatives by donor NGOs, a preoccupation with efficiency and financial sustainability, and a critique of the "rent-seeking" state.[97] It also stemmed from clientelism in domestic affairs. The NGO Affairs Bureau, a government body that oversees NGO activities in Bangladesh, often approves projects based on personal relationships between elites. They direct most of their support to large NGOs running service delivery programs.[98] In addition, the country's many military regimes curtailed NGOs' mobilization activities between 1976 and 1991.[99] Together, they steered development work in the direction of service delivery.

The 2005 NGO survey also finds that most NGOs operate in partnership with at least one government agency.[100] Donors advocate for such NGO-government partnerships. A 1990 World Bank study recommended NGO expansion to supplement government efforts and improved service delivery through competition.[101] Now, the relationship is more collaborative. NGOs enjoy substantial legitimacy among the rural population. Indeed, *The State of Governance in Bangladesh 2006*, a report by BRAC University, shows that NGOs had higher legitimacy than the government itself. More respondents were also satisfied with services that NGOs shared responsibility in delivering, such as health care (66 percent) and education (87.7 percent), when compared to exclusively government-delivered services, such as power supply (23.3 percent) and price of commodities (2.7 percent). While only 31.9 percent trusted politicians and

44.4 percent trusted members of Parliament, 79.1 percent of respondents trusted NGO officials.[102]

The NGO-government partnership model is not without critique. Some argue that NGOs operate as a shadow or franchise state.[103] This is a complicated relationship, especially for a country where aid has been conditional on liberalization. David Lewis writes that "the 1990s have seen a growing emphasis on the so-called new policy agenda of market liberalization and democratic governance," which seeps into NGO strategies through a focus on governance and election monitoring, and donors' willingness to fund these activities under the agendas of good governance and civil society.[104] This focus on political change is reflective of the modernization approach—the idea that economic and political development go hand in hand, and can be accelerated with the right knowledge. Sarah White writes that it echoes the 1960s concerns with political modernization, where the transfer of capital and technology was meant to foster democracy.[105] But the state-NGO partnership receives insufficient credit for Bangladesh's development. NGOs implement programs, study their successes and failures, and replicate them at lightning speed, something that the sheer bureaucratic inefficiencies of state structures would not allow. At the same time, NGOs cannot fulfill the governance functions of the state. Nor can they implement national-level programs without the state's coordination and infrastructural support, which is particularly necessary for multi-donor programs. BRAC's IGVGD (Income Generation for Vulnerable Group Development) program provides a good example of this—while BRAC innovated the program, it was eventually scaled up in partnership with the government.

Many NGO programs distribute services—especially microcredit—through small groups that later become a channel for distributing other resources, such as income generation training and awareness raising. Simeen Mahmud writes that the informal group was believed to be the most effective means for delivering services, both "financial (microcredit) and human resource (awareness raising, health, literacy, skills training) inputs to participating women and households."[106] Groups increase women's physical mobility. As women run small enterprises, they venture into new spaces—for example, markets, local committees, even local government—and build new relationships. They gain confidence and self-esteem as a result of attending meetings, and group members are more likely to venture outside on their own and receive more respect at home and in the community.[107] Lending groups also provide women with an arena to organize outside household and community spaces, where their voices are silenced.

The group-based model's popularity suggests that NGOs have not completely shed their organizational spirit. Nor are they entirely removed from the conscientization approach. The 2005 survey of NGOs found that 93 percent of the surveyed organizations engage in some kind of awareness-raising program. These training programs and schools have aided Bangladesh's capitalist transformation and simultaneously enhanced women's income-generation prospects. Shelley Feldman writes that they have created a class of industrial workers in teaching sewing and handicraft to rural women, creating a venue for them to secure employment in the ready-made garment (RMG) industry.[108] Some NGOs do radical organizing work. Nagorik Uddyog forms women's groups at the UP level, where members participate in intensive two- to three-day workshops on their rights as citizens. Participants share details of their own lives and discuss the lives of women in their communities. They reflect on gender roles and patriarchal informal institutions, such as dowry and child marriage, and deliberate on strategies to counter them.[109] Embracing a social mobilization mission in 1980, Nijera Kori combines training with a savings program to build what Naila Kabeer calls "grassroots citizenship."[110] Although the training itself is an individual service, its purpose is to build collective capabilities so that the poor, both men and women, can understand their rights and claim them.[111] Group members create savings funds, buy collective assets, or fund protests and campaigns.[112]

Women's Movements

Women's movements, too, have shifted from radical organizing to donor-funded programming. South Asia has a long history of women's organization. Historically, the "woman question" held a key place in the nationalist movements and the nation-building efforts.[113] Kumari Jayawardena writes that women's emancipation in the subcontinent is linked to two simultaneous movements—the political movement resisting imperialism and a social movement resisting traditional structures.[114] Women's issues took a central place in identity formation among Muslim leaders and intellectuals in Bengal.[115] Inspired by progressive Islamic states like Turkey, modernists advocated for the adaptation of older customs, such as extreme segregation, and encouraged increased public participation for women. Traditionalists revived old practices and norms.[116] Both groups supported girls' education—one of the earliest reforms—though they viewed it as necessary only in making women better homemakers.[117] One of the key dissident voices was that of Rokeya Sakhawat Hossain, who pushed for social reform and women's education; she critiqued women's subordination, seclusion, and patriarchy inherent in Islam.[118]

By the late nineteenth century, a cadre of English-educated, middle-class women embraced the political sphere. The Indian National Congress permitted women members, and ten women attended its first session in 1889 in Bombay.[119] Jayawardena calls upper-class Bengali women some of the "earliest pioneers of reform and political agitation."[120] By the early twentieth century, women had stepped into nationalist activities, including the *swadeshi* movement, which involved the boycott of British goods and was part of Indian's larger anticolonial movement. They joined the 1908 strikes by Bombay workers, organized *swadeshi* meetings, took the movement's message to village women, boycotted foreign goods, and donated money and jewelry to the nationalist cause.[121] With rising calls for the creation of Pakistan as a separate homeland for Muslims, young women from colleges joined the movement. At the same time, women's issues took a backseat to the nationalist cause. Matters important to the educated urban classes were the only exceptions. This included women's suffrage, which came to pass as provincial legislatures gave women the right to vote over the 1920s.[122] But real social reform remained unaddressed.

In postcolonial Pakistan, women continued to participate in public and political life. Elora Shehabuddin writes that in the immediate post-partition period, women previously engaged in anti-British national activism organized to aid refugees coming across the new border.[123] The movement was led by urban-based upper-class women. Ra'ana Liaquat Ali Khan, the wife of Pakistan's first prime minister, "took the lead in establishing formal women's organisations for emergency relief, social welfare projects, and even national defense."[124] She founded the All Pakistan Women's Association, a state-sponsored national organization led by government officials' wives.[125] Debates raged in the pages of the Bengali women's magazine *Begum* on topics ranging from women's health to the donning of purdah, and the need for women's rights, and especially education, in rural areas.[126] Women's organizations played a key role in the modification of Muslim family laws, and the Family Laws Ordinance of 1961 set the minimum age for marriage and gave women the right to divorce.[127]

In East Pakistan, women's political considerations were intertwined with the movement for autonomy—and later, independence. According to Shehabuddin, demands for women's education—for example, those seen in *Begum*—alongside the simultaneously raging language movement suggest that the writers did not perceive a conflict between their rights as Bengalis and their rights as women.[128] When the AL launched its movement for autonomy, young leftist women organized to free political prisoners, eventually leading to the formation of the Bangladesh Mahila Parishad.[129] In 1952, at the height of the language movement, a group of women protested the deaths at the February 21 rally and joined the demand for Bangla as national language.[130] As the Liberation War raged in 1971, images of women in saris and adornments, singing songs by Tagore, shaped the nationalist narrative. Women came together to assert their Bengali identity, representing Bengali culture in ways that were oppositional to Pakistani identity and thus distinguished the new Bengali nation from its neocolonial past.[131]

Following independence in 1971, Bangladesh's constitution granted women equal rights in the public sphere. And yet, in a manner similar to that in many postcolonial states, the state marginalized them.[132] In Bangladesh, development policies met some of women's immediate needs, while overlooking necessary social reforms. In family matters, religious laws still governed women's lives. Women's organizations pressured the state to adopt and implement new policies. They highlighted the needs of poor rural women, now heightened by the devastation of war, genocide, mass sexual violence, and disaster. As development aid poured into the country, they sought foreign funding for their projects. Nazneen and Sultan argue that increased dependence on foreign funding and the prioritization of donor demands led to their gradual NGO-ization, which they characterize as instances where feminist organizations adopt neoliberal organizational forms and practices of donors and policymakers at the national and global levels.[133] For example, small women's organizations and cooperatives that provided training and relief, and organized cultural activities for poor women, grew with donor funding. Typically operating out of members' households, they professionalized, competed for project funding, and even took on subcontracts.[134] They sought to increase services for their members, but instead moved further away from them and subscribed to a vertical accountability structure.[135]

NGO-ization brought mixed effects. One the one hand, women's organizations have embraced broad international agendas and global platforms. They champion gender mainstreaming and international treaties, such as the Convention on the Elimination of All Forms of Discrimination against Women (CEDAW). They participate in formulating national policies and plans. They have expanded their work and have engaged with large networks, promoting coalition building around particular issues, such as violence against women. On the other hand, they have neglected women's diverse realities and needs.[136] Like women's groups before them, these organizations are led by educated, urban elites who are far removed from the rural women they seek to help. Elora Chowdhury writes that women's organizations face the predicament of carving out "an autonomous space from colonialist discourses of donor-driven development agendas and the state's conflicting ideologies subscribing to these agendas," among other things.[137] And while these new relationships—both national and international—provide scope for new alliances, they also prevent the building of "radically transformative alliances" across communities.[138]

Many larger organizations have retained their autonomous agendas despite relying on donor funds. Some continue their radically transformative work. In their study of women's rights discourses in Bangladesh, Naomi Hossain et al. find that women's organizations emphasize "collective change, solidarity, and inclusiveness," whether through changes in society—that is, informal institutions—or through laws.[139] They use donor funds and alliances strategically while maintaining their core agendas. For example, Mahila Parishad and Naripokkho, both organizations that began on a voluntary basis, maintained their purpose despite taking donor funds; they used these funds to do what they already did, but better.[140]

Women's organizations coexist with other collective movements that involve women's issues among their goals. RMG workers—mostly women—have organized around workers' safety, higher minimum wages, weekly holidays, and the right to unionize, among other concerns. Protesters spill to the streets, blocking traffic and often clashing with the police in violent altercations in key manufacturing areas, such as Savar, in the outskirts of Dhaka. Although RMG workers can now unionize, the fight for wages and safety continues. Workers now receive Tk. 8,000 ($96) a month.[141] In 2011, the Tazreen factory fire killed 112 workers, and in 2013, the Rana Plaza collapse took another 1,134 lives.[142] Although 250 companies signed two initiatives to improve safety in over 2,000 factories, progress has been slow.[143] These organizing efforts challenge the state and capital instead of partnering with them.[144]

Islamic Politics

During the Zia-Ershad years, increasing aid from Islamic sources led to the rise of religious NGOs, many of whom delivered services alongside the secular NGOs. Geoffrey Wood writes that military regimes allied with NGOs and decentralized politics in order to overcome problems of legitimacy and constituency building, especially as they assumed power through military coups.[145] These Islamic NGOs financed new schools (madrasas), hospitals, and other service institutions whose values clashed with that of women's organizations and development agencies. Now, both Christian and Islamic NGOs work on various development projects, including credit provision and gender-related programs. Some reinforce religious and traditional norms and aim to create a new space for Islam in rural civil society.[146] Islamic NGOs have in particular developed a niche of their own; avoiding Western donor-favored sectors like agriculture, infrastructure, and poverty reduction, they have taken up health services and madrasa education.[147] Now, as national and Western NGOs have turned to these sectors, they have become contested terrain.[148] Bangladesh has reached almost universal primary education, and madrasas have played a significant role in this success. Lamia Karim writes that the number of government madrasas grew from 1,976 in 1978—when Zia came to power—to 15,661 in 2002, with a 653 percent rise in enrollment.[149] These government madrasas teach a range of subjects and combine religious studies with the national curriculum. They coexist with private religious schools called Qaomi madrasas that follow the Deobandi school of thought, which only teach the "Quran, *hadith*, *sunna*, and an orthodox interpretation of *sharia* to their students."[150] Wood writes that it is certainly not a coincidence that cultural and religious rejection of Bangladesh's secular founding principles occurred alongside a heightened sense of relative deprivation that arises from the exclusionary growth that urbanization, migration, and mobility have created.[151] Indeed, relative poverty and an absent state may have made religious organizations more attractive for rural Bangladeshis.

Local religious leaders have found new spaces to exercise their authority within this rapidly shifting social structure. The clergy opposed women's newfound mobility as un-Islamic, as it brought women out of purdah. Some groups have responded to NGO programs with violence and intimidation. Between 1993 and 1998, the resistance to NGO activities manifested in violence against women and NGO workers. Ali Riaz describes some incidents from 1994—in Bogra, a fatwa was decreed to close BRAC schools, and in the following days, twenty-five BRAC schools were set on fire; in Kishoreganj, six thousand mulberry trees grown by women were cut down; in Hobiganj, Grameen Bank staff were manhandled, and in Bogra, the bank was told to cease operations. NGO offices were attacked and their workers physically threatened.[152] Lamia Karim writes that in 1993, several women were publicly stoned by members of the local clergy for adultery, and one woman was burned to death. During this time, the clergy also "ostracized 500 families of women who worked with NGOs, forbade women to appear in public without the *burqa*, and forcibly divorced 50 women whose marriages they deemed 'un-Islamic.'"[153] In early 1997, a BRAC human rights initiative that involved fixing 700,000 posters throughout Bangladesh met with opposition from religious groups who tore down posters and organized demonstrations. The attackers teased, rebuked, and physically assaulted BRAC staff.[154]

At the same time, the narrative of secular NGOs as women's saviors and the clergy as their oppressors is a simplistic one. In her study of a conflict between local clergy and the NGO Proshika in 1998, Lamia Karim writes that the clergy in Brahmanbaria had declared a Proshika-organized women's public rally un-Islamic. And yet, ignoring numerous warnings by the clergy and police, Proshika leaders forced their members to attend. Soon, youths and clergy from the local madrasa attacked the rally, beating women attendees and tearing off their clothes.[155] Indeed, in rural Bangladesh, secular and Islamic elites have competed over the "hearts, minds, and souls of poor rural women"—by attempting to control their sexual and social behavior through legislation, their economic behavior by limiting NGO activity, and their political behavior via controlling their electoral participation.[156] The elite cast poor rural women as gullible and thus incapable of making their own decisions. While NGOs claim to liberate them and bring them out of their homes, the religious elite seek to save them spiritually and push them back into seclusion. But rural women act strategically. They join NGOs and work outside of their homes in order to meet their survival needs, while maintaining their piety simultaneously. In a setting where the state fails to meet their basic needs, they adjust their behaviors to the situation. Thus, they make choices "based on both material and spiritual concerns."[157]

Islamic groups have also secured a space in national politics. Since the 1990s, Islamic political parties have grown in number; between 1971 and 2005, thirty-five parties with an Islamist agenda competed in elections, and according to one estimate, between twenty-nine and fifty-three clandestine Islamist groups also operated in Bangladesh at that time.[158] The now-banned JI enjoyed a small but steady following in the past, and formed coalition governments with both the AL and the BNP. Unlike the above groups, JI has sought the support of rural women. In 1996, it campaigned with a reformed election manifesto that proposed changes in employment, inheritance rights, and practices that violate women's rights.[159] At the same time, a more radical form of religious politics has emerged in the form of extremist groups, such as the Hefazat-e-Islam, Jamaatul Mujahidin Bangladesh, Harkat ul-Jihad-al-Islami Bangladesh, and Hizb ut Tahrir.

CONCLUSION

This chapter tells a gendered story of Bangladesh. Until recently, women have appeared in the development discourse only as welfare recipients or actors driving development forward. Their social needs—particularly the need to break with patriarchal norms—have become part of the story only recently. I trace the four—perhaps not so distinct—areas where gender issues appear in the conversation. Bangladesh's governments have embraced an aid-based development strategy that has predominantly addressed gender issues in terms of welfare or women's contribution to development; women's rights and their place in the community have become a priority only recently. As NGOs grew in number, they shifted their focus from collective mobilization to service delivery. Some continue to do anti-oppression work in line with their radical beginnings. NGO expansion appears alongside a women's movement that has increasingly NGO-ized over time. Finally, a growing number of Islamic groups have continued to challenge the work of NGOs, complicating the terrain. In the next chapter, I move on to neoliberal development as it manifests in rural Bangladeshis' women's lives and present PS as an alternative development model.

CHAPTER 3

Poor Women's Politics

When the PS group from Taragonj gathered that day, its leaders informed members that their local UP office had received VGD cards. VGD is a highly coveted service. Unlike seasonal food-for-work programs, which require labor in exchange for services, it comes without conditions. Recipients receive rations along with training in income-generation strategies; while rations help them with daily subsistence needs, training provides long-term economic stability.[1] VGD is also one of Bangladesh's largest safety net initiatives. And yet, many eligible families do not belong to the program. In 2007, it served 750,000 women, a fraction of the 56 million who lived in dire poverty around that time.[2] Impoverished families may hear that new VGD cards have arrived at their local UP. Someone they knew could have received one. However, by the time they visit the UP office, cards often run out. At the national level, ministries allocate cards to localities based on poverty levels; poorer areas receive more cards. But once cards reach the UP, local officials decide who gets them. Historically, the rural elite have used government resources to maintain their political status, distributing services through clientelism—in exchange for labor, votes, and other services.[3] These days, poor families might get them. But rations still end up in the hands of wealthy recipients who sell them for profit.[4]

The women of Taragonj sought to change these patterns. They discussed which villagers most deserved these cards. They made a list of twelve people—seven from the group and five others from the community. They brought these names to their local UP member and asked him to serve the candidates on the list. The member would not take the list. He suggested that the women visit the chairman at the UP office. The chairman gave them the runaround as well. But the women would not take no for an answer. They visited the chairman over and over again, insisting that he serve his constituents. Eventually, he agreed to set cards aside for four people on the list—two PS members and two villagers. He asked that the PS members return with the recipients. They could collect the cards together.

As the Taragonj women bargained with the UP officials, they could have secured some cards for themselves. They were all poor women and thus eligible for the benefit. But they did not take advantage of their PS membership. Instead, they secured cards for needy community members. The women mentioned that some of their own group members were very poor, but strong and able to work; they could feed their families every day. "But many members of our community are unfit for labor," they added. The women chose to help these community members instead. Their behavior takes one by surprise. In rural Bangladesh, NGO and government programs have made ample resources available for those who know how to get them. But these women were not clamoring for services.

This chapter argues that in contrast to neoliberal development programs that rely on individual efforts, PS models a kind of development that centers on the collective. This includes challenging oppressive practices, deliberative decision making, and embeddedness in the community. Neoliberalism manifests most visibly in Bangladesh's national development strategies, which combine economic growth with aid-based rural development. But policies translate into development programs on the ground, which have a tangible effect on poor people's lives. This chapter begins by unpacking neoliberalism as it manifests in poor women's worlds. The second section explores how PS groups challenge injustices. The third section addresses PS groups' deliberative decision-making process. The fourth section sketches out the embeddedness of PS groups in their communities.

In the Field[5]

In the field, neoliberal development manifests most visibly in service delivery programs, many of which provide poor women with credit, employment opportunities, and income-generation training with the objective of bringing them into the market.[6] When benefits extend beyond livelihood programs—for example, services related to health, legal support, or awareness training—their success relies largely on women's individual action. Neoliberal development's focus on women can be traced back to 1975, when the United Nations officially recognized women as a priority for development. As the UN decade for Women (1975–1985) began, a group of policymakers challenged how the development industry viewed women from the global South—primarily in their gendered roles in the household, as daughters, wives, and mothers. These proponents of the Women in Development (WID) approach recognized that women could play a role in society that took them beyond their household responsibilities.[7] They viewed women as an untapped resource for development; they sought to bring women out of the household and into the workforce. Their approach had a dual purpose: by tying women's equality with economic efficiency, one could both emancipate women and contribute to economic development at the same time.[8]

WID theorists placed tremendous emphasis on individual action. They operated within the classic neoliberal space, viewing "individual rationality, self-interest, and profit maximization as quintessential human traits."[9] But human beings rarely operate in isolation from their environment; our actions are influenced by our social relations. For women from the global South, relationships codify particular standards of behavior that society deems appropriate. Women are not free to act as they choose; rather, their actions are shaped by informal institutions—the "rules-in-use." These institutions are gendered, where gender signifies "a feature of institutions and social structures, and a part of the symbolic realm of meaning-making, within which individuals and actors are 'nested.'"[10] They dictate how society views women, speaks of them, treats them, and expects them to behave. WID advocates neglected to consider that women's behaviors are intimately tied to their social worlds, with unequal labor burdens, socially constructed identities, and limited decision-making capacities in the household, as well as the freedom to pursue economic activity.[11]

For example, microfinance institutions (MFIs) give small loans to poor women without collateral, sometimes packaged with training and access to markets. MFIs boast incredible success. They have high loan return rates. The Nobel Prize–winning institution Grameen Bank claims to recover over 99 percent of its loans.[12] Studies have linked microfinance programs with increased income and expenditure, higher school enrollment, reduced malnutrition among children, and better use of health services.[13] However, MFIs' impact on the empowerment of women—their largest target group—remains contested. This is especially true for the poorest recipients.[14] Lending groups can embody existing power relationships in society.[15] In her work on MFIs in Bangladesh, Lamia Karim writes of the microfinance loan manager who views his client as an "autonomous and rational female subject who freely makes choices in the market," whereas in reality she is bound by social relationships and expectations.[16] MFIs administer loans through small groups of borrowers. Because poor women lack the assets to hold as physical collateral, groups provide an avenue for women to hold each other accountable through social collateral, their social relationships. As part of this arrangement, women support each other in their business endeavors. But when it comes to repaying loans, accountability also comes from peer pressure, coercion, and public shaming.[17] As women lack decision-making authority in the household, male family members may interfere with loan use.[18] Thus, they become publicly liable for funds they may have little control over. If they default, their reputation and social worth are at stake. This is particularly dangerous in Bangladesh, where women are the "traditional custodians of family honor," and for a woman to fail on her payments would be the ultimate mark of shame, not just for her, but also for her family.[19]

Institutional challenges limit the gains of neoliberal programs in other sectors as well. A qualitative study of adolescent mothers in rural Bangladesh found that many young mothers depend on their husbands, in-laws, and even fathers to make decisions regarding pregnancy and childbirth. When surrounded by family, the women in the study were unable to articulate their needs and seek appropriate care. Husbands felt uncomfortable with the number of people—especially male doctors—who would attend to their wives.[20] It is likely that young mothers refrain from expressing themselves freely to doctors, as they are expected to practice seclusion—this may include physical veiling, restricted physical mobility, and limited interactions with men, especially outside of the household.

Neoliberalism assumes that individual rationality, self-interest, and profit maximization are the quintessential human traits.[21] These are also deeply individual traits. In *Development as Freedom*, Amartya Sen speaks of human development as enhancing human capabilities—that is, increasing people's abilities to make choices freely—from multiple dimensions, such as the provision of basic services, gender equality, and basic political and civil rights.[22] Sen rejects the idea that economic development alone brings human development. Rather, he argues that people cannot make choices freely when they live without basic resources. Nor can they thrive under oppressive regimes and inequitable institutions. But Sen places tremendous emphasis on individual human action. In a critique of *Development as Freedom*, Peter Evans argues, "Classic liberal exaltation of the individual and an implicit acceptance of individual (as opposed to social) preferences as exogenous" characterize this work.[23] For Evans, the less privileged cannot attain this freedom through individual action alone. Rather, organized collectivities like unions, political parties, and women's groups provide an important space for creating "shared values and preferences, and instruments for pursuing them, even in the face of powerful opposition."[24] The next section explores how PS presents such a model.

CHALLENGING OPPRESSION

PS groups challenge everyday injustices against the poor, especially poor women. Their efforts are organized into four program objectives, which I classify into three broad areas.[25] First, PS groups negotiate with government and NGO service providers to ensure that resources and services reach the rural poor. Table 3.1 presents selective descriptives on PS structure, operations, and activities. It shows that over 98 percent of PS groups undertook at least one drive to access safety nets for community members; the data reflect a one-year period between 2008 and 2010.[26] Some, like the Taragonj PS, pursued services multiple times. In addition to VGD cards, they also approached the UP for twenty-two VGF cards, eventually receiving eleven.

TABLE 3.1

WHAT PS GROUPS DO: STRUCTURE, OPERATIONS, AND ACTIVITIES

		N	Mean
STRUCTURE AND OPERATIONS			
Rural (%)		671	92.996
Independent PS groups (%)[1]		671	18.629
PS age (mean no. of years)		671	7.988 (3.690)
PS size (mean)		670	60.030 (18.864)
Current VO members in PS (%)		534	46.079 (23.381)
Current non-BRAC NGO members in PS (%)		534	29.918 (18.415)
No current NGO membership (%)		534	23.416 (18.780)
Muslim (%)		653	85.860 (27.887)
Hindu (%)		666	12.271 (25.870)
Ranking (%)[2]	A	666	20.871
	B		55.556
	C		23.574
Frequency of executive meetings (%)	<2 months	623	87.319
	2–6 months		9.791
	>7 months		2.889
Frequency of general meetings (%)	<2 months	628	88.535
	2–6 months		9.395
	>7 months		2.070
ACTIVITIES[3]			
Distributive Politics			
Groups pursuing social safety nets (%)		671	98.063
PS members assisted (mean)		671	17.200 (19.456)
Community members assisted (mean)		671	9.218 (16.159)
Rule of Law			
Groups participating in *shalish* (%)[4]			27.720

(continued)

TABLE 3.1

WHAT PS GROUPS DO: STRUCTURE, OPERATIONS, AND ACTIVITIES *(continued)*

	N	Mean
Groups resolving legal issues for PS members (%)	671	15.798
Groups resolving legal issues in community (%)	671	10.879
Local Governance		
Community initiatives for PS members (%)	671	34.873
Community initiatives for villagers (%)	671	31.893
PS members contested local elections (% PS)	437	10.755
PS members elected to UP (% candidates)	52	46.154

Note: Standard deviation in parentheses.

[1] These PS groups run without PO support.

[2] POs rate each PS group as A, B, or C, based on several criteria, such as the ability to hold meetings, invite guests, and bargain for services. The best PS groups score an A; the worst PS groups score a C.

[3] The data reflect a one-year period between 2008 and 2010. For groups interviewed in 2009, this is from 2008 to 2009, and for groups interviewed in 2010, it is from 2009 to 2010.

[4] Only includes groups playing an active role in *shalish.*

PS groups increase poor people's access to the law. They prevent and respond to violence, such as intervening in the case of dowry and child marriage. They record and report cases of extreme violence in the community.[27] They advocate for the poor—and particularly poor women—in informal decision-making spaces like *shalish* (village court). And they connect survivors of violence to legal and medical support, often with the help of BRAC staff—program organizers (POs) from CEP, health, and legal aid programs. More than a quarter of PS groups had active participants in *shalish*, which women typically avoided; 15.798 percent resolved at least one incidence of violence within their own group, and 10.879 percent resolved an issue in the community (table 3.1).

Finally, PS groups enhance women's representation in local governance, sometimes by having their members run for elected local committees—and even the local government—and elsewhere by taking on local initiatives themselves. These efforts place PS members center stage representing the poor in local governance. Sometimes, PS members served as elected members in the UP and local committees. During the 2003 local election, 10.755 percent of PS groups had at least one group member run for local government; over 46 percent of those candidates won (table 3.1). Elsewhere, they do what the local government should, but fails to do. They undertake development projects that range from building roads, mosques, and bridges, to drives that ensure village children attend school. A small number of PS members belong to governing committees set up by NGOs. In the next section, I examine how PS members embrace deliberative decision making.

Deliberation

PS members hold long conversations and debates rooted in practical, everyday concerns. From identifying problems to brainstorming for solutions, they make decisions together. They discuss community issues, identify potential solutions to problems, and pursue a course of action. For example, the Taragonj PS chose potential service recipients in consultation with their community—collectively, transparently, and, since meetings are held in an open space and can attract passersby, perhaps even with a little help from other villagers. Such deliberative decision making differs dramatically from the neoliberal program, where empowerment is an individual responsibility.

Each PS has two governing entities, an eleven-member executive committee (EC) and a larger general body, which includes all members. The groups meet in alternate months. The executive body handles logistical matters, while all critical learning and action happen at the general meeting.[28] Table 3.2 lists meeting agenda items for the last-held meetings; it shows that PS leaders handle logistical matters at their EC meetings, leaving initiatives that require extensive discussion and decision making—for example, welfare, health and sanitation, children's education—for the general body.

A PS group in Chapai Nawabganj had four items on its EC meeting agenda. Leaders tracked progress on current initiatives and chose a date and time for their next general meeting. Then, they discussed their big agenda item. PS groups are required to invite *poramorshodatas* (learning advisers) to lead guided discussions on community issues, such as hygiene, dowry, and underage marriage. The leaders identified a potential adviser. The general meeting was a far more exciting affair. Gathering so many attendees in one place could get chaotic; the average group had sixty members, and meetings required quorum. Leaders typically organized meetings in the open air, perhaps outside the president's home, turning private verandahs and courtyards into public spaces. They took attendance, reported progress on initiatives, and designated responsibilities for

TABLE 3.2

MEETING AGENDAS (N = 671)

Issue	EC meeting (% of PS)	General meeting (% of PS)
OPERATIONS		
Logistics	82.563	61.401
Ensuring attendance	77.347	8.793
Training	2.534	6.259
PS elections	2.385	7.452
INITIATIVES		
Welfare	28.912	61.401
Education	18.331	34.724
Health	13.562	33.830
Community initiatives	16.692	33.532
Human rights violations	6.259	3.577

future projects. General members raised new issues. Learning advisers led animated conversations. Members donated money to a common fund for emergency projects.[29]

PS leaders placed tremendous emphasis on meeting attendance. When EC members reported on their last meeting activity, ensuring attendance came up as an important agenda item, trailing close behind logistics (table 3.2). One group from Thakurgaon picked a future meeting date at the very beginning of their gathering. They settled for November 8, 2019, at 9 A.M. They said, "We did this together so that everyone could attend. We also asked each member to bring at least two members from their neighborhood with them." The act of choosing a meeting date together creates consensus and accountability; now that members had agreed that this time works for them, they were obligated to attend. Indeed, the program's operational guidebook emphasizes the importance of meetings. It states that meetings connect members, and in-person conversations can help the women solve individual and collective social problems. They may learn new life skills from each other.[30]

But large meetings can be difficult to organize. Poor women play multiple roles—they cook, clean, and raise children at home; labor in the field or at other people's homes; and in the NGO era, often run small businesses simultaneously. In a world where women already bear the double burden of labor in the household and outside, attending PS meetings becomes one more thing that they have to do. The women from Thakurgaon decided to divide and conquer. Each EC member would head out on meeting day and knock on people's doors. They would gather members from their own neighborhood and walk to the meeting spot together. This was difficult, the EC leaders said. No one wants to take the responsibility of bringing others. But in the end, the group had its quorum.

PS is not unique in its approach. Lauren Leve and Anuradha Sharma study similar collective behavior within development programs in Nepal and India, respectively; both programs are inspired by Paulo Freire's conscientization approach and embrace critical thinking as an integral component.[31] In *Pedagogy of the Oppressed*, Brazilian educator and philosopher Paulo Freire advocates for a participatory and action-oriented pedagogy for the impoverished, which differs dramatically from what he calls the "banking system of education."[32] Banking education has the teacher assume students' ignorance and bestow knowledge on the student. But it also inhibits creative power. Freire writes, "The former attempts to maintain the *submersion* of consciousness; the latter strives for the *emergence* of consciousness and *critical intervention* in reality." Students uncover problems in their own lives and in the world and feel compelled to challenge them.[33] This kind of learning is deliberative and grounded in reality. It frees learners to develop their own understanding of the world and motivates action that stems from this knowledge. In the case of PS, meetings become a space where members construct a collective understanding of their challenges. Deliberations allow each group to govern based on their particular needs. Sharma studies Mahila Samakhya, a rural women's empowerment initiative that, like PS groups, emphasizes "women's *collective*, anti-oppression-focused political work."[34] Leve studies the work of Development for All in Nepal, a program that combined "community development, literacy learning, and critical empowerment in a way that would transform the consciousness of its participants."[35] In Bangladesh, NGOs like Naripokkho and Nijera Kori have pioneered such collective mobilization. As of 2002, Nijera Kori organized 8,622 groups across the country engaging over 180,000 people. The groups brought together village men and women to learn, engage, and discuss ideas through training and cultural activities. Naila Kabeer writes that through training and social activities, group members grasp some of the theoretical explanations for their condition—and in particular, the deeper roots of oppression—that they can reflect on and analyze, both in relation to their own condition and poor people's struggles.[36] BRAC, too, embraces training as a huge part of its mandate. And while some may find the model of training to be top-down, perhaps even a manifestation of the neoliberal enterprise, how one conducts trainings and what training recipients do with their learnings are an important part of the story. Deliberation allows poor people to take ownership of their own development as well as that of the community. They make and enforce decisions together, independent of external influence.

EMBEDDEDNESS

PS groups are vertically and horizontally embedded in their communities. In *Embedded Autonomy*, Peter Evans defines embeddedness as "a concrete set of social ties that binds the state to society and provides institutionalized channels for the continual negotiation and renegotiation of goals and policies."[37] Evans sets up his work in the context of the 1990s development industry, when the declining influence of neoliberalism paved the way for institutional alternatives. This new body of literature pushed back against neo-utilitarian development models; while the latter examined the state in terms of the rational, utilitarian behavior of individual actors, institutional approaches prioritized relationships between state and society.[38] One can trace the concept further back to Karl Polanyi, who had written in *The Great Transformation* that markets and societies were historically embedded in each other. Man may not necessarily act to protect his self-interest, but rather to "safeguard his social standing[,] his social claims, his social assets."[39] Thus people live in the context of social relationships. For Polanyi, industrial capital seeks to dis-embed our economic and social lives. But embeddedness continues to exist in industrial society. Indeed, as sociological institutionalists would argue, self-interest itself is influenced by one's embeddedness in one's cultural and organizational life. Relationships define the interests that people develop, and in fact, the many relationships that individuals are embedded in would make rational behavior absurd.[40]

Embedded Autonomy explores state-society linkages—particularly relationships between state and industrial capital—at the macro level.[41] At the meso and micro levels, relationships are often encapsulated in social capital, or "networks, norms and social trust that facilitate coordination and cooperation for mutual benefit."[42] Based on his work in Italy, Robert Putnam argues that local organizations have the capacity to create such linkages. In contrast to Evans's embeddedness, which refers to vertical state-society relationships, Putnam's speaks to horizontal linkages between actors in society. In the global South, both vertical and horizontal relationships have created new spaces for negotiation. Anirudh Krishna discovers that in north India, social capital influences participation when enhanced through capable agency. Here, independent agents have filled an institutional gap left by weak political parties; while horizontal associations provide the glue that bind society together, the institutional capacity of villages provides agency, the gear for participation.[43] In rural China, Lily Tsai finds that embeddedness in solidary local organizations—groups with shared moral obligations and interests—along with how encompassing they are allow villagers to hold public officials accountable through informal accountability in the absence of democratic accountability. Tsai measures embeddedness as local officials' memberships in solidarity groups and encompassing as groups that are open to everyone.[44] In both instances, vertical and horizontal relationships

open up spaces for negotiation. Thus, embeddedness extends beyond relationships between state and society, and encapsulates relationships between different societal actors.

In rural Bangladesh, embeddedness manifests in a web of relationships
between actors. NGOs have created new ties that are vertical, horizontal, and
overlapping. They have developed an alternate infrastructure to that of the state,
with offices dispersed in the remotest of locations, community-based staff who
bring services to people's doorsteps, and local-level beneficiary groups that help
administer services. PS groups exist in a world where ample social ties already
exist. They are now part of this changing landscape. Their membership encompasses an extensive set of ties. These relationships expand vertically to service
providers through contacts at the UP and NGOs, and horizontally through connections with other NGO programs. Figure 3.1 compares PS leaders with average PS members on demographics. It shows that over 65 percent of PS members
also belong to another NGO and that over 40 percent are members of the BRAC
VO. In fact, NGO networks are so dense in rural Bangladesh that it is almost
impossible to find women who have never belonged to one.

In the Community

CEP POs set up PS groups after multiple conversations within the community.
When they create new PS groups, they first scope out potential wards based on
levels of poverty. They get to know local stakeholders, including government officials, the local elite, influential families, and staff from other NGO programs
operating in the area. They introduce the concept of PS to the community over
multiple conversations. They emphasize how the group would make poor people's
lives better. Leaders from one PS group said, "BRAC *bhai* (brothers) came to our
area and talked to some of us about creating Polli Shomaj. They sat down with
us a few times." Subsequently, BRAC officials gathered the local elite. By attending discussions, the local elite would be endorsing the group.

Some PS groups identify men as important allies. A small percentage
(4 percent) had one or more male members. Others invite men to meetings or
seek their advice from time to time. One group mentioned that men found
their discussions interesting; they wanted to know more about child marriage,
dowry, and other social issues. When asked how men react to their work,
another group remarked that men are "very" interested in their activities. Men
would show up at meeting venues and watch enthusiastically. The women's
response conveyed a hint of sarcasm, suggesting that men wanted to keep tabs
on women's activities. But these PS groups also recognized the benefit of letting
men in. Male allies helped embed them in spaces like the UP that typically kept
women out.

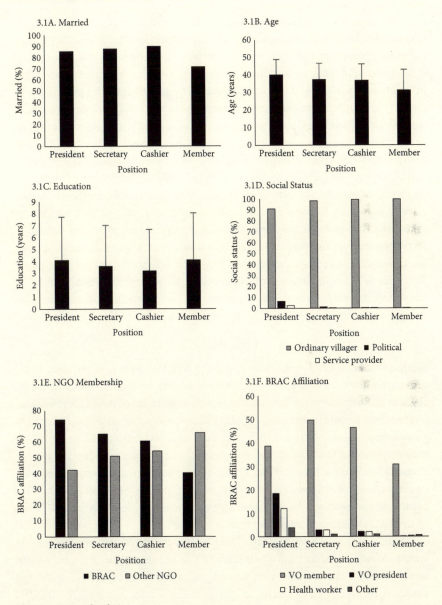

Figure 3.1. Leadership

Leadership

PS groups elect leaders who are embedded in their communities. Figure 3.1 shows that presidents are of higher socioeconomic status than general members; they are more educated, economically better off, and more likely to come from influential families. PS members choose these women deliberately, as vertical connections open up access to the UP. They also pick eloquent and confident leaders—typically wealthier, educated members—who can negotiate with decision makers. Socially connected leaders improve their groups' performance. CEP staff rank their PS groups into three categories—A, B, and C—based on how well they operate. A higher percentage of leaders from A category groups come from influential families (7.469 percent) compared to leaders from B (4.018 percent) and C (2.375 percent) category groups. Leaders who lack vertical networks build them. They embed themselves into governing processes by forging relationships with UP officials, and sometimes having a group member run for office. Indeed, many successful groups had a PS member in the UP. A 2005 RED report found that PS groups with leaders as elected UP members acquired more resources.[45]

PS groups also elect leaders with extensive horizontal networks. These women know community members and display compassion toward the poor. When asked why they have elected the same woman as president term after term, one PS from Jamalpur said that their president stood by others during times of trouble and could connect with everybody.[46] Another PS had re-elected their president Amena multiple times, because "everyone knows her and she always helps the poor." In both instances, leaders' horizontal embeddedness in and compassion for the community were integral to realizing poor peoples' needs.

PS and BRAC

Being a BRAC program embeds PS groups in NGO networks. At the same time, groups are divorced from the larger enterprise, partly by design and partly by chance. Initially, the program brought together members of the VO, the village-level women's lending group for BRAC's microfinance program. Although PS groups draw women well beyond the VO now, they collaborate with other BRAC programs in their localities. BRAC programs like health and legal aid may engage PS groups to disseminate services. Often, when community members need particular services, PS members bring them to the CEP PO, who facilitates further connections—for example, by connecting survivors of violence with BRAC legal or health clinics at the subdistrict level.

PS members belong to multiple NGOs. But the BRAC influence remains strong. Many PS leaders have belonged to the VO or served as BRAC health workers at some point, even performing leadership roles before being elected executive officers (figure 3.1). One PS group in Madargonj, Jamalpur, elected the same president repeatedly. Its members felt that Momena knew how to gather members for meetings. Momena was a VO president for ten years. Her experience with the VO had made her a good organizer. And perhaps running a small business with her microfinance loan increased her interactions with the community. PS members probably came to meetings under her leadership because they knew her.

Despite strong ties to the BRAC family, the women ran the organization freely. The group was intended to operate this way. In the words of a senior CEP official, the ultimate goal would be for all PS groups to exist independently of any BRAC support. Once some groups ran on their own, the program could divert support to setting up new groups. This does not mean that PS operates without any oversight. POs help PS leaders run the organization. This mixed governance model is not unlike Sharma's Mahila Samakhya in India, which embraces both state bureaucratic procedures and feminist action as a vehicle for subaltern women to hold the state accountable.[47] In this case, switch the Indian state with the largest development organization in the world.

A number of groups run without PO support. In the field, POs call them independent PS groups.[48] But even supervised groups often saw limited PO engagement. POs are tasked with administrative matters only. They help organize meetings, maintain records, connect members with local institutions, and submit written documentation to BRAC offices. But some PS groups are so far removed from the organization that PS members could not identify their PO by name. In order to get the BRAC side of the story, the research team interviewed POs and BRAC staff at local offices. There was consensus among BRAC staff that POs were seriously overstretched in their responsibilities. They spent their days traveling between the office and meeting spots, rushing from one meeting to another, and scurrying back to the local office by early afternoon, where they would write reports for the headquarters and preserve them in registers and files. But BRAC local staff felt that POs could provide the support that PS groups needed.

Still, PS groups remain locked in a power struggle with their POs. This manifests in record-keeping procedures. Groups maintain meeting records in a register, ideally stored close to the meeting spot and accessible to officers at all times.[49] The task of writing in it often falls on the group's young adult member, a *kishori netri* (youth leader), chosen from BRAC's Adolescent Development Program. Many PS members could not read or write. But with *kishori netris* keeping records, the group could assert ownership over their registers. Some groups maintained years-old registers with worn-out sheets and filled-in pages. They documented their work well, some going as far as recording the names of service recipients. Elsewhere, registers were missing or brand new, with little information beyond a handful of meeting dates. Older registers had disappeared with staffing changes; when POs left, they took registers with them. The women resented this. They wanted some material assistance from BRAC—for example, a supply of register books and space in the BRAC office to store it—but desired autonomy over their own affairs.

CONCLUSION

PS groups present an alternative to the neoliberal development model. The two approaches differ in their goals. While neoliberal development centers on service delivery, PS challenges oppression and injustices against the poor, and especially poor women. The two models are not entirely indistinguishable; in the field, programs often blend the best characteristics of both. Indeed, the PS story suggests that it is possible to implement alternative development models without challenging or competing with service delivery programs. The collective development model's success rests on two additional factors. Deliberative decision making turns development into a discursive process. PS groups discuss new information—including BRAC messaging—and apply it to their everyday problems, creating room for mobilization in a way that individualized awareness raising campaigns rarely can. Finally, groups are deeply embedded in their communities, which becomes instrumental to their performance, as I write in later chapters. Such embeddedness occurs by design, strategic choices that members make, and context. By design, the group is established in consultation with local stakeholders. Its members choose connected leaders deliberately. And the NGO-infused villages of Bangladesh create a world where women find themselves in overlapping personal networks. Indeed, service delivery programs have created a development infrastructure that is crucial for PS operations.

The last two chapters have set the stage for the rest of the book. Part II moves on to scoping formal and informal institutions. These chapters explore the rules-in-use—the dos and don'ts on the ground—and gauge whether something different is happening in PS areas. To begin, chapter 4 addresses distributive politics.

Formal and Informal Institutions

CHAPTER 4

Clients, Rules, and Transactions

Anowara was a fortunate woman. She had recently received a VGF card from her local UP office. VGF is a government-run social safety net program that provides ration cards for low-income and female-headed households. Recipients use cards to pick up free food grains every few months. Anowara was a good candidate. She lived in Sirajganj, a district where the river Jamuna and its tributaries erode vast swaths of land, displacing vulnerable households every year. She belonged to a poor and rather large family. At twenty, Anowara was a young mother. She worked as an informal day laborer, doing housekeeping work for better-off villagers. Rural Bangladeshis refer to her profession as *grihosthali*, a job reserved for the poorest women. Having attended school for a mere two years, she was not qualified for much else.

Bangladeshi villagers rarely got government services without knowing the right people. One would typically rely on a neighbor or relative with links to the local government. Despite her obvious eligibility, Anowara lacked such social connections. Two of her acquaintances sought her advice in the matter. Now that she had acquired cards for herself, perhaps she could help them as well. Like Anowara, the women came from poor families. They would certainly qualify. Anowara suggested that her friends visit their female UP member, Jahanara.[1] "Tell her [Jahanara] about your troubles. She is a good person. If she sympathizes, she may give you VGF rice," she instructed. Anowara mentioned during her interview that her friends had visited Jahanara. "They told her about their difficult and painful lives [in poverty], she gave them VGF rice."

In Patuakhali, Shiuli found herself in a different situation. She had requested a VGD card from the local UP office. At one point, Shiuli's sister-in-law said to her, "I've heard that you put down your name for a VGD card." Shiuli confirmed that she did manage to get on the list, but had to pay the UP office for it. Shiuli's sister-in-law insisted that Shiuli ask whether another card could be acquired. She was willing to pay. That same evening, Shiuli took her to the UP office and urged their local UP member to add her name to the list of potential beneficiaries. "She is very poor," Shiuli pleaded. Eventually, both women received cards.

Both Anowara and Shiuli qualified for government safety nets. Their family incomes were similar. Shiuli's family earned Tk. 57,000 (US$680) yearly, whereas Anowara's family earned Tk. 67,400 (US$804) yearly. At twenty-four, Shiuli was only slightly older than Anowara. She had five years of formal schooling compared to Anowara's two years. And like Sirajganj, Patuakhali is highly vulnerable to river erosion. But their experiences were far from similar. In Sirajganj, Anowara trusted her female UP official to follow the formal rules for distributing welfare goods. She expected that Jahanara Parvez would give out services to the most eligible candidates, and that her two acquaintances might receive VGD cards if they could convince Jahanara of their precarious situations. But in Potuakhali, Shiuli's advice to her sister-in-law bore an expectation that in her area, services did not come for free.

This chapter argues that in rural Bangladesh, distributive politics—decisions regarding who gets services and how—embodies multiple, overlapping institutions, and that these practices are fundamentally different in PS areas. First, the rules-in-use—the dos and don'ts on the ground—can embody both formal and informal rules. Sometimes, providers distribute resources based on formal rules. Anowara's experience fell within this category. But often, the rules-in-use deviate from formal rules. They embody informal institutions, which, in Shiuli's case, involved a one-time monetary transaction. I identify two kinds of informal rules, clientelism and transactionalism, that coexist with formal rules.

When PS members receive goods, the rules of the game are different from those applying to the control group. PS members are more likely to acquire services via transactionalism over clientelism. When the quality of PS groups is taken into consideration, a higher percentage of exchanges involving members of better-performing PS groups embody formal rules. PS members are also embedded in a wider network of relationships, which manifests in how they receive services. In Bangladeshi villages, services come from both government and nongovernment sources. Government providers include the UP, schoolteachers, and government health workers, whereas nongovernmental sources include NGO offices and field staff. These providers make decisions every day regarding who receives what goods and services. Instead of approaching UP staff directly, villagers now acquire services through diverse personal networks. These variations are more prominent among PS members.

The first section of this chapter explores the rules-in-use—clientelism, transactionalism, and formal rules. The second section explores how PS groups differ from the control group. I compare the service networks of both groups followed by types of exchange.

Figure 4.1A. Types of Exchange (N = 4,723)   Figure 4.1B. Types of Clientelism (N = 605)

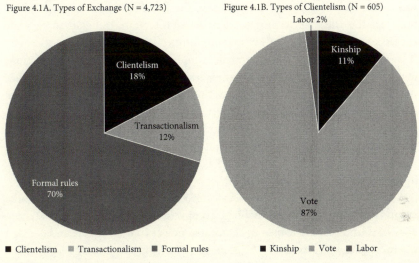

■ Clientelism   ■ Transactionalism   ■ Formal rules   ■ Kinship   ■ Vote   ■ Labor

Figure 4.1. Types of Exchange

Rules-in-Use

Rural Bangladeshis access services through multiple and overlapping practices. Figure 4.1 illustrates how respondents have received services; the numbers reflect a two-year period between 2007 and 2010.[2] While the vast majority of exchanges involve formal rules—service providers distribute them free of cost, without conditions, as they are expected to—informal institutions persist. A range of services are distributed through traditional clientelist practices and what I identify as transactionalism, a short-term monetary transaction whereby recipients secure services through a payment.

Clientelism

Historically, clientelism dominated distributive politics in Bangladeshi villages. It still exists despite the many societal changes that NGOs, migration, industrialization, and capitalism have brought (figure 4.1a). In its broadest iteration, clientelism refers to an unequal relationship between patrons (the rural elite) and clients (villagers) grounded in some kind of political support. This relationship can be face to face or network-based, binding or nonbinding, short- or long-term, may involve votes or other support from the client, and can exist in both election and nonelection periods. James Scott defines the relationship between patrons and their clients as "a largely instrumental friendship in which an individual of higher socioeconomic status (patron) uses his own influence and resources to provide protection or benefits, or both, for a person of lower status (client) who, for his part, reciprocates by offering general support and assistance, including personal services, to the patron."[3] Scott's conceptualization sees the client as seeking security and protection, things that the state should provide, but often fails to in communities with poverty or a weak state.[4] It takes a broader approach, where client support takes place in both elections and beyond. This is important for Bangladesh, where patrons maintain influence through traditional and elected positions, and the rural poor—potential clients—navigate intricate personal networks to pursue services. As figure 4.1b illustrates, clientelism manifests in a range of exchanges; the rural poor receive services due to kinship ties, labor relations, and in exchange for votes. But these varieties of clientelism are not mutually exclusive—they have been historically intertwined.

Previously, rural Bangladeshi service providers formed clientelist networks around tight-knit kinship and political groups. In the early 1980s, the RED study *The Net* found that a few men concentrated power in their hands and decided whether villagers received services or employment, or exercised their legal rights. These men relied on their personal wealth, supporters, thugs, official positions, and a "complex net of co-operative connections with other powerful men including the government officers."[5] They controlled food supply for patronage, for example, by distributing goods from the food for work program among their relatives and faction members, and closing off access for rivals or dissenting groups.[6] Another RED study, *Who Gets What and Why*, outlines similar patterns in the village of Dhankura, where leaders of the two biggest kinship groups—those having common ancestry—headed two political factions and maintained connections with union and thana-level politics. These officials could "guarantee whether one's land documents are legal and upheld, whether one gets the employment one seeks, whether one can avail institutional sources of credit whether one's life and property are secure, whether one's rights under law are upheld and much more."[7] These patterns resemble neopatrimonialism in Africa, which, too, "originates in the African extended family, with the dominance of older males and strong interpersonal ties," and now invades political institutions in the form of big men and personal political relationships.[8]

At the time, many of these big men maintained power through land ownership, which granted status and labor patronage.[9] Some held elected office, whereas others were *shomaj* heads, traditional leaders who maintained control over kinship and neighborhood groups.[10] They built a client base from hired labor who worked the land. All landowners who employed permanent workers maintained a political orientation and practiced factional politics. In addition to wages, they gave their clients financial assistance, social support, legal advice, and connections to public resources, among other things. In turn, clients provided labor, services, and political support.[11] Thus, the clientelist relationships extended beyond election periods. Sometimes they spanned generations. Kinship ties dominated these exchanges.[12] Landowners typically hired their kin to work the fields—they were easily available during times of acute labor shortage—and also employed neighbors from time to time. Thus land became a political investment, and labor, kinship, and factional politics intersected in intricate ways.[13]

Typically, the patron-client relationship embodies reciprocity. Some scholars— including Scott—depict clientelism as a mutually beneficial friendship that is distinct from coercive bonds linked to land or debt.[14] And yet, given the entangled nature of land, kinship, factional, and electoral ties of the past, traditional clientelism can trap the poorest families in coercive relationships that transcend time. In their study on engaging elite support for a BRAC program catering to the ultra-poor, Naomi Hossain and Imran Matin write that social relations are still organized along hierarchical patronage lines. While the moderate poor can access these networks, the ultra-poor cannot. For the ultra-poor, such support comes at the high cost of free or highly subsidized labor, which may "endure over generations" and be "unusually demeaning or arduous."[15]

Now, NGOs have changed how rural Bangladeshis receive resources. Many compete with the local government to distribute both donor and government-funded benefits as parallel providers, government partners, or subcontractors. Old clientelist relationships are also shifting. With a wealth of resources and multiple hands distributing them, the net has gradually opened up and dispersed the power once concentrated within closed networks. NGOs have forced the rural elite to maintain their power in diverse ways. David Lewis and Abul Hossain studied three villages in 2004—almost thirty-five years after the two BRAC studies—and found tremendous variation in power structures. They argue that the "net" is becoming more open and less constraining for poor people. At the village level, decision makers include both formal and informal power holders— gusti [kinship group] patrilineages, samaj [society or community] social groups, informal leadership, mosque/temple committees, shalish informal courts, philanthropic activities, local gherao movements, and social movements.[16]

These changes are not due to NGOs alone. Rather, they emanate from broader transformations in livelihood mechanisms; increased migration (for example, to work abroad or in cities), access to education, shifting landholding patterns, and the capital and skills that NGOs inject into rural society. Over time, and in conjunction with increasing landlessness, land- and kinship-based loyalties have given way to new relationships that are centered on employment and the market.[17] Ashram Village, another RED study, finds that these shifts began as early as the 1970s. Although the resource structure in rural Bangladesh was still primarily based on land, increasing landlessness was pushing people to other forms of sustenance.[18] At the time, kinship ties remained strong because diversified income avenues did not exist. As the resource structure shifted, these traditional relationships ceased to dominate rural life—for example, if landless labors began trading, they would rely less on their wealthy kin.[19] These changes freed both the rural poor and the rural elite from a codependent relationship; the former could access resources in diverse ways, and the latter no longer needed to provide charity, especially during crises.[20]

Now, distributive practices have diversified beyond the old clientelism—a binding, long-term relationship based on land and kinship—to a new electoral clientelism based on votes. Figure 4.1a illustrates that generational labor obligations (2 percent) and kinship (11 percent)—typically embodying coercive relationships—make up a very small percentage of exchanges. These relationships still exist. A 2002 study finds that when it comes to the chronically poor, those who are "connected to local elites mostly as house-helps or their husbands as potential election helps and/or managing agricultural labour during the peak *boro* [type of rice cultivation] harvest season" receive VGD cards.[21] But providers also distribute a large percentage of services free of cost and through electoral clientelism (figure 4.1a, b). This marks a major shift in service delivery patterns from the way the BRAC series portrays 1970s Bangladesh.

As old ties disintegrate, they make room for the less-binding and less-coercive electoral clientelism. Figure 4.1b illustrates that among the different types of clientelist exchanges, the vast majority entail swapping services for votes (86.446 percent). Indeed, some scholars study clientelism specifically through the lens of electoral mobilization, where clients promise votes for services both during and beyond election periods.[22] For example, Susan Stokes defies clientelism as the "proffering of material goods in return for electoral support."[23] Herbert Kitschelt and Steven Wilkinson argue that in many countries, including the advanced industrial democracies, accountability does not come from politicians delivering collective goods or improving incomes. In contrast to the typically Western model of responsible party government, where parties and candidates that draw voters using their policy platforms, citizen-politician linkages are based on material exchanges in clientelistic societies. And instead of democratic accountability, one finds clientelistic accountability, which "represents a transaction, the direct exchange of a citizen's vote, in return for direct payments or continuing access to employment, goods, and services."[24] But electoral clientelism is not a simple one-time trade. Nor does it resemble binding, coercive relationships of the past. In her study on rural Pakistan, Shandana Khan Mohmand defines clientelism as "an asymmetrical but instrumental, short term, quid pro quo relationship in which clients are in face-to-face contact with a local patron of higher status, but with whom they are able to strategically exchange and negotiate their vote for access to certain benefits."[25] By Mohmand's definition, electoral clientelism allows bargaining on the part of the client. Thus it acknowledges clients' agency, which is lacking in the binding and coercive old clientelism. In addition, recipients who engage in electoral clientelism are not necessarily part of the provider's patronage networks. Thus, clientelist relationships are getting looser with the unraveling net, and old traditional ties—coercive, perhaps transcending generations—are in decline.

Transactionalism

Transactionalism—a new informal institution—has emerged among these overlapping practices. In transactional exchanges, poor candidates access resources for a material cost, often a designated fee. Such monetary exchanges are not unusual in places with ineffective service delivery mechanisms. Jennifer Bussell writes that in many patronage democracies, there is strong demand for such informal routes to obtaining services, particularly through "influential intermediaries." Citizens may engage in "petty corruption, including the payment of 'speed' money," or involve intermediaries, including politicians or local-level organizations.[26] Transactionalism is an informal institution. Like clientelism, it defies formal rules; it can even be categorized as an illegal exchange[27] or a type of corruption.[28] It comes with conditions—a monetary cost for the client. But unlike clientelism, it is not based on political support. Rather, clients partake in a one-time exchange with no political or behavioral obligations. Unlike traditional clientelism, it is encompassing and allows poor people like Shiuli to access services that would otherwise be out of their reach. And very often, recipients pay for services willingly, as the benefits outweigh the cost.

When their local UP received some latrines, Maya's friend Neela asked her for a favor—could Maya reach out to the UP on her behalf? Neela lived in another village, and the two women knew each other because their husbands worked together. She complained that she had to visit other people's homes to use the toilet. Maya should know how cumbersome this was. Maya's cousin was a UP member and would perhaps listen to her. Maya responded, "There is no latrine without money here." Neela agreed to pay. She had brought money with her and handed it over to Maya, who later enacted the transaction. Because Maya's relative was their UP member, Neela expected that Maya would have a direct line of contact to the UP. But even with this personal connection, Neela was prepared to pay a price.

Maya's response suggests that the transaction was more than a behavioral irregularity; it was an established and expected practice. A similar pattern emerges in Shiuli's story. Underneath the informality of transactions lay distinct rules—perhaps even set rates for particular localities. Sometimes the payment served as insurance; it secured the recipient a place in line. Elsewhere, payments could not guarantee benefits. UP officials would accept money and eventually claim that they had run out of services. In each of the above instances, the women found a connection to the UP despite being outside patronage networks. And while they paid money, they owed no political allegiance or long-term commitment to the provider.

Formal Institutions

Informal institutions have not only diversified beyond traditional clientelism; they have also given way to formal rules. Now, formal institutions dictate the vast majority of exchanges (figure 4.1a). And yet, exchanges rarely follow a consistent pattern. Both the government and NGOs allocate benefits in abundant supply. But safety nets do not reach every family in need. Most villagers qualify as recipients, creating overwhelming demand that far outstrips supply. In the absence of prescribed rules, UP officials use their judgment and distribute services in an ad hoc manner. This discrepancy is not unrecognized by the government; the country's own national welfare strategy advocates a move away from this "discretionary" approach.[29] Without concrete guidelines and with insufficient benefits, potential recipients get benefits when they bargain persistently and evoke the provider's sympathy.[30] For example, Anowara's story suggests that speaking up pays off. Her acquaintances pleaded that poverty had made their lives unbearably difficult. Beneficiaries still belong to poor families. But when services reach the persistent and articulate families among the poor, they leave out the most vulnerable—those who are unlikely to possess bargaining skills or the resources for repeated follow-up.

While formal rules appear in exchanges across all kinds of services, they occur much more frequently in the case of services distributed outside of the UP. In the past, services were concentrated in the hands of UP officials—the big men, who kept them within the confines of the closed net. Now, rural Bangladeshis get services from a range of providers. Ideally, government services would be handed out by local government officials—UP members and chairmen, subdistrict-level officers, schoolteachers, health workers, and nurses—and NGO services from NGO field offices or field staff. Figure 4.2 compares PS members and the control group on their service networks—the first point of contact as they sought a service, categorized by seven service types. It demonstrates that with the diversification of providers, the UP office no longer holds unadulterated power. Potential recipients follow an intricate path spanning personal relationships involving neighbors, friends, kin, and other community members; they have multiple interactions before approaching the provider. These interactions take service delivery from the singular actor and disperses it within a network far wider than the net of the 1970s. They create an encompassing network that involves more people, and consequently, provides access to information and other resources for villagers.

Sometimes, potential recipients ask friends and family members for assistance. One respondent said that UP member Sadek Ali was her uncle. She had asked him to secure a card for a relative, "a very poor person," she added. "So my uncle gave me a card." The woman went out of her way to advocate for her poor relative. Another respondent, Kariman, mentioned that her neighbor had

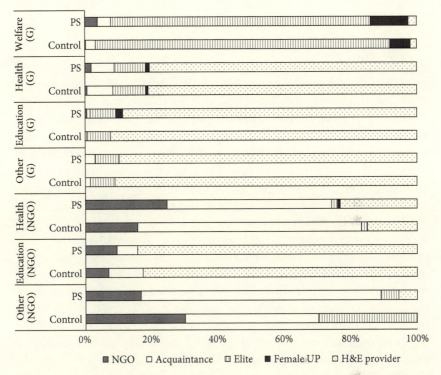

Figure 4.2. Service Networks (PS vs. Control)

come over to borrow some rice. While bantering about their lives, the woman asked Kariman if she could put in a good word for her with the UP chairman. Kariman said, "She told me, *apa*, you know the chairman, it would be very helpful if you could ask him to arrange for a card for me." Kariman agreed that it was a good idea. She asked her husband to arrange a card for this woman. She added, "I know my husband has a good relationship with the chairman and can arrange for a card if he wants. So my husband took [my neighbor's husband] to the chairman, who listened to him and issued him a card."

In the above cases, exchanges followed formal rules. Individuals with connections to the UP used their personal relationships to assist disenfranchised community members. Neither respondent sought any benefit in return. Recipients owed them nothing. These new distributive patterns are only possible because of the unraveling net, which has diminished UP officials' ability to use safety nets solely for maintaining political power. It is within this context that PS has emerged as a new political actor. The following section explores differences between PS members and the control group on service-seeking behaviors. I begin by tracing the contacts through which PS members and the control group receive services.

ARE PS AREAS DIFFERENT?

Networks

Within this unraveling net, PS members receive services through wider personal networks than the control group. Figure 4.2 illustrates a shift from the UP-dominated distributive patterns of the 1970s. As a whole, male UP officials no longer serve as sole providers; recipients now get their services from a range of contacts. The vast majority of government welfare goods still come from men—UP officials and local traditional leaders. Women providers dole out some services, often indirectly.[31] Government health and education services follow a fairly consistent path; books and education stipends come from schoolteachers and administrators, and medical services, like immunization and birth control pills, come from government clinics.

Women rarely approach service providers directly. Rather, they navigate their personal networks, reaching providers through intermediaries—friends, relatives, neighbors, and fellow villagers. Personal networks are particularly prominent for NGO services, including health and education benefits. This is unexpected. NGOs have created a dense infrastructure in rural Bangladesh with their intricate networks of offices and staff. In addition, rapid urbanization and a growing population—both of which bring people into closer proximity—should increase direct access to resources. But this is not the case.

PS's embeddedness in the community allows its members to create intricate and overlapping social ties that replace the clientelist net. PS members acquire benefits through a wider network compared to the control group; this pattern is most prominent for government welfare goods and NGO-distributed health services. On welfare, a higher percentage of exchanges involving PS members come from women UP officials and NGO contacts. In comparison, a higher percentage of exchanges involving the control group come from "big men" of the past—UP members, chairmen, and members of the traditional rural elite, such as the *matobbor* (informal village leader), the *shomaj prodhan* (leader of community or society) and the *gosthi prodhan* (leader of kinship group). For PS members, approaching women officials may be a strategic decision. They develop close relationships with these women through PS work—for example, when the latter attend general meetings, lead discussions as learning advisers, or help out with local projects. Sometimes, PS members—both current and former—hold these designated seats themselves. They may also view UP members as more sympathetic to poor people's problems than male officials, who often dismiss them. Approaching women does not increase the likelihood of getting services—in fact, the opposite may be true. In Bangladesh, women officeholders lack decision-making power at both the national and local levels. However, their presence as a secondary contact suggests the emergence of new distributive networks that women create around themselves.

Personal networks become particularly prominent for NGO-distributed health services. PS members access these goods directly from providers—POs and health workers—whereas those in the control group pursue them through personal networks. Acquaintances provide access to valuable information. Generally, news of services travels by word of mouth. Villagers may not even know that government services exist or how to acquire them. Women who receive birth control from the government or NGOs typically receive it from health workers. Clinics and NGOs dispatch health workers to visit women in their homes or address them at the community level in order to share information and deliver health services to women in the comfort of their localities. But in many instances, women sought birth control after being encouraged by an acquaintance who also used it. Newlywed women approached their married neighbors or relatives for advice. Newly relocated to live with their in-laws, they would not know clinics or health workers in the area. Sometimes, women accompanied each other to the service provider. Najma's neighbor Saleha—belonging to a family of five— struggled because she came from a very poor family. "But her husband has not taken any initiative to keep her family small. I explained things to her and took her to a government clinic one day." By "things" Najma alluded to the intimate details of how birth control works. She introduced Saleha to their local government health worker, who gave Saleha three months' supply of birth control pills. Such friendships can extend beyond information sharing—they can provide solidarities when women have to step outside their prescribed gender roles. From Najma's perspective, Saleha sought birth control, as her husband had failed to act. This was now Saleha's responsibility. Najma's advice, personal connections to the clinic, and willingness to accompany Saleha to the clinic physically became a source of support for Saleha.

Exchanges

PS members and the control group receive services differently. These differences vary by the type of service—and, consequently, who distributes them.[32] Figure 4.3 illustrates how PS members and the control group receive services across seven service types.[33] In line with historical patterns, clientelism features most prominently in exchanges involving government welfare goods, which still come out of the UP office. At the same time, providers handing out education (government and NGO) and health (NGO) benefits—teachers and health workers, respectively—are most likely to follow formal rules. The rest of this section focuses on benefits with the most variation between PS members and the control group—government welfare goods and NGO health services, resources that come directly out of the UP and NGO offices, respectively.

UP officials still use welfare services to maintain their political position. However, this occurs less frequently for PS members. When it comes to government-distributed welfare goods, a larger percentage of exchanges involving PS members

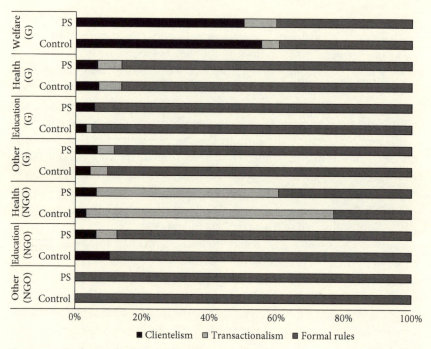

Figure 4.3. Exchanges by Service Type (PS vs. Control)

embody transactionalism when compared to the control group, where clientelism is more prominent. The difference is statistically significant. Transactionalism is an unintended and undesirable outcome. It violates formal rules and can even be labeled a corrupt practice. However, it allows poor families to access services when they lack political networks and without the cost of political support. PS intervention does not just lead to transactionalism; in well-performing groups, it can lead to formal rules. CEP classifies PS groups into three categories based on performance—A, B, and C, with A being the best-performing. Figure 4.4 illustrates the types of exchange for PS members based on ranking, for all welfare goods. It shows that a higher percentage of exchanges involving respondents from A-category PS groups receive services based on formal rules. These are the most active groups. They meet frequently, have strong leadership, and undertake multiple initiatives each year. Thus, PS intervention shifts distributive practices from clientelism to formal rules when we consider the strongest PS groups only.

As distributive patterns shift, they move away from a particular kind of clientelism. Traditional clientelism is resilient to change; this is particularly true of kinship networks. Figure 4.5 shows welfare–related exchanges by type of exchange, the latter broken down to illustrate varieties of clientelism. It compares PS members with the control group and PS members only by ranking. Of traditional clientelism, relationships based on labor—often binding and

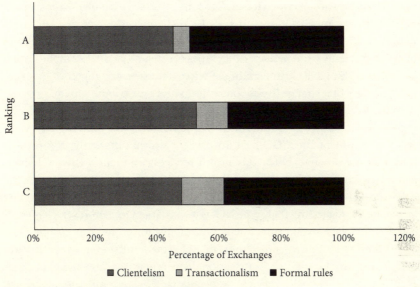

Figure 4.4. Exchanges by Ranking (Welfare)

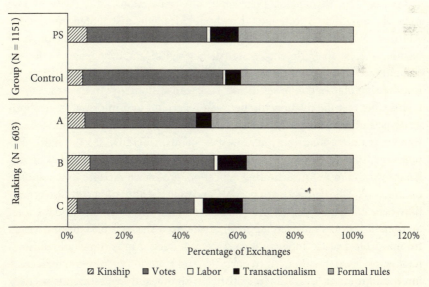

Figure 4.5. Varieties of Clientelism

coercive—have all but disintegrated. They are completely absent in exchanges involving members of A-category PS groups. At the same time, kinship dictates a small but consistent number of exchanges across all groups. A lower percentage of exchanges involving members of A-category groups embody electoral clientelism when compared to less-effective groups. But they do only a little better than B-category groups when it comes to kinship-based exchanges. Thus, grass-roots collective mobilization shifts electoral clientelism far more easily than dissolving kinship obligations. Indeed, if traditional clientelism evolved from ownership of land—and perhaps other types of capital—grassroots mobilization cannot alone lead to its disintegration. Rather, it must be accompanied by structural changes that change livelihood patterns and redistribute capital.

When it comes to health services, a higher percentage of exchanges involving PS members embody formal rules when compared to the control group. Generally, government and NGO health workers perform differently; government health services are free, but NGOs' health services cost money. This could happen for two reasons. Some NGOs may charge fees for services. For example, women paid money for 88.7 percent of all exchanges involving NGO-distributed birth control, suggesting that some NGOs may charge a fee. However, NGO staff could also violate formal rules and charge money for profit. This is confirmed by the finding that birth control pills do not skew results; even when they are removed from the picture, transactionalism remains a prevalent mode of exchange for NGO health services (appendix table A.3). Transactionalism also appears in the case of latrines, a good that NGOs typically distribute free of cost; 36.5 percent of all exchanges for latrines involve transactions. Thus, NGOs appear to be charging money for goods that should ideally be distributed free of cost. At the same time, transactionalism occurs less frequently in PS areas for NGO health services. The difference is statistically significant, even when birth control pills are taken out of the analysis.[34] Thus, for particular NGO services, PS intervention may lead to fewer incidents of transactionalism in PS areas.

I further test the relationship between PS groups and informal institutions using Generalized Linear Mixed Models (GLMM) with a multinomial logistic link function.[35] I focus on social welfare goods, where we see the most pronounced difference.[36] Control variables include demographic measures of vulnerability and mobility, including education, profession (service as *grihosthali* or household labor), practice of purdah, and political affiliation. The two groups have been compared on baseline indicators—both demographics and the total amount of services received (appendix table A.1). The data have been checked for multicollinearity. Table 4.1 includes two models. Model 1 includes a three-level empty model with no fixed variables and a randomly varying intercept.[37] The random-effect covariance is statistically significant, suggesting the need for a multilevel model to account for variance across various levels—that is, we expect there to be differences across wards as well as across individuals that a multilevel model will take into account.

Model 2 estimates the effect of PS membership on type of exchange. It holds clientelism as the reference category, since it seeks to measure changes away from existing institutions. Holding formal rules as the reference category imagines imposed standards as an ideal. The model confirms earlier findings that

TABLE 4.1

MULTILEVEL MULTINOMIAL LOGIT MODEL OF TYPE OF EXCHANGE (WELFARE)

	Model 1		Model 2	
	Formal vs. clientelism	Transaction vs. clientelism	Formal vs. clientelism	Transaction vs. clientelism
Intercept	0.129(0.127)***	0.722 (0.077)***	1.241(0.302)	0.145(0.472)***
PS membership (yes = 1; no = 0)			1.198(0.157)	1.960(0.273)**
Education (years)			1.029(0.025)	0.926(0.050)
Occupation (Grihosthali = 1; other = 0)			0.792(0.275)	0.855(0.407)
Purdah (yes = 1; no = 0)			0.836(0.150)	0.939(0.260)
Political affiliation (yes = 1; no = 0)			0.200(0.191)***	0.609(0.281)*
Random Effect Covariance	1.236(0.211)***	1.267(0.328)***	1.069(0.212)***	1.325(0.340)***
N	1151		1135	
Level 3 cases	801		793	
Level 2 cases	1098		1082	
Overall % correct	88.0		86.3	
AIC	8862.204		8891.964	

*p<.1

**p<.05

***p<.01

exchanges involving PS members are more likely to embody transactionalism over clientelism. Thus, PS intervention shifts distributive politics in favor of the rural poor by increasing access. On control variables, measures of vulnerability— occupation, religion, and marital status—have no effect on types of exchange. Because the entire sample is drawn from impoverished communities, there may be insufficient variation between individuals (see baseline demographics in appendix table A.1). Education helps respondents hold the local government accountable. An extra year of schooling decreases respondents' odds of engaging in transactions over formal rules. Finally, contrary to what one might expect, purdah has no statistically significant effect on type of exchange. This debunks assumptions of Muslim women as subservient and politically disengaged. Finally, political affiliation emerges as an important control variable. Exchanges involving respondents who belong to political networks are far more likely to embody clientelism and transactions as opposed to formal rules. Women belonging to the clientelist net who would have received services in the past are now entrapped by it. They receive services for political support while their peers negotiate with providers to abide by formal rules. As state-society relationships are changing in rural Bangladesh, they remain caught within older power structures while others are finding ways to escape.

Conclusion

This chapter examines whether the closed service delivery net that character- ized traditional clientelism shifted with the vast influx of NGOs in rural Ban- gladesh, and if these relationships are different in PS areas. Exchanges between rural Bangladeshis and their service providers embody multiple and overlapping institutions, both formal and informal. Rural Bangladeshis still find themselves in clientelist networks, though providers also distribute services by formal rules. At the same time, an intermediary relationship has emerged. Transactionalism, the exchange of material goods for services, marks a midpoint between clien- telism and adherence to formal rules. It deviates from formal rules, but allows poor rural women access to services without the binding cost of political sup- port. All three kinds of relationships appear across government and NGO ser- vices. Documenting these diverse relationships, and particularly identifying behavioral practices that deviate from formal rules, is the first step to discover- ing whether informal institutions exist.

This chapter also explores whether something different is happening in PS areas. First, the dismantling net appears more prominent in PS areas. PS mem- bers engage a wider network of contacts including women officials and NGO staff, many of whom are also women. Thus, the net is being replaced by women- centered networks. In addition, service recipients are better able to hold provid- ers accountable in PS areas. The two groups differ on the nature of exchanges.

On welfare, exchanges involving PS members are more likely to embody trans-actionalism than clientelism. While transactionalism involves paying a fee, recipients are not bound to a patron for political support. When it comes to NGO health services, exchanges involving PS members are more likely to embody for-mal rules. Stronger PS groups ensure even better adherence to formal rules; PS members from wards with A-category groups are more likely to receive services free of cost.

Rural Bangladeshi society is in transition. PS groups are riding this wave. NGOs have created an extensive infrastructure with their offices, field staff, and incredible volume of services that provide ideal conditions for women's mobili-zation programs to succeed. Women in rural Bangladesh are now more con-nected to each other than ever before. These personal networks have helped PS groups prosper, creating an organizational infrastructure that members can navigate as they mobilize. This chapter also illustrates that programs like PS can have unintended consequences such as transactionalism, as women mobi-lize but find themselves engulfed by the myriad informal institutions that char-acterize rural societies. In the following chapter, I explore formal and informal institutions in the legal system.

CHAPTER 5

Rule of Law

Only two people knew what happened that morning. The man was dead. Then there was the woman, Meena, who said that he had raped her. She was about forty-five years old. Villagers had seen her sitting by the roadside. She had wounds on her face and arm, and as her torn clothes would reveal, all over her body. Later that morning, she approached some local men gathered at a nearby street side stall. She inquired about a man who often hung around there. Meena said that she did not know his name. But that man had accosted her as she walked through mist-laden rice fields in the early morning. He was cutting the harvest, hidden amid paddy stalks in the dense fog that had wrapped around the village. No one would have seen her being attacked. If she had screamed, villagers would not have heard her.

As PS members told the story, some of the women claimed that the *matobbor* (village leader) rushed to the scene. Others insisted that Meena visited the *matobbor* herself. They did agree that the local elders responded swiftly. Meena belonged to the community. People knew her and wanted to help one of their own. The *matobbor*, later joined by the local UP member, sent some village men to locate the alleged perpetrator. When asked to identify her attacker from a lineup, Meena recognized Ram Deb, a local Hindu man. Village elders proceeded to resolve the issue in *shalish*, an informal village court. The *shalishkar* (decision makers) found Ram guilty. They declared that as punishment, some local men would shave Ram's head and strip him naked. Locals tied a brick to his exposed genitals and beat him ruthlessly.

Later that evening, Ram Deb drank poison and killed himself. The crime he was accused of never made it to the state's legal system, but his death did. Ram's family filed a murder case with the police. In the coming months, local police raided the village repeatedly. At one point, they arrested Meena. According to PS members, they coerced a retraction of her original statement. In a new confession, she declared that the UP member had paid her Tk. 20,000 to concoct the rape allegation. "She lied because she was afraid of the police," PS members said. As they spoke, the women did not say the word "rape." Instead, they used the Bengali word *noshto* (spoiled; ruined; in this context, even destroyed). Their language embodied the taboo nature of sexual violence in Bangladesh; society inhibits discussion of it, and so we do not use precise words.[1] In addition to the trauma of sexual violence, Meena had endured damage to her reputation. She would forever be known as a raped woman. Now, she was also in legal trouble.

Meena was not alone. The case involved the entire village. In the months since the attack, the community had been on edge. Police visited the village frequently, seeking those associated with the incident, and in the words of PS members, "arresting whomever they could get their hands on." Men left their homes in the evenings, fearing arrest. Women, home alone with their children, spent their nights petrified that the police would knock on their doors. Eight men, including the local leaders who had delivered Ram Deb's *shalish* verdict, awaited a murder trial in jail.

The Bangladeshi legal system is messy and difficult to navigate. People avoid courts due to outrageous costs, large backlogs, delays, corruption, and a tendency to favor the wealthy and politically connected. Villagers often resolve local disputes via *shalish*, an informal judicial avenue presided over by the local elite— elected UP officials, nonelected government officials, the traditional elite, religious leaders, men and women from established families, and sometimes NGO staff.[2] *Shalish* can take numerous forms—traditional and informal elite-driven adjudication, official UP-administered village courts (*gram adalot*), or NGO-administered mechanisms. Stephen Golub describes it as a "community-based, largely informal Bangladeshi process through which small panels of influential local figures help resolve community members' disputes and/or impose . . . sanctions on them."[3] Decision makers resolve problems through deliberations. They draw on formal and informal institutions, sometimes a mix of the two. As opposed to legal action, violations are punished through social sanctions, where community members hold defendants publicly liable for their actions. Most incidents pertain to disputes over property or family—for example, violence, dowry, inheritance, polygamy, divorce, financial upkeep of one's wife and children—while serious crimes may pass through *shalish* and end up in court.[4]

In the above incident, *shalish* procedures violated formal rules on two counts. Although rural Bangladeshis often try criminal cases in *shalish*, this violates state law. The *shalishkars* should have handed the case over to the police. They also punished Ram Deb with physical damage and public humiliation. According to the penal code of 1860, rape is a criminal offense punishable by ten years to life, and based on the Suppression of Violence against Women and Children Act of 2000 and the 2003 amendment, survivors receive civil reparations.[5] Ram Deb should have gone to jail. Meena should have received compensation.

Legal systems—whether formal or informal, and handled by the police, courts, or local elders—are also disproportionately biased against the vulnerable, particularly the poor, women, and minorities. Both Ram Deb and Meena came from poor families. And while the villagers intended to provide Meena with justice, the verdict drew on an informal practice that deprived Ram Deb of his right to a trial. Ram Deb belonged to the minority Hindu community. This raises additional questions about whom informal institutions favor and how the complexities surrounding them are amplified for the most vulnerable. Finally, as the incident had turned into a murder case, the police tormented not just those involved, but the entire village community. We do not know whether Ram Deb's family had sought support from powerful factions, but at this time, the police—those with authority—penalized the entire village community for the *shalish-kars'* infractions.

This chapter explores the rules-in-use, the dos and don'ts around legal issues—dowry, child marriage, violence against women and the rural poor, and issues related to property, love, marriage, and family. It takes the first steps to identifying informal institutions, asking whether we see outcomes in accordance with the informal institution we seek to identify.[6] It argues that in rural Bangladesh, legal issues are resolved through a mix of formal and informal rules. These diverse rules-in-use embody power relationships within the community; they are both gendered and disenfranchise the rural poor. It also argues that the rules-in-use are different in PS areas compared to the control group. PS members are more likely to resolve certain kinds of legal disputes when compared to the control group; some resolutions are based on formal rules, others are reconciliatory and socially sanctioned. They are also more likely to represent women's voices in legal proceedings. Finally, PS members are embedded in personal networks that open up channels for accessing legal resources.

The first two sections of the chapter unearth the rules-in-use around legal issues. I discuss *what* rules people typically follow and *why* they follow them, paying particular attention to appropriate or expected behavior. The first section speaks to dowry and child marriage—the two types of issues that people resolve in the privacy of their homes. The second section discusses types of incidents that appear prominently in *shalish*—violence against women and girls (VAWG), "unsocial" activities, other forms of violence, and disputes over property.[7] The third section examines differences between PS members and the control group.

Private Spaces
Dowry

Although dowry defies parchment rules, it remains the rule-in-use.[8] It refers to the transfer of resources from the bride's family to the groom's family during

wedding negotiations and festivities, most often in cash, but also in jewelry, fur-
niture, bicycles or motorbikes, and even securing documents for the groom to
emigrate abroad for work.[9] Dowry places tremendous financial burdens on young
girls' families. It is a precursor to domestic violence.[10] It is also illegal; according
to the Dowry Prohibition Ordinance of 1980 and the Dowry Prohibition (Amendment) Ordinances of 1982 and 1986, those giving or taking dowry can receive
five years' imprisonment, a fine, or perhaps both.[11] The government and NGOs
run extensive anti-dowry campaigns and programs. In fact, in Bangladesh's contested rural terrain, both Islamists and secularists condemn dowry; women's
rights groups prohibit it for its devastating effect on women's lives, and religious
groups claim that it is un-Islamic.[12] The extent of dowry practice is particularly
astonishing when one considers Bangladesh's remarkable human development
achievements for women and girls—higher employment and school enrollment,
reduced wage gaps, and better health outcomes.[13] And yet, it is an accepted practice. Bangladesh is not unique in this regard; studies have found similar patterns in Kerala, India, where dowry exists in spite of much activism and is seen
as the only way to secure a good marriage.[14]

There was a general understanding among village folk that in their localities,
all weddings require dowry. In Dinajpur's Chirir Bondor *upazila*, one woman
recalled paying dowry for her daughter's wedding five years ago. She worked as
a day laborer and had never attended school. Despite having two breadwinners—
the woman and her husband—the demand was a hefty sum for the family. But
she insisted that if not for dowry, her daughter would not have found a husband.
In Dinajpur's Parbotipur upazila, another woman mentioned that one could not
even imagine a wedding without dowry in their area. She, too, worked as a day
laborer. She had both given and taken dowry. She was forced to pay dowry for
her daughter's wedding. "Why should I not take money for my son's wedding?"
she asked. "Based on this rule I took Tk. 50,000 dowry for my son's wedding,"
she added. When describing dowry, she used the word *niyom* (rule), suggesting
that this was just how things were done. And one may speculate that perhaps,
as she paid her daughter's dowry, she took comfort in knowing that one day she
would recover the funds taking dowry for her own son.

As an institution, dowry has survived vast education campaigns by the government and NGOs alike. One may be tempted to associate its tenacity with
history—it would appear logical that dowry is an age-old institution that has
survived the times. However, the prevalence of dowry is fairly recent among Bangladesh's Muslim population. Capitalist development has injected new resources
into rural society and contributed to increasing dowry demands. Rahnuma
Ahmed finds that as far back as 1987, patterns of resource exchange were shifting, reversing from *denmohor*—resource transfer from the groom's family to
the bride's family as part of Islamic marital contract—to dowry. She finds it to
be a new form of "gift giving" that has become more and more expensive over

time.[15] Elora Shehabuddin notes that among the women she interviewed for her book *Reshaping the Holy*, most claiming to have paid dowry were married in the last twenty years; in contrast, older women said that they received gifts when they got married.[16] The easy availability of microfinance loans has provided new financial avenues to meet dowry demands; people often borrow from MFIs for family weddings, where expenses can include dowry payments.[17] The nature of dowry has also changed with increasing women's mobilization. With more women working away from home, husbands often appropriate working women's salaries. Farah Deeba Chowdhury writes that this has become a new form of dowry.[18]

Given its illegality, most dowry talks occur behind closed doors. During negotiations, people rarely use the Bengali word for dowry, *joutuk*. They say *dabi*, *aabdar*, or the literal English translation of these words, "demand."[19] Indeed, this use of language normalizes transactions, as the word *joutuk* is associated with breaking the law. Also given its illegality, some grooms' families ask subtly—for example, demanding goods instead of cash. One woman in Sunamganj's Chatok upazila was caught unawares during her daughter's wedding talks. Her now son-in-law's family had asked for nothing at first. However, once the two families started to plan the wedding, the groom's family asked for the bride to be "adorned" (*shajiye dawa*); she needed to be decked in gold. Once married, she would move to her in-laws' home, bringing the jewels into her new family. Perhaps her husband or mother-in-law would confiscate them. It was most likely that the jewelry would belong to her new family. Eventually, the family spent Tk. 50,000 on wedding expenses, including the gold.

Child Marriage

Despite the illegality of the practice, Bangladesh has one of the highest rates of child marriage in the world.[20] The Child Marriage Restraint Act of 1929 and its 1984 amendment set the legal age of marriage at eighteen for women and twenty-one for men.[21] And yet, according to the Bangladesh Demographic Health Survey of 2011, more than 75 percent of the marriages in the country involve underage brides or grooms.[22] A study on global child marriage trends put the number at 82.3 percent in 2007 for all women aged 18 to 49, making it the highest incidence among the sixty countries in the report, and placing Bangladesh at twice the average for South Asia.[23] And while child marriage has seen some decline—it was almost universal before 1970, and incidence is lower among younger women—it remains the "rule-in-use."[24]

The prevalence of child marriage is startling given government and NGO advocacy around the issue. In August 2018, a National Plan of Action to End Child Marriage was launched by the Ministry of Women and Children's Affairs and UNICEF Bangladesh. The plan engages multiple stakeholders and seeks to eliminate child marriage in stages—by 2021 reducing by a third marriage under the age of eighteen and ending marriage under the age of fifteen for girls, and by 2041 ending child marriage altogether.[25] UNICEF has been one of many NGOs engaging in multipronged advocacy on the ground—for example, engaging communities (adolescent girls and their families, especially fathers), involving key decision makers, and incorporating information into mainstream development programs.[26] Microfinance providers such as BRAC and Grameen Bank educate their borrowers regarding the potential dangers of child marriage. Some NGO programs have made a difference. Education—of young girls, their potential husbands, and even their fathers—has had the strongest impact.[27] Amin, Ahmed, et al. find in their study of the Population Council's Balika project, which provides education, gender awareness training, and livelihood training to young girls, that program participants who met with peers and trainers weekly in training centers were a third less likely to be married early than those in a control group.[28] Other kinds of programs have had less of an impact. Cash transfer programs have had some effect, but are unlikely to transform underlying social norms.[29] And while microfinance has been hailed as a magic bullet for women's empowerment, there is little evidence that it has altered community perceptions and behaviors regarding child marriage.

Gendered Institutions

Dowry and child marriage are gendered institutions; they subscribe to "stereotypes about men and women's attributes, experiences, and abilities, and symbolically valorize masculine traits, especially hegemonic ones, over feminine ones."[30] Gendered norms subscribe to the bounds of women's appropriate roles and behaviors—how a woman should be and what she should do. A woman's position is tied to the socially desirable goal of marriage and playing the ideal daughter, wife, and mother. As such, rules that dictate her behaviors as well those of her family exalt her reputation, marriageability, chastity, and the importance of maintaining her marital status. Before marriage, she is an obedient daughter. After marriage, her primary responsibility would be *shongshar kora* (the act of living a domestic life), a term that encompasses the sum total of her marital duties, ranging from household maintenance to sexual and reproductive obligations.[31] While her husband would fulfill his role as provider, she would run the household and play the nurturer.[32] Thus, dowry and child marriage are visibly gendered institutions, where notions of masculinity and femininity determine the actions of not just potential brides, but also their families. A woman needs to be married, even if it is before reaching the legal age of eighteen. And since marriage is her ultimate destiny, getting her there ends up being parents' primary responsibility.

As families seek to fulfill their parental obligations, they hesitate to let go of a *bhalo chele*—a good boy.[33] In Magura's Sripur upazila, one woman said that a potential groom's family had come to see her sister-in-law, Kajol. They had liked

Kajol and claimed to have no "demand." However, they asked that the family adorn the bride. The woman protested. At seventeen, Kajol should finish school. But her husband, Kajol's elder brother, put his foot down. He argued that the young man had a good job. "We cannot find a good boy like this so easily." Eventually, the wedding took place. For Kajol, there was a trade-off between marriage and education. She had most likely left school. But her family had married her to a good provider. Girls' families prioritized this quality. A working man was considered good. A man with a secure job was even better. But a wealthy family with landed property was ideal. Indeed, Farah Deeba Chowdhury finds in her study of one Bangladeshi village that "economically solvent" men are viewed as good bridegrooms.[34] Sonia Dalmia and Pareena Lawrence discover a similar pattern in India, where dowry was the price paid for a good match.[35] Thus, when parents pay dowry, they make what Sarah White identifies as "patriarchal investments," where marriage becomes a structural alliance between two families and dowry an investment toward enhancing the groom's economic prospects.[36] In his new married life, he would be the provider while his wife manages the home, and dowry would be his in-laws' contribution to getting him there.

Parents' obligations toward a girl's *shongshar* (domestic life) also drive child marriage. One study found that when a girl remained unmarried, both she and her parents suffered from guilt. Such daughters became burdens; their parents described them as fish bones stuck in one's throat.[37] Families also feared that their daughters would miss their window for marriage if they waited too long. They would not be wrong. Typically, grooms' families seek younger girls, viewing them as submissive and more willing to be an obedient wife.[38] Younger girls are easily moldable into a *shongshari* wife—one perceived as having the mindset and skills to live a domestic life. Younger girls also pay lesser dowry.[39] Shahnaz Huda writes that like dark-complexioned girls, who are not viewed as conventionally attractive, older brides are undesirable and married at a higher cost.[40] Thus parents were desperate to get their daughters married early, when prospects were better and costs were low. They hesitated to let go of a good match when it appeared, and as with dowry, justified child marriage with the claim that good men are hard to find. One woman, Dinajpur Sadar, mentioned that she arranged her daughter's marriage when the girl was fifteen. "I saw the boy's family situation and got her married that young," she said.

SHALISH
Violence against Women and Girls (VAWG)

According to a report by the Sustainable Development Goals fund, two out of three women in Bangladesh experience gender-based violence in their lifetime.[41]

Recent legislation protects women from violence, both at home and outside. Existing laws recognize "the infliction of physical injury, rape (with the exception of marital rape), provoking suicide, trafficking in women, kidnapping of women, and murder" as crimes and punishable by law.[42] The Domestic Violence (Prevention and Protection) Act of 2010 protects women from physical, psychological, sexual, and economic abuse, giving them protections, rights to a shared home, access to support networks, and civil reparations. The law does not permit *shalish* to handle criminal matters. As such, when rape and other forms of sexual violence come to the attention of local elders, they eventually end up in the courts. But generally, incidents of violence against women and girls tend to go unreported.[43]

Ruma came from a poor family in Kurigram's Rajarhat upazila. She was married eight years ago with Tk. 10,000 dowry. "I was fine for five months" she said, "but then, the physical assaults began." Her husband worked in construction. When he was out of work, he coerced her into getting money from her father. "If I do not, he punches and kicks me, he beats me with a stick and throws me out of the house." Her father, an agricultural laborer, could do little to help. Ruma approached UP officials for assistance. The member came to her house and spoke to her husband, but the violence continued. Eventually, the member asked her to file a case. Ruma refused. "I am silently bearing the pain," she added.

Ruma's story is fairly common. Women rarely seek help when they experience violence at home. A study conducted between 2000 and 2004 finds that 66 percent of survivors endured abuse in silence.[44] They feared that reporting would further intensify violence and jeopardize their reputation as well as their family's honor. The authors found high acceptance of violence and stigma associated with reporting. Women believed that their husbands were justified in their use of violence.[45] Shehabuddin finds a similar scenario where women believed that their economic dependence on their husbands gave the men the right to violence. They claimed to learn of this "right to discipline" from their families, communities, and religious sources.[46] Thus, a woman is socialized to accept violence. Playing the role of a "good" wife—submissive and dependent on her husband—she is expected to endure abuse. And her husband's role as breadwinner entitles him to perpetrate violence.

"Unsocial" Activities

Jasmine's neighbors had accused her of being a sex worker. As a PS member from Rangpur Sadar told the story, she mentioned that the girl had a bad character. Her liaisons ruined the general atmosphere (*poribesh*) of her neighborhood. And so community members approached local elders to call a *shalish*. At the trial, *shalishkars* decided that Jasmine's family would have to leave the village before the day was over. The woman telling the story claimed to have pushed back.

"I protested and said that Jasmine can go but the mother and her two children must stay here." She said that she helped the mother, but Jasmine, "with her bad character, had to go." Jasmine was only seventeen, still a minor.

Matters of love and sex often veer into the unacceptable in rural Bangladesh. Although laws do not forbid premarital relationships, extramarital affairs, elopement, marriage without consent of elders, and even sex work, romantic and sexual affiliations prior to and outside of marriage defy social norms. Such incidents come to *shalish* often. In Bangladeshi villages, young women are expected to refrain from romantic and sexual relationships until marriage. Chastity is an expected and integral component of being an ideal bride. When a woman engages in a relationship, she risks more than her heart. She also risks her reputation and possibly her future. The details of Jasmine's case remain unclear. The teenager could have been in a romantic or sexual relationship. She could have been involved with multiple men, simultaneously or sequentially. She could have been engaged in sex work. Any of these actions would have earned her a reputation of being sexually promiscuous. But sexual activity—and even sex work—do not violate laws. In 2000, the Bangladeshi High Court ruled prostitution as legal, following a case filed by one hundred sex workers dislocated when the government raided and closed down their brothels.[47] Being a minor makes Jasmine's case even more complicated. *Shalish* had punished a child for alleged sex work and failed to identify the men involved. By law, men involved in procuring or trafficking minors are in violation of the Repression of Women and Children Act, which prevents forced trafficking. If Jasmine was a sex worker, her clients should have been tried as well.

When the community adjudicates matters of love, sex, and marriage, women bear stronger penalties than men, and the poor more than the wealthy. In Sirajganj's Raiganj upazila, Malek and Rania had fallen in love. But they were married to other people. The lovers wanted to divorce their current spouses and marry each other. Malek had made his intentions clear. But his family opposed the match. Rania came from a poor family. One night, Rania's brother caught Malek sneaking into her room. He locked Malek inside and informed his family. When the family arranged for a *shalish* the next day, folks blamed Rania for the affair. Community members beat her brutally in public. According to the women telling the story, Malek's wealthy family had *shalishkars'* favor. Rania had two things working against her—she was a woman, and her family held low socioeconomic status. She was powerless to oppose the verdict and paid the penalty alone.

Violence against the Poor

Rural Bangladeshis often faced assault by the wealthy and politically connected, including the police. In Gaibanda's Sundarganj upazila, retired soldier Amin visited his local chairman to request a VGD card. The chairman brushed him off and asked him to come back another day. Amin returned again and again. On his third visit, the chairman had his thugs beat Amin and hand him over to the police. Although Amin had not committed a crime, the police took him into custody. His family reached out to village elders for help. The local *matobbor* intervened. He accompanied Amin's family to the police station. Together, they brought him home.

If formal rules were followed, the chairman would have been arrested. But he had the police on his side. Amin's family took no further action. They probably considered themselves fortunate. Without the *matobbor*'s help, Amin could have become embroiled in a long, drawn-out case or remained in jail indefinitely. The rural elite engaged in this kind of violence often. Villagers accepted it to the extent that they hesitated to retaliate against powerful community members. The police—often in alliance with local power holders—inflicted violence themselves. Thus, ordinary people feared that seeking justice would cost them dearly. Their inaction marks both an expectation that such violence is normalized and fear of further violence—the threat of social sanction. Both of these factors make such violence acceptable.

At the same time, *shalish* provides an avenue for justice that eludes the formal legal system. When perpetrators came from wealthy families, the village elite playing *shalishkar* were in a position to resolve cases through reparations and social accountability—for example, the promise to refrain from further violence or monetary reparations. One respondent had sold a large chunk of her family's inherited land. She grew some trees in the remaining plot. But an influential man by the name of Bulu Miya confiscated this land. Land-grabbing is now well documented in Bangladesh; the wealthy and powerful would often occupy land that belonged to the poor or indigenous groups or was allocated by the government for occupation by the landless.[48] As the family confronted Bulu Miya, he attacked the woman's husband and broke his arm. The couple approached the local elite—the UP officials, *matobbor*, and chairman—who eventually gave a judgment to return the family's land and trees. The decision makers required Bulu Miya to pay Tk. 3,000 in damages. Unlike Amin, this family received reparations for the violence inflicted on them.

Property

Someone raided Monir's house in the middle of the night. Bhanu thief, the nickname that he had earned himself now that his identity was public, had taken the family's bicycle, jewels, TV, and saris, robbing the family of most of their possessions. But then he made the unfortunate decision to sell the stolen goods at a local market. It did not take much time for the village folk to recognize Monir's belongings. They grabbed Bhanu thief and took him to the chairman. "Through the [UP] chairman, *chowkidar*, all things were recovered and Bhanu thief was handed over to the police," said the respondent.

In another incident, PS members spoke of a mobile (phone) store close to a nearby upazila. A local man by the name of Mohsin had borrowed a phone from the store on the pretext of making a call. Initially, Mohsin stood nearby as he talked on the phone. But as he spoke, he shuffled around, pacing back and forth. At one point, he casually walked away with the phone in hand. When the store owner tracked him down, Mohsin refused to return the phone. He insisted that he would return it later. The store owner informed the UP member, who reached out to the chairman. The latter called a *shalish* with "respectable people in the area." Mohsin admitted to taking the phone and ended up returning it.

Many cases that came to *shalish* involved similar scuffles over property, including inheritance, theft, gambling, or property destruction, for example, in the form of one person's animals venturing onto another's land and destroying their crops. Typically, elders resolved these conflicts—sometimes in *shalish*, and elsewhere informally—by evaluating documents and verbal statements. But for criminal offenses, including petty crimes like theft as in Bhanu thief's case above, *shalishkar* collaborated with the police. *Shalish* is often the first stop for reporting legal conflicts of all kinds. Since *shalishkar* cannot try criminal matters legally, they hand the more serious cases over to the police. But villagers prefer to keep the police out of their lives. Thus, *shalishkar* may resolve less serious incidents informally, adjudicating solutions that may involve monetary reparations. In doing so, they subscribe to the law, which prescribes fines or imprisonment for theft. Adjudications are more complicated in inheritance cases—for example, brothers or cousins fighting over ancestral land. In such instances, *shalish* may go on for weeks, with the display of documents, oral testimonies, and even land surveys. In most property-related disputes, laws are followed, and outcomes may resemble what one would see in courts.

Rule of Law

Shalish often reflects existing power dynamics in rural society. And yet, it provides an opportunity for justice in the absence of the state. *Shalish* decisions draw on a combination of laws, local customs, and extensive deliberations. Because it is grounded in the community and seeks to maintain justice and harmony simultaneously, decision makers attempt reconciliation as a first recourse. This is especially true for family matters, including domestic violence cases. Aleya's drug-addicted husband beat her ruthlessly. Her mother-in-law would watch and cheer him on, sometimes joining her son in hitting her. At one point, Aleya was sent back to her parents' house. Her return foreshadowed the looming threat of separation; it implied that her husband had rejected her because she had failed to fulfill her wifely duties. Aleya's mother was a PS member. Instead of pleading with Aleya's in-laws to take her back, she brought her concerns to a PS meeting. The group met with local leaders and requested a *shalish*. Aleya's in-laws were asked to attend the proceedings. The *shalishkars* commanded reconciliation.

They ordered Aleya's husband to take her home and treat her well. But the man started beating Aleya again. Eventually, he threw her out of their home, and Aleya returned to her parents' house. Unable to ensure compliance with the *shalish*'s decision, the chairman asked Aleya's mother to file a police case. Once Aleya's husband discovered that a police report was in the works, he begged the chairman for forgiveness. Initially, Aleya's husband avoided legal recourse due to the social norm of keeping marriages intact. *Shalishkars* attempted to hold Aleya's husband accountable through social sanctions; he was expected to attempt harmonious marital life (*mile mishe thaka*) under the watchful eye of the community. When social sanctions failed, the family took legal action.

Despite its reliance on social norms, *shalish* does not always hurt the disempowered. Sometimes it provides justice when the law fails. This is particularly true for divorce, where men typically have the upper hand. Men decide whether and when to end a marriage. Some remarry while still married to their first wives. Shehabuddin writes that marriages in rural Bangladesh are often unregistered, making divorce difficult. And yet, men often divorce women without cause. Sometimes they do so verbally, uttering the word *talaaq* (divorce) three times. If the man wishes to follow through legally, he can inform the local government office in writing, and a *shalish* is arranged within thirty days. If the *shalish*'s attempts at reconciliation fail, divorce is granted within ninety days of the wife being informed.[49] Women may initiate divorce under certain conditions based on the Muslim Marriages Dissolution Act, but few women know of this right.[50] Under these circumstances, *shalish* provides an avenue for women to seek annulment.

Kushum's husband hit her on a regular basis. He demanded dowry money, threatened divorce, and like Aleya's husband, sent her to her parents' home often. Neighbors had seen Kushum tied up outside her house, sometimes in the brutal cold. Her husband did not work. Rather, he spent his time drinking and smoking *ganja* (weed). Kushum was the family's sole earner. But she had little control over financial decisions; her husband demanded that she hand him all her earnings. Eventually, Kushum's father asked their local UP member and *matobbor* for a *shalish*. Following deliberations, the *shalishkars* arranged for a divorce (*chharachhari*) and directed Kushum's husband to return her dowry.

Often *shalish* provided women with civil reparations for damage inflicted on their reputation and well-being. One PS member recalled a romantic liaison between a man and a woman from her village. The man had lured his lover with the false promise of marriage. Then he ended the relationship. The young woman showed up at his home, insisting that she would marry nobody but him. Village folk gathered to watch the incident unfold. The woman's father, who had accompanied her, proceeded to report the incident to the chairman. It is not certain whether a formal *shalish* was held, but the chairman decided that the man would have to pay the woman Tk. 30,000 in damages. While this decision had no basis in formal law, it provided reparations to the young woman for the damage to her reputation. The chairman monetized her loss, grounded in the gendered norms that deem her less marriageable than before. Thus, *shalish*—and the informal institutions that often inform decision making within it—is not always unjust. Sometimes it provides justice in places the state fails to reach.

Are PS Areas Different?
Rules-in-Use

In this section, I compare PS areas with control areas on whether different rules-in-use are exercised on legal matters. Given the multiple rules in existence—both formal and informal—it is nearly impossible to separate formal from informal rules. Instead, I look for whether legal disputes are resolved, where resolution can indicate adherence to formal rules as well as informal measures, such as reconciliation. I examine three types of incidents: dowry and child marriage, where resolution indicates adherence to formal institutions, and violence against women and girls (VAWG), where resolutions could be formal or informal. The latter may be resolved through reparations, imprisonment, or reconciliation.

Figure 5.1 compares PS members and the control group on the occurrence and resolution of incidents.[51] Respondents answered whether such incidents took place in their families, and if so, whether the issues were resolved. Of incidents that occurred, a higher percentage were resolved in PS households compared to the control group. Disaggregated by incidents, the largest difference occurred in the case of child marriage. The pattern does not appear in the case of dowry or VAWG, where the differences are statistically insignificant.

Dowry, violence, and child marriage are all informal institutions tied to expected behaviors—that of women as "good wives" and men as providers and authority figures. And yet, child marriage is the only practice that PS members challenge and overturn to a greater degree than the control group. One may speculate on a number of reasons for this. Massive information campaigns have made rural Bangladeshis aware of the physical and emotional dangers of child marriage. Mothers can seek help to keep their daughters safe. One mother from Natore's Lalpur upazila mentioned that she had secured her daughter's marriage alliance with a matchmaker's help when the girl was only fifteen. "She was not fit for marriage" she said. "I knew that she might have trouble if she gets married too early." The mother added that her daughter had no idea about *shongshar* (domestic life) at fifteen. She understood that her daughter was too young for sex and childbirth, as well as household responsibilities. When her relatives insisted that she should not spoil a good match, the woman gave in. But there were others who stood their ground.

Young brides' families may have a hard time keeping impending weddings a secret. They must take girls out of school and make wedding preparations,

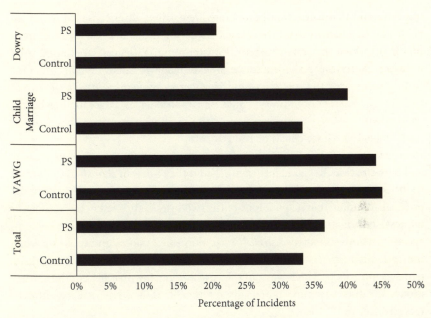

Figure 5.1. Incidents Resolved in the Family (PS vs. Control)

neither of which they can conceal. In comparison, dowry arrangements and domestic violence take place behind closed doors. The public nature of child marriages provides community members with the opportunity to intervene. The damages from dowry are less visible. Initially, it is not the bride but the family that bears the monetary obligations. The cost to the bride—further demands, violence, and separation—comes much later. Protesting domestic violence is even more difficult. As I discuss above, intimate partner violence is an accepted social norm and part of the marital contract. Women face the burden of defending their families' honor by making their marriages last. In an ethnographic study of PS members, Farah Nawaz found that women were unwilling to publicly disclose sensitive information around their own experiences with violence; they were more likely to tell their stories during in-depth one-on-one interviews. These women accepted their husbands as guardians and viewed violence as their husbands' right.[52] They likely felt that public disclosure would defy the normative practice of being a good wife. However, the study also found that women who were educated or had attended PS-organized training had experienced less violence at home.[53]

Representation

Shalish deliberations are often biased against women and the poor. They also silence women's voices. Respondents shared that in their communities, it was unacceptable for women to attend public events. When asked why, women typically said that this is just how things were. Their absence was an expected behavior—the rule-in-use. One woman said, "Villagers have bad ideas about us [if we go]." Women were chastised for attending. Villagers sanctioned their behavior by shaming them and causing damage to their reputations. One respondent feared that society would view her as spoiled (*noshto*), a woman of bad character. Her community would reprimand her by attacking her honor. Even when women attended sessions, they rarely spoke. When they tried to participate, the village elite interrupted them.

Figure 5.2 compares PS members and the control group on *shalish* attendance and participation. Respondents were asked if they knew of *shalish* in their area, whether they attended the event, and what role they played—*shalishkar*, silent or vocal attendant, participant (one of the two sides embroiled in the conflict or witness), or not attending. Compared with the control group, a higher percentage of PS members attended *shalish* when they knew of one, and spoke up when they attended proceedings. PS members also served on the decision-making panel as *shalishkar*, which was not the case among any members of the control group. The differences are statistically significant. Thus women's representation was stronger in PS areas.

PS members also took action in higher numbers when it came to gender-related violence in their communities. Respondents were asked if incidents—dowry, child marriage, and VAWG—had occurred in their household and community, and if so, whether they had responded. Figure 5.3 illustrates respondents' actions in three areas—dowry, child marriage, and VAWG. A larger percentage of PS members took action against child marriage when compared to the control group, but they fell behind on VAWG. The difference between their engagement within and outside of *shalish* suggests that women have difficulty confronting legal issues alone; they may be far better equipped to fight this battle as a group.

Embeddedness

This section explores whether PS groups seek help differently from the control group. Because groups are embedded in both state and society, I expected that PS members would have better access to resources. Figure 5.4 shows the first two points of contact for respondents who reacted to violence in their households and communities. The analysis shows contacts as the percentage of responses—that is, the number of times a respondent sought a contact. Across both groups, women intervened directly or approached an acquaintance; this involved friends, neighbors, or family members. Thus, they tried to resolve issues within their close-knit circles. This suggests a reluctance to approach service providers, who often exist outside of poor rural women's trusted friend and family networks. At the same time, a higher percentage of contacts among PS members involved reaching out to service providers directly—NGOs (including BRAC programs),

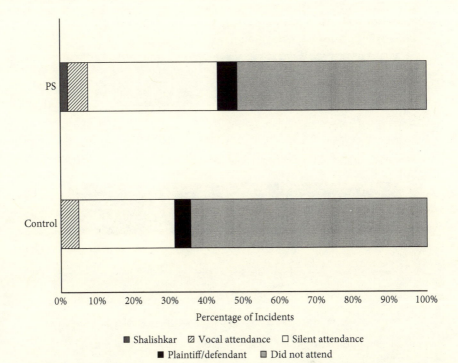

Figure 5.2. Role in Shalish (PS vs. Control)

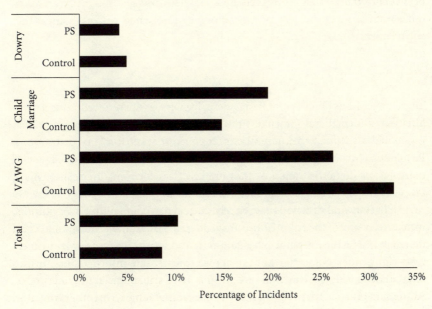

Figure 5.3. Action Taken on Incidents in the Family and Community (PS vs. Control)

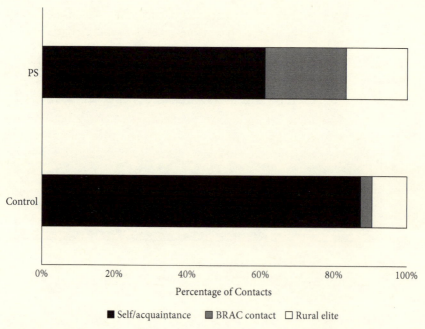

Figure 5.4. Support Networks for Incidents in the Family and Community (PS vs. Control)

health workers, hospitals and clinics, the UP, and the rural elite. These PS members ventured beyond their immediate social networks and sought direct assistance from service providers, possibly dipping into the network of resources that BRAC offers.

Conclusion

This chapter finds that in rural Bangladesh, legal issues are resolved using a combination of formal and informal rules. Often, complex and overlapping rules-in-use make it difficult to differentiate between formal and informal institutions. Resolutions involving formal institutions are evident in the case of dowry, child marriage, or domestic violence. They are less clear for romantic relationships, property-related conflicts, and other minor scuffles. Sometimes solutions involve reconciliation, and decision makers rely on social accountability over punitive measures. Many of the rules-in-use are gendered. For example, dowry and child marriage rest on the roles and expectations that society has carved out for women. And yet, gender inequities appear across formal and informal institutions alike. Indeed, informal institutions are not always inequitable or undesirable. Sometimes they can fill in the gaps left by formal institutions that are inequitable, unjust, or simply ineffective. This becomes particularly clear in the case of divorce, which women can initiate based on Muslim law, but rarely do.

The rules-in-use are different in PS areas, where more legal issues were resolved, women's voices were better represented in *shalish*, and people reached out directly to service providers. These numbers vary for types of incidents. Resolutions were more likely for child marriage than for dowry or violence. Indeed, women's prescribed roles as the ideal wife and the related obligation to preserve their marriage and their honor prevent them from challenging such incidents. In part III I delve deeper into the dynamics of these practices, and in particular, how PS shifts them. Chapter 6 returns to distributive politics.

Negotiating with State and Society

CHAPTER 6

Changing Distributive Politics

It had caught Marium's attention that her son Shohag was not bringing home his full education stipend. He had qualified for the PESP program, which supports primary education for poor children.[1] In 2010, the grant serviced 7.8 million students in 62,087 rural schools.[2] Of late, Shohag had been short on his allowance. News of this discrepancy eventually reached Baby Begum, the PS president from Marium's ward. Baby speculated that Shohag's teacher had been siphoning funds. She gathered some PS members and confronted the teacher.

On the day of their meeting, Baby Begum asked the teacher why Shohag received less money. "Because he misses school regularly and does not study," the teacher complained. Baby Begum responded, "If the student may not study, does that mean you will give him less money?" PESP conditions require that students maintain regular attendance and good performance. But if Shohag failed to meet these conditions, the program would eliminate him. Poor performance did not allow teachers to withhold funding. After a prolonged exchange, the teacher agreed to give Shohag his full stipend. Subsequently, Baby Begum inquired whether other students from her ward had also received partial *upobritti* (education stipend) money. It appeared that there were quite a few. PS members made a list of these students—there were seven—and showed up at the teacher's office once more. They asked, "Which rule says that you give less money if the child misses school and does not do well?" The teacher had no answer. She promised that she would no longer withhold funds.

PS is tasked with helping impoverished community members acquire government and NGO resources. As their interaction with Baby Begum demonstrates, they also ensure equitable service distribution in the community. Over 98 percent of PS groups had pursued safety nets in the previous year; on average, they served 17.2 of their own members and an additional 9.2 individuals from the community. Chapter 4 established that in rural Bangladesh, distributive politics embodies multiple and overlapping institutions. Old clientelist networks have disintegrated, making room for formal rules and transactionalism. The clientelist net is less resilient in PS areas, where exchanges are more likely to embody transactionalism and—for the best-performing PS groups—formal rules. This chapter examines PS efforts to shift distributive politics. I argue that PS groups enact institutional change by negotiating with state and society. They negotiate with the community to change expectations regarding who gets services, with the state through electoral accountability centered on morality, and with NGOs to ensure effective targeting of resources. Embeddedness plays a crucial role in this process by providing access to information and opening up spaces for negotiation.

This chapter follows the sequence of events as PS groups seek services. The first section explores how embeddedness enhances access to information and negotiation spaces. The second section unveils how deliberation can shift expectations in PS meetings. The third section explores negotiations with the state. Then I explore the nature of moral sanctions placed on government service providers. The last section discusses PS interactions with NGOs.

EMBEDDEDNESS

PS groups' embeddedness in state and society provides access to crucial information and new negotiation spaces. By embeddedness, I refer to personal relationships as they manifest in extended family, kinship, neighborhood, and NGO-based networks. James Coleman identifies the potential for information sharing as an important form of social capital. He writes that information is "important in providing a basis for action."[3] It is costly to acquire, but one way of doing so would be via relationships that formed for other purposes.[4] Mark Granovetter writes that our acquaintances, with whom we have a loose connection, move in different circles than we do and can provide better access to information than our close-knit circle of friends.[5] These relationships fill massive information gaps common in the rural global South. In this context, social capital can facilitate knowledge transmission about numerous things, including others' behavior, technology, and markets.[6] For example, a study based in rural Uganda finds that social capital facilitates information exchange among farmers regarding improved seeds and practices.[7]

Embeddedness also opens up new spaces for negotiation between state and society. In *Embedded Autonomy*, Peter Evans writes that developmental states—states that have played a role in industrial transformation—are embedded in "a set of social ties that binds the state to society and provides institutionalized channels for the continual negotiation and renegotiation of goals and policies."[8] For example, in the Indian state of Kerala, the Communist Party, built from peasant movements and associations led by members of the Congress Party, maintains connections with actors mobilizing on the ground while the state remains independent due to its financial reliance on the national government.[9] In Egypt, the Shaa'b or common people forge networks that help them influence the allocation of goods; these networks allow people to create public spaces and "connect individuals and communities to state bureaucracies, public institutions, and formal political institutions."[10] In Iran, street dwellers, the unemployed, immigrants from the same place, and squatters developed formal associations or informal contacts to seek autonomy from state institutions and influence the redistribution of social goods and opportunities such as acquisition of collective consumption, public space, and opportunities for survival.[11] In all of these instances, linkages open up spaces for negotiation between the state and various groups in society.

PS groups maintain extensive social ties. These relationships diffuse vertically through state and nonstate providers and horizontally through village communities. They engulf rural society in a complex, interwoven web, sometimes without clear demarcation between actors and groups. Generally, news of services travels by word of mouth. Villagers may not know that government services exist or have been deployed. Neighbors could tell them that new services have arrived at the UP office. But due to high demand—poor people need them, officials use them to maintain their political power, and wealthier families acquire them to sell as goods for profit—benefits run out very quickly. Embeddedness gives PS groups early access to this information, allowing them to act quickly.

Typically, the CEP PO tells their assigned group when new resources reach the UP. PO Mokbul oversaw a number of PS groups in Rangpur's Peergonj. He informed them when welfare goods arrived in their area. He reminded them of their mandate—to identify beneficiaries and advocate for them. POs like Mokbul create a bridge between PS groups and the UP. Some PS leaders visit the UP office regularly. Indeed, the PS operational guidebook identifies regular contact with the UP office as a key responsibility.[12] It was through one such visit that a PS president from Pabna's Faridpur discovered free winter clothes. When she brought this news to a subsequent meeting, members expressed concern that a particularly harsh winter had left two PS members without sufficient clothing. Others agreed. The group's leaders then asked the UP officials to provide some warm clothes for these women.

Often, groups acquire information via horizontal community networks. In Sunamganj Sadar, the members of one PS informed their leaders of the imminent arrival of ration cards at the general meeting. The women made a list of deserving candidates right away, choosing from individuals who could not earn a living—in their words, the helpless. In Tangail's Mirzapur, another PS member mentioned newly available VGD cards at a general meeting; she had heard this through word of mouth (*lokher mukhe*). It was in a similar way that a PS leader in Nilfamari Sadar discovered that villagers would get work through the one hundred days employment program, a seasonal employment program that connected jobs with building rural infrastructure. She then alerted general members. Together, they made a list of thirty-two eligible women. In Rangpur Sadar, a PS president's nephew informed her that the UP would hand out winter clothes at Rangpur *pouroshova* (municipal council). And in Nogaon's Badalgachi, PS members discovered through local people that their UP had received VGD cards; they went on to make a list of five people in their general meeting.

Embeddedness creates access to closed negotiation spaces. PS groups do well when their leaders maintain direct connections to service providers. Sometimes, vertical embeddedness emerges organically from personal networks. Elsewhere, PS leaders create it. Their kinship networks can extend to the UP. In Sunamganj Sadar, a PS leader's uncle was their UP member. He would let her know when new government services arrived. A PS president's brother was the chairman in Manikganj's Harirampur. She had arranged VGD cards for her community's poorest members through him. In Kurigram, the UP member lived close to a group's president. He informed them when food aid arrived. The group's leaders mentioned that they never had problems acquiring benefits. As neighbors, they knew the member well. A PS president from Khanshama was a UP member herself, elected in the designated seat for women. Her group members felt that despite being an elected official, her loyalties remained with PS. In the past year, she made a list with PS's help and gave it to the chairman. He accepted these names because he knew her.

Embedded groups perform better on service distribution. Figure 6.1 shows two scatterplots. The y-axes show the number of services that PS acquired for PS members and villagers, respectively, and the x-axes show the percentage of PS members who belong to NGOs. Both figures illustrate a moderately strong positive linear association between services received and the percentage of group members who belong to NGOs. The importance of horizontal networks is also illustrated by the fact that larger groups perform better. Table 6.1 shows services acquired in the past year based on selected group characteristics. It illustrates that groups with over sixty members obtain more services than smaller groups. Larger groups may have more hands on deck to share the work. But they also have a much larger set of relationships expanding both vertically and horizontally. The same holds true for vertical embeddedness; groups with socially connected leaders acquire more services on average than those without (table 6.1).

SOCIETY

PS groups change expectations in rural society regarding who gets what. Shared expectations are often the clearest manifestations of informal institutions. By asking how "actors themselves understand the informal constraints they faced" one may identify the informal rules that enhance or bind their actions.[13] For

Figure 6.1A. Villagers Assisted

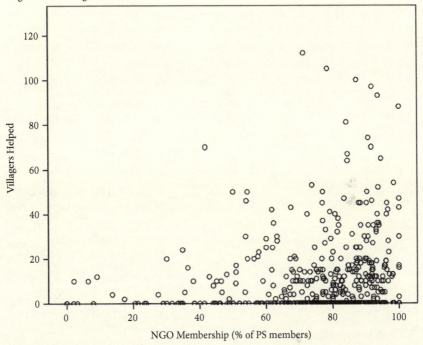

Figure 6.1B. PS Members Assisted

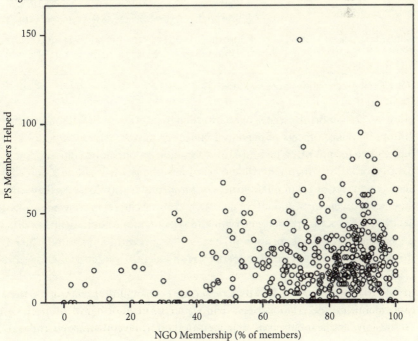

Figure 6.1. Service Distribution by NGO Membership

TABLE 6.1

SERVICES ACQUIRED BY PS GROUP CHARACTERISTICS (N = 671)

		PS members	Villagers
Age of PS (years)	1–3	13.862 (18.413)	6.105 (14.193)
	4–6	16.444 (19.053)	9.605 (17.899)
	7–9	19.179 (19.893)	10.203 (17.099)
	10–12	18.232 (19.755)	10.235 (16.091)
Size of PS	1–30	7.720 (14.493)	4.760 (11.174)
	31–60	14.091(17.620)	8.438 (15.566)
	60+	22.103 (20.952)	10.649 (17.172)
Social status of PS leaders	Ordinary villager	16.757 (18.556)	8.503 (14.666)
	Influential	21.058 (25.873)	15.449 (25.057)
Independent	Dependent	15.755 (18.910)	7.932 (14.534)
	Independent	23.512 (20.598)	14.832 (21.055)
Context: Liberal or conservative?	Conservative	17.739 (23.396)	5.000 (11.485)
	Liberal	17.181 (19.323)	9.367 (16.287)
Context: Can men and women meet?	Yes	19.792 (22.971)	7.667 (15.639)
	No	17.104 (19.327)	9.275 (16.187)
Context: Wealth status of locality	Rich	0	0
	Poor	14.723 (16.133)	7.798 (13.104)
	Well-off	16.891 (17.706)	9.814 (16.176)
	Ultra-poor	23.188 (25.585)	12.042 (21.364)
Context: Urban or rural?	Pouroshova	23.340 (20.374)	13.064 (20.875)
	Union	16.737 (19.323)	8.928 (15.730)

Note: Standard deviations in parentheses.

example, Daniel Brinks writes of an informal institution in Brazil that permits killings by police officers of perceived violent criminals. Although police killings violate formal rules, he finds an expectation among police officers that in the case of killings involving violent criminals, the law will not be enforced.[14] Shared expectations signal the presence of informal institutions. As they shift, they can instigate institutional change. Such expectations often converge around behaviors that actors perceive as right and good. James March identifies these understandings as logics of appropriateness, the core intuition around which is that "humans maintain a repertoire of roles and identities, each providing rules of appropriate behavior in situations for which they are relevant."[15] Actors identify appropriate behaviors based on their own positionality in the world—their roles, identities, and relationships—and act accordingly.

As PS groups negotiate with their communities in general meetings, they create new understandings about what is right and good. Institutional changes often come out of "a particular event or collective experience, a gradual accu-mulation of experiences, or the existence of a mechanism through which to coordinate expectations."[16] PS meetings provide this opportunity. When the women meet, they deliberate their mandate, community concerns, and projects. Over time, they create a series of collective experiences that shape their under-standing of poor people's rights. Their deliberations often begin with BRAC messaging that they receive through multiple sources—their operational guide-book, which states that one of the group's objectives is to help "the area's poor who are fit for getting government and NGO resources—especially women and children—acquire them"[17]—and VO meetings where microfinance recipients chant "eighteen promises" about poor women's rights. At general meetings, learn-ing advisers (*poramorshodata*) lead discussions on women's rights and respon-sibilities. Through these deliberations, PS members connect abstract ideas with their own circumstances and identify pathways out of oppression.

These collective experiences lead to negotiations regarding who gets what. PS groups are required to create and maintain a list of potential service recipients in their communities.[18] Once the women hear that new resources have arrived in their locality, they identify candidates and submit their list to the respective ser-vice provider. Such community-based targeting has numerous historical examples—the English Poor Laws, which till 1834 had local parishes hand out poor relief; the 1994 efforts of the Uzbek government to hand out social assis-tance through "quasi-official, quasi-religious" groups called *mahallas*, and Alba-nia's economic support safety net of the early 1990s administered through local communes.[19] BRAC implements a thorough targeting process for its program for the ultra-poor, which draws on local knowledge through rapport building and inviting local residents to a Participatory Rural Appraisal.[20] The women picked the most deserving candidates. In their language, this included the help-less, downtrodden, and neglected—particularly individuals unable to work or lacking the connections and bargaining skills to pursue services themselves. In Rangpur's Kaunia, one group mentioned that they chose people who could not approach the chairman and make demands openly. Their candidates lacked the confidence and skills to advocate for themselves. "In this case, these people can talk to us openly. That is why we take their demands to the chairman." Because these women come from the community, people feel comfortable sharing prob-lems with them. Another group from Rangpur Sadar said that it chose those who are completely helpless and could benefit at least a little bit from government ser-vices. "Look, all PS members are poor. They all want assistance. But we took recommendations during the general assembly to select beneficiaries."

As the women pick candidates, they create a shared understanding that ser-vices should go to the poorest, most deserving candidates and not to those who maintain political connections or advocate the loudest. They draw on extensive community knowledge to decide who is the most helpless and who can wait for the next round. Considering the group's recommendations creates a collective experience that crystallizes expectations and forms shared understandings regarding a kind of service distribution that is equitable and pro-poor—it targets those with the greatest need. The women attending meetings no longer assume that the most vocal or connected individuals will make the list. Instead of scrambling to get resources for their own families, they embrace their role as community leaders, listening to people's concerns and helping identify potential candidates in their wards. As their expectations shift, so does the logic of appropriateness—helping the most disenfranchised becomes publicly acknowledged as the right thing to do.

Institutions are not just practices; they are established rules. Violating them comes at a price. Indeed, Louise Chappell writes that the logic of appropriateness is not "impermeable" but it is "difficult to unsettle as it is perpetuated by institutional actors who 'embody and reflect existing norms and beliefs' and who seek to maintain the rules."[21] Here, the logic of appropriateness shifts from acquiring resources for oneself to acquiring them for the poorest families. However, as PS groups seek to shift institutions, their very own members push back in an effort to maintain existing practices. These disaffected members place sanctions on the group. They express their disapproval upon discovering that PS membership would not bring them material benefits. Familiar with other NGO programs—including those BRAC runs—they would have heard that BRAC programs hand out material goods to their members.[22] A PS group from Bajedpur, Kishoreganj district, said, "You cannot protect everyone's sentiments by doing this kind of work. We have no problem getting cards, but our members are dissatisfied if we do not get enough." Another group from Joypurhat's Akkelpur *upazila* mentioned that they had to take everyone's opinion into consideration when making their list. And so, when two of their members got a card and three others did not, the latter came to the president and said "bad things" (*kharap kotha*). "They said, we took money to give Bithi and Bhanu cards. They taunted that if we had told them [about paying bribes] we would have paid too," the women added. A third group from Khetlal, Joypurhaat mentioned that some disaffected members yelled at the PS leaders. "But we cannot make everyone happy, obviously," they acknowledged. Some of these women left the group. Others expressed their disaffection aggressively. They yelled at PS leaders, accused them of taking bribes, and spread rumors in the community that the women engaged in corrupt practices. The dissatisfied women resisted PS efforts to change expectations. They punished PS leaders through social ostracization, by publicly challenging the group's reputation. Sanctions can help identify the presence of informal institutions. But the above example illustrates that they can also signal moments of institutional change. In this instance, PS groups faced sanctions for their attempts to shift existing distributive practices.

THE STATE
Resisting Clientelism

As PS groups negotiate with the state—government employees and elected offi-cials at the UP—they push back against clientelist practices. UP officials give them the runaround. Often, they tell the women to go home, promising to look at the lists later. The lists gather dust at the UP office, forgotten until the next visit. As the women wait to meet with officials—sometimes for hours at a time—office staff taunt them, inferring that the UP is no place for poor women. PS leaders follow up with the UP repeatedly. One group from Sirajganj's Belkuchi visited the UP fifteen times before the women received cards. They said, "They [UP officials] don't see our list, they just pretend to see it. They want to avoid us, sometimes they get angry and say not now, come later." When PS members arrive at the UP, they often sit around at the office all day with little certainty of get-ting a meeting, while bearing the taunts and demeaning gaze of officials and employees. "[The] member does not want to sign the list," the Belkuchi women added. Sometimes officials hand over a small number of cards to appease the women. One PS from Dinajpur's Nobabganj said their UP member would not give enough cards. "He said, we gave you three, where will I get more? Should I make up cards? Give you all the cards?" The women pleaded with him; they said that one of their candidates was very poor and could not work properly. He should at least give her a card. The UP member said that they should take what he offered at the moment. He would deal with the other candidate later. He never did.

Clientelism—like many informal institutions—is resilient. UP officials try to avoid PS members, possibly as they save services for clients, sell them for profit, or keep some for their own families. Indeed, PS groups recognize the intracta-ble challenge of clientelism; they accept that officials will siphon cards for them-selves. One group spoke of an animated general meeting where they chose candidates. As PS members competed to get their names on the list, the presi-dent offered them some calming words. She said, "There are thirty-four cards this year, and the chairman and [UP] member are also included in this. Other villagers are also candidates." She expected that UP officials would distribute some cards via clientelist networks; this was standard practice. Another PS from Chirir Bandar echoed similar sentiments. Its leaders mentioned that theirs was a poor area, with hundreds of poor people waiting for VGF. "Some of them were members' people, some chairman's people, some related to this political leader and that powerful person." They admitted that they had to work in this sce-nario from the very start, and it was most stressful. These women expected that clientelism was the rule-in-use on the ground and difficult to get around.

And yet, UP officials rarely deny the women cards up front. They avoid meet-ing PS members. They negotiate hard. They even try to appease them with a small number of cards. But they rarely refuse the women to their face. Elected officials seek their constituencies' support. PS members from Rangpur's Kaunia upazila said that their chairman took their list, but avoided giving them a definitive answer. "Because elections are coming up" they added. The women returned a second time, and once again he said nothing. A few days later, he handed a few cards to the president and asked her to take those for now. He promised more cards later. The women seemed to understand that the chairman was afraid of losing votes. This was particularly important during the data collection period (2009–2010), a year into a new AL national government and a year from new local elections. Until 2015, when the Cabinet of Ministers passed a decision to hold local polls on a partisan basis, local government elections were vigorously fought. Even if UP officials did not recognize PS as a political organization, having their constituents turn up at the office day after day, in a large group, waiting and bargaining, was not a good look for a political candidate.

UP officials violate formal rules when they distribute cards through clientelist networks or for profit. In order to enforce formal rules, PS groups resort to sanctions. Some groups threaten UP officials directly, while others imply it. Sanctions work in multiple ways. The previous section establishes that PS leaders themselves face sanctions for defying informal institutions in distributive practices. However, as they bargain with UP officials, they, too, threaten sanctions to enforce formal institutions. Thus, as actors attempt to change rules—both formal and informal—they punish each other for violations of the rules that they seek to enforce. As a consequence, multiple actors impose sanctions that are simultaneous and compete with each other.

PS groups threaten or impose sanctions that draw on a particular kind of democratic accountability based on morality. Voters hold candidates accountable based on the distribution of collective goods to the poor. Unlike democratic accountability in the established Western democracies, where citizens elect candidates based on policy successes, rural Bangladeshis choose candidates based on moral performance.[23] When candidates provide collective services to the poor, voters view them as good people. Lily Tsai examines how solidarity groups in rural China increase the accountability of local governing institutions. In the absence of democratic accountability, local governments deliver goods to earn respect and good reputation. She writes, "Even when formal accountability is weak, officials may still have a strong incentive to provide public goods when they are subject to obligations and institutions set by social groups."[24] For Tsai, moral standing refers to the esteem or respect granted for good performance that the people regarded as morally good.[25] There is ample evidence that politicians care about serving all citizens, even in societies where clientelism runs rampant. Jennifer Bussell finds that in India, high-level officials provide services to their constituents irrespective of citizens' political preferences, partisanship, or ethnicity—in fact, they are willing to serve all kinds of citizens. Naomi Hossain and

Imran Matin study the work of Village Assistance Committees, formed in order to support BRAC's comprehensive program for the ultra-poor in rural Bangladesh. The committees include ultra-poor representatives of the program, BRAC staff, members of PS, and local influential persons. The study highlights the importance of village leaders' "demonstrated capacity and willingness" to provide for the poor; their committee leadership frequently stressed the link between their committee work and other charitable acts.[26]

PS groups stake their claims as voters. In Manikganj's Ghior upazila, one PS group visited the UP three times. As the member kept turning them away, they negotiated, "Why won't you give us a card? We are poor people, we voted for you." They insisted that he should investigate the impoverished circumstances of their ward and evaluate their candidates himself. The member relented. He promised seven cards and delivered four in the end. In Gaibanda, another PS kept being turned away by their UP member. So they went straight to the chairman. The man told them he would not give anyone a card. "Why won't you give us a card? We are poor people. We voted for you. You have to give us a card. If you do not, we will go to the UNO," the women responded. They received six cards. In both of these instances, the women claimed that they had voted for the officials who were now compelled to serve the poor. The officials were being sanctioned through their accountability to their constituencies—and in particular, whether they assisted the poor.

When officials refuse services or demand money, PS members see them as immoral. Conversely, they recognize officials who serve the poor as good people. The women associate goodness or moral behavior with a general concern for poor people's welfare. PS members in Potuakhali Sadar mentioned that they had no problem while acquiring VGD cards. "Our ward's member is a very good person, understanding of the poor." Another PS from Rangpur Sadar said that their ward's member was an advocate for PS. He was a van driver; being poor himself, he understood the plight of the poor. In Panchagar Sadar, one PS explained that their ward commissioner, Ripon, was an extremely honest man. He understood poor people's pain and sadness (*dukkho koshto*). In all of these instances, PS members' conceptions of moral behavior—goodness and honesty were the words that came up—were tied to the candidates' compassion for the poor and willingness to serve them.

For rural Bangladeshis, a local government official's electability is tied to their compassion toward the poor collectively as perceived by their constituency.[27] The rural poor care just as much for their communities' collective benefit as their own private gain. When individual respondents—both PS members and the control group—were asked to explain their choice of candidate in the last-held local election (2003), only 21.2 percent voted hoping for individual benefits. This is only slightly lower than the 23.2 percent who expected that the entire village would benefit. A mere 5.5 percent claimed to personally know and like the candidate.[28] Qualitative data illustrates that voters choose candidates whom they perceive as helpful toward the poor. Respondents mentioned candidates' previous record and current campaign promises. They highlighted both public and private goods—welfare resources, infrastructural development, and justice in *shalish* (village court). Below are some common responses:

> I voted for the chairman and (UP) member who gives more rice and wheat. They help more. Through this chairman we will get relief aid so I voted.
>
> If the chairman and member are elected, they will build roads and arrange *shalish*. That is why I voted for the chairman and member.
>
> Before the election, the chairman promised that if he wins, he will arrange for us to receive various opportunities and benefits like relief, old-age allowance, latrines, *khas* land. We voted for him with the hope of receiving these benefits.

In all of these instances, respondents voted for individuals who promised services to their localities as a whole. Even when they referred to private goods like safety nets, their responses conveyed hope that the entire community would benefit. Local officials may serve PS members because they hesitate to turn away members of their constituency, but they may also fear losing their reputation as benefactors of the poor. As punishment for turning away PS members, they could be voted out of office.

Transactionalism

Sometimes, PS groups fail to shift clientelist practices in favor of formal rules. As they negotiate with the UP, they end up with the unintended consequence of transactionalism—exchanging goods for money. Transactionalism is an established practice, sometimes with predetermined service rates. Safety net cards can cost between Tk. 100 and Tk. 2,000, sometimes higher. One PS group from Kurigram's Roumari upazila said, "Problem is that whenever we give a list they demand money. There is no relief without money." Their response—that no exchanges occur without money—suggests that transactionalism is repetitive, resilient, and expected. Another PS from Rangpur said that their leaders had approached the UP member for a widow's allowance card. The member told them to check back in ten days. When they returned, he asked them for money. "You will need to pay Tk. 500," he said. His language—that one needs to pay—suggests that this is not a request; it is a requirement. It took the women three trips, two weeks, and Tk. 500 to get their card. For another PS from Haluaghat, the fee was an exorbitant Tk. 2,000.

PS groups expect and abide by transactionalism. But they do not approve of it. Many PS members identify it as a normal but immoral practice. They rarely use the word corruption. This echoes Steven Pierce's conceptualization of corruption in Nigeria, where people view acts such as "bribery-seeking, extortion,

and embezzlement" not as corruption, but rather as oppression—"acts that were *wrong* but that were nonetheless a common quality of people in government."[29] For Pierce, conceptualizing corruption as misuse of government office is a technocratic idea.[30] It takes on different meanings when local understandings are considered. In rural Bangladesh, the meaning of corruption extends beyond breaking rules. It signals bad character traits—greed, dishonesty, and oppression. In Rangpur Sadar, a PS member said, "Actually our member is a bit greedy. He does not want to give a card without money." The women recognized the practice as wrong, but added that poor people had no choice. They could use whatever little assistance they got. They took money from their potential recipient and handed it over to the UP office. "If we pay money, the member gives cards quickly," they said. Her comment suggests that the fee could guarantee or expedite services, and that the poor had no choice but to accept this.

Transactionalism is an unintended consequence of PS negotiating efforts. Thus, as PS groups fight clientelist practices but entangle themselves in the norm of paying for goods, their actions shift from one informal institution to another. Transactionalism still provides the poor with access to otherwise unavailable resources—for some, this is better than not receiving services at all—it deviates from formal rules. For development programming purposes, this is an undesirable outcome. However, institutions are both stabilizing and dynamic.[31] Institutional changes are not predictable; they cannot be externally imposed and pushed toward a predetermined outcome. Very often, they take actors to unexpected places. As old practices stand firm, change occurs in increments as actors shift and adapt their behaviors.[32] In the process, they may end up somewhere entirely unanticipated.

Embeddedness

PS groups are vertically and horizontally embedded in their communities. Their embeddedness plays a crucial role in negotiations. Horizontal embeddedness gives PS groups access to information regarding eligible candidates. It also provides credibility and legitimizes their decisions. When UP officials push back, the women claim that they come from the community and are thus better equipped to choose beneficiaries than elected officials. A PS group from Taragonj said, "Our PS members are poor to begin with, but some at least do not have to starve." They were meticulous in choosing not just the poor, but the completely helpless, who could not work to make a living. They claimed that PS was very detailed in making these decisions. "Since PS is a poor people's organization, PS knows who deserves VGD cards," they added. When they took their list to the chairman, he turned them away. The women objected. They insisted that he take the list. They said that they were poorer than the member and knew more poor and helpless people. "Eventually, the chairman had no choice but to take our list," they added. Numerous PS groups insisted that they could do the

work of the local government much more effectively than UP officials because of their embedding in the community.

Vertical embeddedness opens up access to closed negotiation spaces. Women with direct linkages to the UP or party networks can acquire services far more easily than leaders without such contacts. Sometimes, PS members are themselves elected into office. We are left with the lingering question of whether these women engage in clientelist politics themselves or use PS for their own political gain. If PS members are linked to local political networks, then embeddedness may provide a channel for local power structures to infiltrate the group. Hossain and Matin's study found that Village Assistance Committees had mixed effects on ultra-poor peoples' lives. In some cases, program participants with the closest ties to committee members benefited most. However, the committee also brought program participants into a larger social network, inviting them to events, exposing them to exclusively male decision-making spaces, sometimes having members accompany women to get services such as health care, and generally expanding elite protection to encompass more of the rural poor.[33] Thus, elite-poor linkages can have dual effects: they expand patronage, but they also provide the excluded with advantages that patronage provides.

The deliberative nature of PS groups can protect the community from inequitable service distribution. First, PS members elect vertically embedded leaders precisely because these women can increase access to the UP. Even when leaders hold elected UP positions, they continue to serve the group. In Shirajgonj's Kamarkhand, one PS maintained the same leadership committee for years. The women said that their current PS president was the female UP member and perfectly fit for this position. Indeed, in almost every case where a PS leader belonged to the UP, the group expressed confidence in her leadership abilities. When a leader did not present these qualities, she could always be voted out. The deliberative nature of PS groups may also prevent leaders from securing goods for themselves or their acquaintances. Because of the public nature of decision making, the leader remains accountable to the group.

NGOs

PS groups provide a platform for other NGO programs to allocate services, especially when the goods come from BRAC. The women ensure that resources reach the right recipients, both within and outside of the NGO's own membership. One PS from Chirir Bondor upazila in Dinajpur mentioned that one of their members did not have a latrine. The women discussed the issue at the meeting and planned to get her a latrine through BRAC. They informed the CEP PO, who facilitated the process. In Tangail's Madhupur, PS President Rahela went around the village and made a list of twenty-eight people who needed sanitary latrines. She

submitted the list to the BRAC WASH program. The office called a month later, and BRAC staff came to verify the list. They visited eighteen people and gave them latrines. In creating a first draft of the list, PS members collaborated with the WASH program; they assisted WASH staff in choosing beneficiaries in the same way that they helped the UP. Such community-based decision making gives the service delivery process greater credibility than if it were done by the NGO alone. These PS members said, "We chose those who had no latrines, defecate in open fields." Villagers did not cooperate at first. According to the PS members, they complained that lists are always being compiled, but the people get nothing. They were wary of NGOs and tired of cooperating without being given anything in return. Since PS members came from the community, they helped bridge this gap.

Conclusion

This chapter establishes how PS groups shift distributive politics. It argues that PS groups negotiate with the state and society to enact institutional change. The women of PS groups negotiate with society when they choose potential service recipients through deliberations. They change the expectation that being vocal will get them resources—rather, they establish the practice of allocating safety nets to the most deserving candidates. In turn, poor candidates begin to expect that they, too, can get typically out of reach services. When the women negotiate with the state, they threaten or imply sanctions based on democratic accountability; local government officials face the potential threat of being voted out of office if they deny demands that come from their constituencies. Finally, the women work with NGOs to ensure proper targeting of resources. Here, the relationship is often one of mutual collaboration.

In thinking about institutional change, this chapter asks what compels actors to pursue one set of rules over another. In the PS story, institutional shifts occur in two ways—by changing expectations and by imposing or threatening sanctions on actors. Informal institutions like clientelism or transactionalism—and even less institutionalized practices such as relentless bargaining for resources—are resilient. Their very robustness becomes apparent when PS members face sanctions for attempting to remove them. Some group members castigate them by yelling at them, accusing them of corruption, and spreading rumors. At the same time, PS members themselves hold UP officials accountable by threatening sanctions—in this case, the subtle warning that failing to serve their constituencies might result in officials being voted out of office. Sanctions indicate the presence of informal institutions. But this chapter suggests that they can also signal institutional change. One may identify a period of imminent institutional change via multiple and overlapping sanctions placed by numerous parties, some seeking to maintain old institutions, others hoping to enact new ones.

From a policy perspective, community-level targeting of safety nets can change how providers distribute services. When conducted through local organizations embedded in rural society, its benefits extend beyond efficient targeting—often the focus of development programs—to encompass long-term shifts in the relational aspects of distributive politics. In the following chapter, I explore similar institutional shifts in the legal domain.

Negotiating Justice

When Shornali's family discovered her romantic relationship with Neel, they visited his family with a formal wedding proposal. As local PS members described the love affair, they used the word *prem*, signifying romantic love but ambiguous on sexual involvement or the intentionality of marriage. The story unfolds in neighboring villages outside of Tangail city, an urban hub adjacent to the capital, Dhaka. Shornali's family may have desired a quick wedding. Most parents of young women would find this situation worrisome. Whether the relationship had turned sexual was perhaps irrelevant; her frequent meetings with a young man put her reputation at great risk. This was unbecoming by social standards. People would talk. And if the relationship fizzled, she would have a difficult time finding another match.

Initially, Neel's family accepted the proposal. But at the peak of wedding planning, his mother made a significant demand—Tk. 50,000 in dowry. If Shornali's family refused, wedding preparations would likely come to a halt. In the words of PS president Sabiha, the alliance would break (*biye bhanga*). Sabiha gathered a group of PS members to visit Neel's mother. The women warned her that dowry was a crime. "If we let the police know, you will be punished," they cautioned. With the lingering threat of legal action, Neel's mother withdrew her demand. The wedding proceeded as planned.

In much of rural Bangladesh—where romantic relationships are expected to result in marriage—*prem* brings significant risks for any young woman. She may expect marriage, but her partner could end the relationship. He would have little to lose. Society does not hold men to the same standards of chastity as it holds women. Wedding talks are fragile. The two families may disapprove of the relationship. They could seek better matches for their children. Here "better" refers to potential brides and grooms who come from wealthy families or meet the socially accepted standards of beauty—tall, fair, and slender. If the families come from the same area, they could be embroiled in conflicts or rivalries with each other. Wedding preparations might proceed until families disagree about costs, logistics, and gifts. But dowry poses the biggest threat to wedding talks. Whether a young woman marries depends on her groom's demand and what her parents can afford.

Informal institutions such as dowry, child marriage, and domestic violence are well entrenched in rural Bangladesh. They remain resilient in the face of formal legislation. In chapter 5, I argue that legal issues in rural Bangladesh are resolved through both formal and informal institutions, and that the rules-in-use are different in PS areas compared to the control group. This chapter delves further into the informal institutions surrounding the legal system. I explore how PS groups engage with and change them. This chapter argues that PS groups make rule of law accessible, representative, and equitable toward the rural poor. As PS groups negotiate with society, they seek to change the logic of appropriateness around young women's prescribed behaviors, and impose social and legal sanctions. In doing so, they create the space for a different kind of justice—one that involves both formal and informal institutions—in spaces where the state does not deliver.

RULE OF LAW

Bangladesh has long suffered from weakly performing formal institutions. The legal system is no exception.[1] Across much of the global South, rule of law is elusive. By rule of law, I refer to the fact that "whatever law exists is written down and publicly promulgated by an appropriate authority before the events meant to be regulated by it, and is fairly applied by relevant state institutions including the judiciary (though other state institutions can be involved as well)."[2] It has at least three broad elements—whether laws are (1) accessible to all; (2) valid in that they are written, recognized, and equitable; and (3) democratic, in that they are implemented consistently and equitably, and provide the opportunity for all voices to be heard.[3] In Bangladeshi villages, access to justice—the ability to "appear before formal state courts or otherwise draw on the judicial and legal structures of the state"—is a rare luxury.[4] The rural poor may lack information regarding laws, human rights, and the logistics of seeking legal aid. Md. Abdul Alim and Tariq Omar Ali write that those seeking justice face a complex landscape which they may navigate "through different routes" such as formal district courts, the UP (which includes village courts and the Arbitration Council), *shalish*, and other alternate dispute mechanism processes administered by NGOs, including BRAC.[5] Many areas lack district courts; when they do exist, the poor avoid them due to costly backlogs and bias toward the wealthy, powerful, and politically connected. The police demand bribes to register complaints, and they fabricate and drop charges for money. Upon filing cases, they require further payments to protect arrestees from torture while in custody or to protect complainants from regular harassment.

In the absence of the state, the rural poor turn to traditional and informal mechanisms for their legal needs.[6] With the formal legal system out of reach, *shalish* becomes an avenue for administering justice. Dina Siddiqi describes it as an informal village community hearing, "an enduring and fundamental feature of rural society, and one that has been neither displaced nor endangered by the introduction of the formal justice system."[7] Thus, it serves an important function in addition to the established legal mechanisms of the state. It has deep roots, beginning with the traditional *panchayat* system that predates colonial rule. Siddiqi compares it to the *khap panchayats* of North India or the *loya jirgas* in Afghanistan and Pakistan, which are all "legitimate nonstate modes of adjudication."[8] Bangladesh is not unique in this regard. Guillermo O'Donnell writes that in many Latin American countries, the legal system fails to reach certain areas. Formal law has limited or no application in these places; it is encompassed by and overlaps with informal law. These "brown areas" are "subnational systems of power" that coexist with a seemingly democratic system at the center."[9] In these contexts, rule of law can fail, among other reasons, due to a "sheer lawlessness" when formal rules do not reach peripheral segments of society and informal institutions dictate solutions to legal disputes.[10] Thus, people can access rule of law in both state-made and traditional spaces, and justice can rely on both formal and informal institutions.

In Bangladesh, rule of law lacks validity. Laws—even when written down and widely acknowledged—are not consistent. The legal system is a "mixed arrangement" of indigenous Indian, Mughal, and British laws—a legacy of its complex historical past.[11] Following independence, the country adopted this "vast mixed body of jurisprudence" under the Bangladesh (Adaptation of Existing Bangladesh Laws) Order 1972.[12] This inconsistency spills over into *shalish*. Elora Shehabuddin writes that in the absence of a strong legal system enforced by the state, multiple legal codes operate, often in tension with each other. When it comes to family law, for example—and *shalish* covers family disputes extensively—there exists the "state's own reformed Muslim Family Code, which is derived from Islamic Law; the state's secular criminal code; Islamic laws, which tend to be interpreted very differently by the urban-based Jama'at and rural religious leaders; and a more international human rights perspective that is espoused by numerous secular development organizations."[13] As a result, a "hodgepodge" of laws operates in shalish, both formal and informal, and arbitrarily applied.[14] Tobias Berger writes that they create a kind of legal pluralism where multiple "normative and legal orders overlap and coincide within a given socio-political space."[15] According to Dina Siddiqi, these multiple sources of law are deeply entangled in one another, and "as likely to collude as to collide."[16] But *shalish* provides room for a different kind of justice—one based on deliberation. Seeking to preserve harmony in the community, it allows for the incorporation of local customs and practices, and embraces reconciliation instead of punishment.[17] Verdicts oscillate between formal and informal rules. Because they rely on open and transparent deliberations, the community accepts them as legitimate. This enmeshing of formal and informal institutions resembles how indigenous and state laws intersect in Latin America, where formal and informal institutions sometimes compete with and at other times accommodate each other. Van Cott writes that sometimes formal laws may not concede to informal norms, "but elsewhere, states are recognizing the informal systems and community authorities are reshaping their own norms and procedures to adjust to the new regime of 'legal pluralism.'"[18]

Finally, rule of law is undemocratic; it lacks both representation and fairness. Legal codes can themselves discriminate, particularly against women. The Constitution of Bangladesh guarantees equality to women, but simultaneously recognizes the multiplicity of laws, including religious laws that give men the upper hand in matters of family, such as divorce, inheritance, and child custody and maintenance.[19] *Shalish* embodies local power structures. Typically, decision makers belong to the rural elite.[20] They often ignore formal laws or implement them unfairly, favoring wealthy, dominant, or politically connected groups. As a result, they discriminate against the poor, women, and minorities. The rural elite can use *shalish* for social control. In their study of a village in North Bangladesh, Alim and Ali find that the rural elite often used *shalish* to maintain authority over local residents.[21] Villagers who sought justice outside of *shalish*—for example with BRAC's legal aid program or courts—faced social sanctions. Village leaders would alienate them or fail to cooperate with them in the future.[22] Shalish is also deeply gendered, in both representation and adjudication. Women are discouraged from speaking out or even appearing at the margins of the event.[23] They hold back out of fear and rarely serve as *shalishkar*.[24] In conflicts involving poor women, judgments can be excessively punitive and reflect "personal (and highly patriarchal) interpretations of texts and community norms" instead of laws.[25] Certain issues are so gendered and deeply entrenched in rural society that they may not even make it to *shalish*. The community views them as standard practice, and they remain confined within the family. The next section addresses two such issues—dowry and child marriage.

In Private Spaces
Access

PS groups increase poor rural women's access to the law by bringing the law into private spaces. Dowry and child marriage are intimate matters, limited to the confines of the household. Typically, a bride has little freedom in choosing her partner. She may agree to the parents' chosen match—sometimes reluctantly—unaware of her rights, where to seek help, or the threats that dowry or child marriage pose for her safety and well-being. Concerned community members stay out of others' family affairs. PS members would hear of such incidents by word of mouth. As parents arrange their children's marriages, they share the good news with friends and family. Often, wedding details spread throughout the community. This includes the bride's age and dowry amount. PS groups' embeddedness in the community opens up their access to this information. Between all members, they have extensive reach.

When PS members discovered impending dowry and child marriage in the community, they gathered to plan an intervention. They understood the time sensitivity of weddings, often scheduled for the same week, and sometimes the very same day. They did not have the luxury of waiting until the next meeting. The women approached the involved families to stop the incident. They provided information regarding the dangers of dowry and child marriage. If the families did not listen, they brought in community members for accountability. When all else failed, they threatened legal action.

Informal Institutions

Dowry and child marriage are accepted and expected practices in rural Bangladesh. When PS members intervene, they are often told that "this is how things are done here." In recalling events, they use the words *reeti* (practice or tradition) and *niyom* (rule), marking regularity in behavior. In Kurigram's Rajarhat, PS cashier Shefali tried to speak to a young man's father who had taken Tk. 60,000 in dowry. The father responded, "These are the traditions of the times. So I will take it." He refused to budge from his position. After extensive conversation and persistent bargaining, Shefali gave up and left. In Dinajpur Sadar, a prospective groom demanded Tk. 85,000 from a PS member for her daughter's wedding. As news of the wedding spread throughout their locality, the local PS president approached the groom's family and explained that taking dowry was a crime. She mentioned that the groom's father gave her a hard time. He said, "This is a social practice, it is not wrong." The women recalled showing him books to prove that dowry was illegal. It was not clear what books they showed the man—perhaps it was BRAC leaflets or newspaper articles. But he tried to legitimize his demand by claiming that it was a social practice, and thus the right thing to do despite being illegal.

Dowry and child marriage are the rules-in-use in rural Bangladesh. When families fail to abide by them, they face sanctions—further indication that an informal institution exists.[26] The costs of avoidance are particularly high for young women; society deems them unmarriageable. Their families are chided, ostracized, and become the subject of gossip and ridicule. Dowry amounts ranged from Tk. 20,000 to Tk. 70,000, a big ask for poor families. And yet, brides' families rarely negotiated demands; they feared that they would risk the match.

Nor did they seek legal assistance. Elora Shehabuddin writes that the law dictates that both families would be held responsible if a case is filed, which disin-
centivizes legal action.[27] Rather, families have found ways to cope. One woman
from Chapai Nawabganj Sadar had secured a good match for her daughter. During wedding talks, the groom's family visited to "see the girl." *Meye dekha*—an
integral part of wedding arrangements—refers to the practice of the groom's
family visiting the bride's home to see the bride in person and gauge her beauty,
physical desirability, and homemaking qualities. During this particular visit, the
groom's family demanded Tk. 25,000. When the bride's mother insisted that she
could not afford the sum, the family left abruptly. Later, she heard that the family
had found another bride for their son. The mother would not make the same
mistake again. When a second marriage prospect materialized, she took out a
loan to pay the Tk. 20,000 demand. Another woman from Dinajpur's Parbotipur upazila promised her daughter's prospective in-laws Tk. 50,000. She borrowed from multiple sources to fulfill this obligation. Their behavior is not
uncommon. Often, poor families find themselves in debt paying dowry. They
promise a specific dowry amount during wedding negotiations and pay the sum
in installments, borrowing from several sources over time. There is also some
evidence that microfinance loans have become a source of dowry funds. Studies
have found that people use microfinance loans to fund family weddings, where
expenses can include dowry.[28]

Dowry and child marriage survive because actors keep them alive and construct their behaviors around them. These practices benefit young men and their
families, but parents of both men and women perpetuate them. When women's
families pushed back, their resistance became a violation of institutions. They
were punished and their behaviors sanctioned by the community. Grooms' families employed multiple strategies to hold brides' families accountable for dowry
payments. Sometimes they made demands at the wedding venue. Marriage festivities span multiple days, and the bride's family typically hosts the wedding. A
broken alliance was shameful enough—it would jeopardize future marriage
prospects for the bride to-be—but having this event unfold in the presence of
wedding guests was especially humiliating. To save face, brides' families caved
and promised dowries that they could not afford. Once they gave their word, they
took out multiple loans to fulfill their obligation. Some families paid the promised amount over time. Others fell short. When the bride's family failed to pay,
her in-laws ridiculed, beat, or trapped her in the household. Sometimes they sent
her back to her parents' house and instructed that she should only return with
the owed money. In some cases, they demanded even more money.[29] If her family
could not pay, her husband could show up at their doorstep to demand his
due. There would be a public and humiliating scene. Sometimes the husband
threatened divorce. All of these moves served as sanctions to coerce the bride's
family into submission. The price for noncompliance would be damage to the

woman's reputation—a broken alliance, divorce, or simply being sent back home. These sanctions shame her for being a "bad" wife, incapable of fulfilling her marital role.

Parents of young girls face or fear similar sanctions for failing to marry their daughters at an early age. Many expressed concern that society would label their daughters unmarriageable. This was especially true for young women who lacked the socially accepted standards of beauty. Families also feared for their daughters' safety. Thugs—typically belonging to wealthy or influential families as well as political parties—often harass young girls while going to school, coaching (tutoring), or other activities. In rural Bangladesh, girls typically walk to school—often in large groups, but unaccompanied by elders. Akhter Ahmed and Taniya Sharmeen find distance to be one of the causes of secondary school dropout; secondary schools were located three times as far from students' homes as primary schools.[30] Distance becomes particularly debilitating for adolescent girls in a country with a high incidence of VAWG. Sometimes the men propose relationships or marriage, and rejection leads to further harassment, assault, kidnapping, and even acid attacks. Parents also marry their daughters early as premarital romantic or sexual relationships—consensual or coerced—could jeopardize a girl's marriage prospects. She would no longer be considered pure or honorable, and her marriage prospects would dwindle. Because a family's honor is tied to their women's reputations, the family would lose face.[31]

Thus, parents often pull their daughters out of school to be married. In Bangladesh, despite reaching remarkable goals in girls' education—girls surpass boys on both primary and secondary school enrollments—most girls drop out of school during puberty.[32] Simeen Mahmud and Sajeda Amin find that over a third of girls entering secondary school drop out before completing tenth grade.[33] Education can increase economic prospects; in Bangladesh, women enjoy higher returns on education compared to men.[34] Indeed, parents may be willing to send girls to school, particularly if they perceive the type of schooling to "enhance the possibilities of securing a good marriage by improving a girl's appearance, personality, and social skills."[35] If education increases girls' economic and marriage prospects, parents should want to keep their daughters in school. But Amin and Mahmud find that this is only the case among better-off families.[36] Waiting for a good marriage was a luxury that only wealthy families could afford, and it was often girls from poor families who dropped out to get married.[37]

Logics of Appropriateness

Dowry and child marriage are gendered institutions; they push women into socially accepted behaviors when locked into gendered roles, first as obedient daughters, and later as wives and mothers. Women's husbands are expected to protect them. Their parents hold the ultimate responsibility of securing good marital prospects for their children; this is expected and appropriate behavior.

In meeting their parental obligations, families marry their daughters early and with dowry. But marriage also absolves parents of their guardianship. Once their daughters are married, they are no longer responsible for their safety and honor. This charge now falls on her husband. He is expected to protect and provide for her.

Dowry and child marriage subscribe to particular logics of appropriateness. When brides' families give dowry, they play the role of good parents. As chapter 5 illustrates, they obtain loans from multiple sources, believing that that the money will secure their daughters' happiness. Indeed, Farah Chowdhury finds that in rural Bangladesh, brides' parents typically believe that dowries would serve as a form of insurance against divorce. Families that agree to pay dowry feel that a woman who brings money into her in-laws' family would be treated with respect, and that a large dowry would ensure their child's well-being.[38] As parents, securing a good life for their daughter remains their biggest obligation. And their perception of security is tied to her marriage—a girl's foremost responsibility and her ultimate destiny. Similar logics of appropriateness drive parents' decisions to marry off their underage daughters. People generally know that child marriage endangers young girls. The government and NGOs have undertaken extensive campaigns and training programs to educate community members on its physical and emotional dangers. But parents do not comply with the law. They often fake their daughters' ages in legal documents to avoid hassles with the police or registration. When PS members object, parents arrange marriages in secret.

In Hobiganj's Neyamatpur, a PS president discovered that her fourteen-year-old neighbor Ruma had wedding talks in progress. She knew the family and tried to reason with them. But the mother argued that her daughter was pretty. If she sent the girl to school or kept her at home for too long, a mishap might occur at any time. "So while we have our honor and respect, we should get her married." By mishap, the mother could have referred to a romantic liaison, a sexual relationship, a pregnancy, or simply an instance where a local thug would have his eyes on her. She could be kidnapped and married against her will—perhaps even raped and killed. "We will not listen to anyone," the mother added, and "when we find a good boy we will get her married." When they spoke, the PS group expressed their disappointment. They claimed to have learned that women cannot be married under the age of eighteen. "We have to send them to school. Ruma was only fourteen, this was the age for her to go to school, not be married," the PS president added. "That is why we stood by her side." But in attempting to protect her, PS members were pitted against an adamant mother. The rules dictated that her daughter should remain pure and untainted until marriage. Her role, as Ruma's mother, was to protect the family's honor by ensuring that the marriage took place.

As part of their socially designated roles, grooms' families are expected to take dowry. Gendered norms place the two families on hierarchical and unequal terms. When a marriage is arranged with dowry or an underage bride, the two families involved may be equally poor. But the groom's family has greater authority and bargaining power than the bride's family. They decide the terms of marriage, including the amount of dowry. In child marriage cases, the groom is often an adult. He dominates discussions, as his role as provider and protector is valorized.[39] Parents place their vulnerable young daughters at risk, unwilling to let go of good marriage prospects—potential grooms who are wealthy, employed, or employable, and are expected to protect their daughter both financially and physically.

Negotiations

PS groups negotiate with families to stop weddings involving dowry or child marriage. They shift practices in two ways—by presenting competing logics of appropriateness and threatening sanctions. When the women visit homes during wedding preparations—and sometimes during the weddings themselves—they convey the illegality and dangers of both practices. They warn parents that early marriage could jeopardize their daughters' physical and emotional health. To families discussing dowry, the women explain the complex relationship between dowry and domestic violence. In these conversations, they challenge the logic of appropriateness around marriage as every woman's ultimate goal. They emphasize the value of education and encourage families to keep their daughters in school instead. Thus, they create a new discourse around appropriate behaviors. For the parents of young girls, these behaviors involve protecting their daughters from dowry and child marriage, and securing their futures through education. For young men, it involves shaking the old customs.

In Taragonj, the local PS group's secretary was slapped with a dowry request during her daughter's wedding festivities. The groom's family had asked for Tk. 50,000 (US$595). The mother insisted that she could not afford this sum. But the groom's family threatened that they would break off the alliance if she could not pay. They made their demand at the wedding venue after the guests had arrived. No young woman's parents would want a *biye bhanga* (canceled wedding) on the wedding day. It would damage their honor and tarnish the bride's reputation. PS leaders said, "When we discovered what was going on, we started thinking about the weak points of the groom's family." While deliberating on a solution, PS members came to know that the groom was smitten with the bride; the couple were in love. They attended the wedding as if nothing was amiss. Once at the venue, they pulled the groom aside. PS leaders said that they asked him if he was planning to marry the money or the girl. They recalled, "The boy got embarrassed and married the girl without the dowry." His family was upset and threatened to leave the wedding. But PS members walked over to the groom's house and stated that dowry is *haram* (un-Islamic); they were given plenty of gifts instead. They added, "The girl is pretty. Why will you not agree?" The women negotiated with the groom on a competing logic of appropriateness. They shamed him on two counts—that of being inconsiderate to the woman he loved and adopting un-Islamic norms. Thus, they compelled him to shift his behavior to a new appropriate course of action.

Institutional change occurs in a complex terrain with overlapping norms and standards. As such, no logic of appropriateness—the understanding of one's role, course of action, or the situation at hand—can be untangled from other standards of behavior in the community. While the PS group pushes back against dowry, a gendered institution embedded in deep-rooted, systemic patriarchy, it is important to mention that in this particular instance they also resort to ideals that subscribe to such gendered logics. They negotiate with the groom's family claiming that the bride is pretty, drawing on traditional ideas of beauty—fair skin, slender build, long hair—that make a woman marriageable. This story illustrates the complexities surrounding logics of appropriateness—one may calculate one's actions based on their role in a certain scenario, but their behavior exists in the context of enduring norms and standards. Logics of appropriateness do not just conflict with each other during periods of negotiations and change; they are also in conflict within actors' own decision-making processes. As we figure out who we are and what we should do in any given circumstance, we weigh our options, and while we may know the "right thing to do," our minds may simultaneously be burdened by competing norms.

When negotiations fail, PS groups attempt to hold parents socially accountable by engaging community members, such as UP officials, their BRAC PO, or other NGO staff. Ruma's parents arranged her marriage when she was fourteen. When the PS women visited her home, they informed her mother of the many physical dangers that child marriage can pose for young women. Ruma's mother did not listen. The women then visited their BRAC PO. "We returned to Ruma's house, bringing PO *bhai* with us." After much deliberation, Ruma's parents finally agreed to halt the wedding. "They put their hand on PO *bhai*'s head and swore they would not marry her. They would send her to school," the women added. By bringing their PO into Ruma's home, the group had turned the family's private matter into a public issue. Other PS members would have been present, and perhaps neighbors would have gathered to watch the drama unfold. In putting their hand on the PO's head and making an oath, the family had committed to stopping the marriage in the presence of the village community. They were now socially obligated to follow through.

When all else fails, PS groups threaten to call the police. One PS in Magura's Mohammadpur stepped in when Komola's father promised Tk. 15,000 to her prospective groom but failed to arrange the funds after the wedding. Her husband pressured her to go home and collect the money. Eventually, he sent her back to her parents' house for good. Once Komola had been at her parents' house for three months, her husband came by once more to demand the dowry money. Seeing no way out, Komola's mother, a PS member, approached the group for help. The PS president then took two other members to visit Komola's husband. They threatened to file a police case against him; the women asserted that BRAC would help them. "We wanted to scare him," they said. Komola's husband took her back.

In Dinajpur's Parbotipur upazila, a PS cashier discovered that fourteen-year-old Amena Begum was to be married. When she told the PS president, the two women went to visit the girl's mother. "We talked to the mother about child marriage," they said. They pleaded with her to stop the wedding. They told her that the families could go to jail. They even explained that a young bride is always ill and that if she has a child, both mother and child will suffer from malnutrition. The mother seemed to understand. She agreed to stop the wedding. Once some time had passed, the PS group learned that the wedding was still on. Amena's mother had given in to family pressures. The women went back to Amena's house and threatened to file a police case. "I said that if they do this, I will take the marriage papers and hand it over to the UP office," the PS president said. "The mother stood by our side," they added. "She had wanted this but it was not possible for her to do it on her own." The groom's family had influence in the area. They were wealthier than Amena's family, making it difficult for her family to break off the match. They threatened the PS president. "The boy said to me, I will get married, what is it to you? Don't interfere," the PS president said. She claimed to have responded that he was self-sufficient and could not support his wife. She added, "The boy got even angrier, and I said, if you marry this girl, I will make sure you eat rice in jail."

SHALISH

Access

When PS members come across legal disputes, they increase women's access to the law by calling for *shalish*. PS members from Faridpur's Boalmari intervened when they heard that Sohail assaulted his wife often. They tried to reason with him, but failed. At one point, Sohail physically attacked the PS president. Seeing no other way to resolve this, the president called a *shalish* with the member and *matobbor*. Based on *bichar* (justice), Sohail paid Tk. 3,000 in reparations. We can assume from the monetary reparations that the couple separated. In *shalish*, Sohail's wife found justice that she could not expect from the state. In Nogaon's Dhamoirhaat district, a PS member advised a local woman, Hosneara,

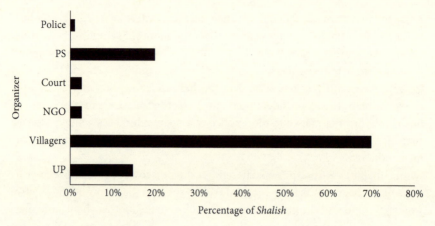

Figure 7.1. *Shalish* Organizers

to approach the local UP member when the latter shared that her husband beat her. He did not work and had stopped providing for her. The couple fought every day. Hosneara ended up getting a *shalish* hearing.

Through *shalish*, PS groups provide poor women with access to justice outside of formal courts. Approximately 58.4 percent of all PS had participated in at least one *shalish* session between 2008 and 2009.[40] Figure 7.1 illustrates that PS organized around 20 percent of the *shalish* in the surveyed areas during the preceding year. The data capture multiple responses, as more than one actor could have organized *shalish*. Thus PS groups not only played a community leadership role in administering justice, they also connected poor people to the informal legal system. Some of these cases went on to formal courts. Figure 7.2 breaks this down by type of *shalish* and shows that the vast majority of *shalish* that PS helped organize related to family matters—divorce, upkeep, marital conflicts, and so on—followed by conflicts over games. The latter includes sports, such as cricket and football, as well as playing cards and other forms of gambling. When PS members served as *shalishkar*, it was mostly for these two types of incidents as well (figure 7.3). Family-related conflicts often draw on religious laws; when resolved in the household, they often favor men. When such conflicts arise, women are unlikely to seek external assistance. By bringing them to *shalish*, PS groups open up this judicial space to poor rural women whose voices and concerns go unheard by the legal system. Thus *shalish* becomes an avenue for providing justice where the state fails—in this instance, for cases pertaining to women's domestic lives. Indeed, PS members often referred to *shalish* as *bichar*, a verb referring to the process of justice provision as well as a noun addressing the judgment. They would claim that justice took place or was provided— irrespective of whether formal or informal rules were followed—when the process and outcome exhibited fairness. At the same time, PS members engaged

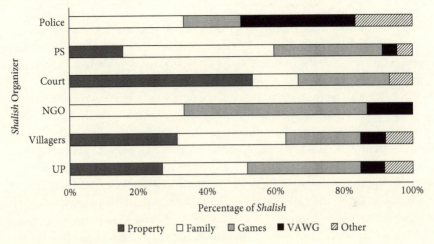

Figure 7.2. *Shalish* Organizers by Type of Incident

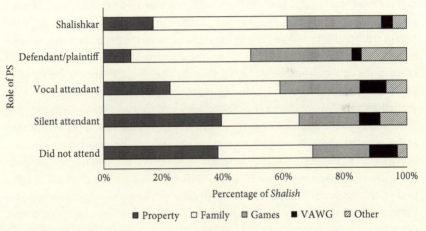

Figure 7.3. PS Role in *Shalish* by Type of Incident

in particular types of gender-related cases. A very small percentage of their interventions—both as organizers and *shalishkar*—involved cases of VAWG.

Representation

PS groups represent the interests of the vulnerable during shalish proceedings. They advocate for the poor—especially women—and create space for women's voices to be heard. Despite being accessible and affordable, *shalish* can be inequitable in its treatment of the vulnerable. PS groups defend the poor during deliberations. Well-known PS members serve as *shalishkar* along with the rural elite. PS president Duari from Rangpur's Kaunia was invited to a *shalish* involving a

man, Aziz, who had sold a tree from his ancestral land. His son had initially
opposed the sale. Upon discovering that Aziz had sold the tree, the son beat up
his elderly father. Duari defended Aziz. She insisted that Aziz's son hold his feet
and ask for forgiveness. In doing so she advocated for the elderly man, possibly
financially dependent on his son and thus beholden to him.

Shalish is a deeply gendered space; it does not welcome women. In Faridpur's
Nagarkanda, a man had beaten his wife and divorced her verbally. When locals
arranged *shalish*, PS members did not go. "Men do shalish," they said, "they do
not let us attend." Rural women cared about the affairs of village court. Those
who could not attend sessions recalled cases in vivid detail; they had heard stories from their husbands, neighbors, or relatives. Some observed from behind
trees or walls. Sakina, a PS member from Chandrapur village, remembered a
conflict between two women. One had borrowed three kilograms of rice from
the other and failed to return it after many requests. Sakina had attended the
event. But instead of sitting in the open space before the mediators, she listened
from behind a bamboo screen that divided the meeting spot and adjacent houses.

When women attend meetings, *shalishkar* refuse to let them speak. One PS
group attended a *shalish* involving a well-known domestic abuse case. They tried
to join deliberations, but the village elite disregarded them. The women refused
to back down. They insisted that they were PS members, trying to claim their
space in the conversation by clarifying that they belonged to an established local
organization and were thus valuable members of the community. The men
replied angrily, "What even is Polli Shomaj?"

When PS members spoke up, they were staunch defenders of the vulnerable.
In Manikganj Sadar, Asma got into an argument with her mother-in-law over
household responsibilities. Her husband worked abroad, leaving her at home
with the older woman. Such living situations were quite common. In the
household, gendered hierarchies extend beyond power exerted by husbands over
their wives. Asma's mother-in-law, being the mother of the provider, would have
decision-making authority in the household. Asma was expected to take over
household responsibilities once she moved to her in-laws' after marriage. Perhaps Asma refused to do the work and her mother-in-law hit her as a consequence. Her husband was not there to defend her. Asma asked for *bichar*. PS
members showed up in a large group and advocated on her behalf. Decision makers heard both sides of the story and tried to make amends. Eventually, Asma's
mother-in-law asked for forgiveness.

Reconciliation

Attempts to provide justice often begin with efforts toward reconciliation.
Shalish adjudications involve a mix of formal and informal rules. But informal
does not necessarily equal unjust. Siddiqi writes that such "parallel, community-
based modes of dispute resolution" take community interests into consideration;

they are face-saving rather than adversarial, and embody restorative justice as opposed to punishment.[41] Indeed, the *shalish* cases that we encountered favored the preservation of order over punishment. This differs from the kind of justice one would see in formal courts. Violations were punished with social instead of legal sanctions. When Asma's mother-in-law asked for forgiveness, she made a public commitment to treat Asma well in the future. She would think twice before forcing housework on Asma under the watchful eye of the village community. Defying a *shalish* verdict could lead to a retrial and further public humiliation.

From time to time, *shalish* draws on formal rules. This is easy when the rules are clear—for example, in the case of property-related matters, such as theft, land grabs, and inheritance. But gender-related matters are far more complex. On family law, legal codes themselves encroach upon women's rights and interests. The power dynamics within *shalish* intersect with the assortment of laws and their ambiguous interpretations to amplify women's disadvantage during adjudications. As a consequence, resolutions favor reconciliation as a first step.

A PS in Tangail's Sakhipur attended a *shalish* involving divorce. The women said that Shila did not like her husband. Although they did not specify why, one could imagine a breadth of scenarios ranging from domestic violence to a forced marriage that she had no choice in. Shila had moved to her father's house, and her husband asked for a *shalish* to bring her back. The couple's relatives attended the event. The village *matobbor* and some PS members were also there. At first, PS members tried to get the couple to reconcile. "We told the girl, you have only one husband. Go to his home." Their position likely stemmed from concern that marriage was a better option than divorce for a woman. As a divorcee, she would lack the status and protection—both economic and social—that her husband could provide. But when Shila did not agree to staying in her marriage, *shalish* delivered a verdict for the couple to separate. Shila received Tk. 7,000 in reparations.

When reconciliation fails, *shalish* provides an avenue for women to initiate divorce. Rabeya got married two years ago. "But her husband did not like her," said a group of PS members. He did not support her financially. And so Rabeya reached out to BRAC legal aid; BRAC staff arranged a *shalish* to initiate divorce. Rabeya's relatives attended, along with the *matobbor*, the member, and PS members. The PS women claimed that they were very vocal. They defended Rabeya, who was eventually granted divorce along with Tk. 33,000 in reparations. Although the story does not mention domestic violence directly, it is implied when PS members mentioned that Rabeya's husband did not like her. In both of the above cases, the *shalish* verdict coincided with the stipulations in the Domestic Violence (Prevention and Protection) Act of 2010, which gives women civil reparations, along with other protections. Thus, *shalish* provided women with an opportunity to access an otherwise elusive rule of law, and a verdict that aligned with formal rules.

Conclusion

This chapter argues that PS groups make rule of law accessible, representative, and equitable toward the rural poor. As they negotiate with state and society to enforce rule of law, they embrace a kind of justice that draws on both formal and informal institutions. This chapter also illuminates why PS groups were successful in resolving certain human rights situations over others. In rural Bangladesh, dowry and child marriage remain the rules-in-use despite the relentless efforts of the government and its NGO partners, most of whom engage in extensive training at the individual and community levels. But many inegalitarian informal institutions are deeply entrenched in rural society. Defying them comes with a price. Especially when it comes to incidents in one's own household, individual action becomes nearly impossible. Indeed, this is the position taken by sociological institutionalists, who argue that institutions are hard to change, as those who need to take action are themselves trapped within the rules. This is where external actors become integral to institutional change. As this chapter illustrates, it takes a village to fight inegalitarian informal institutions. Mothers might oppose dowry or child marriage when it comes to their daughters, but lack the authority to resist when a potential marriage alliance is on the horizon. From a programmatic perspective, this finding provides room for intervention. It suggests that beyond training and informational sessions, NGOs can mobilize grassroots organizations to combat dowry and child marriage.

When it comes to legal issues, resolutions can involve both social and legal sanctions, and reconciliation over adherence to the law. When PS members engage in *shalish*, they aim to provide justice (*bichar*) for the disenfranchised. They open up access to justice, advocate for the poor (particularly women), increase women's representation in decision-making processes, and sometimes challenge and even overturn inequitable legal practices. In *shalish*, PS groups often support reconciliation based on deliberations; supporting informal rule of law draws on both formal and informal rules and fills a gap in the legal system. Reconciliation is not unique to places where PS exists, and nor are PS actions uniquely democratic. In some instances, PS groups remain silent, and even help enforce inegalitarian norms. At the same time, they make rule of law accessible, representative, and equitable, while overturning norms and institutions that treat the vulnerable unfairly in the legal sphere.

CHAPTER 8

Governing Locally

In 2003, Bangladesh held its seventh election for the UP, its lowest tier of local government. Some PS members competed for a seat in this election. About a third of those competing ran for a general seat against established, typically male opponents. Others ran for reserved seats designated for women. As part of the Local Government Amendment Act of 1997, the UP reserves three such spots. Women are elected to these seats alongside the general positions—one chairman and nine general members, men or women.

A PS from Hobiganj found itself running a difficult campaign. This PS performed well; it fell into the "B" category. Created during the program's earliest phase in 1999, it was already five years old. The group employed a strong workforce for the campaign; it was one of the larger groups we encountered.[1] The women lived an active and mobile life. Over half of the members belonged to other NGO programs, attending meetings, running small businesses, and interacting with others regularly in their communities. They also belonged to extensive personal networks to mobilize for the campaign. But the Hobiganj PS members came from poor families. They were competing against establishment candidates from the rural elite. These men and women typically usurped UP seats, and reserved seats were no exception. Elite political families often recruited women from their patronage networks into these positions. They had the money, power, and influence to win the election. With odds stacked against them, the women chose Rabeya as their candidate. "Our PS member Rabeya Begum is one of our most educated members. She is matric pass from the Pakistan era," they said, referring to the secondary school exam. The women emphasized that Rabeya had achieved this prior to the country's independence, when women had even less mobility. This implied that she was exceptionally qualified for the position. Also, Rabeya belonged to a wealthier family. Community members viewed her as a benefactor of the weak. She had bought poor families latrines, built them houses, and given them money for their children's education and to bury loved ones when families could not bear the cost. PS members chose her because she felt compassion for the poor. "[We felt that] this person is a PS member, and PS is a poor person's organization, so if they win, they will help the poor."

The women divided into groups. They spread out to cover the entire locality. As they went door to door, they told residents what PS did. "Particularly, we said that PS helps poor people." They told voters that PS helped poor people receive government services, such as food aid cards, which UP members often pilfered for their own people. They stepped in when human rights violations occurred in the community—for example, domestic abuse or child marriage. They insisted that they had already done this work with no support. If elected, they could do so much more. During the three months of campaigning, PS members helped Rabeya with household chores so that she could spend her time in the field.

People doubted them at first. Voters did not think that elected officials would help the poor. Some villagers mocked them; they said that even the government cannot prevent dowry, so how could PS do it? Others had little faith in NGOs, and PS's connection with BRAC did not help. These NGOs take poor people's money, voters retorted, referring to the interests that microfinance programs charge for their loans. "What motivation would they have to prevent dowry?" they would ask. Campaigning took a physical toll as well. The women would be on their feet for hours, sometimes after long days laboring in the fields or other people's homes. Explaining PS's work to one household after another was exhausting. But Rabeya won. "We fought such adversity," the group told us, "but we won the election!"

This chapter is about women's representation in local governance. Beyond their negotiations with state and society, PS groups also engage in governance matters directly, challenging the norms, practices, and beliefs that keep women out of decision-making spaces. Their work expands the meaning of governance beyond local government—it extends to all decision-making processes involving who gets what and how.[2]

This chapter argues that PS changes the nature of women's representation in governance within the UP, independently of it, and within NGO committees. PS members campaign for UP seats, challenging expectations regarding who governs. They take on community initiatives providing both public and private goods—development endeavors that typically fall under the UP's domain. Finally, they designate services as members of NGO committees within an alternative governing infrastructure. The chapter is divided into four sections. In the first section, I discuss the challenge of women's participation in Bangladesh. The second section examines PS campaigning in local elections. The third section explores the independent community initiatives of PS groups. The fourth section speaks to the involvement of individual PS members in local committees.

WOMEN AND PARTICIPATION

Although Bangladesh has a long history of women's activism, women have yet to play a substantial role in government. Women vote in high numbers.[3] According to the 2008 *State of Democracy in South Asia* report, 81 percent of Bangladeshi women reported voting in every or most elections, and another 15 percent voted in some elections.[4] In the Polli Shomaj survey data, which captures the participatory behaviors of poor rural women, 97.2 percent of respondents reported voting in the 2008 national election and 82.9 percent in the 2003 local election.[5] These numbers illustrate that Bangladeshi women are generally inclined to participate in politics. Some literature suggests that this participation may not be for the right reasons. Across South Asia, poor rural women may vote because as they are aggressively mobilized by political parties and do little else to participate in other avenues.[6] But mobilization by parties does not strip women's participation of its significance.

When it comes to politics, women's representation presents a paradox in South Asia.[7] Women have held high leadership positions in the national government, including that of head of state—Sirimavo Bandaranaike in Sri Lanka, Indira Gandhi in India, Benazir Bhutto in Pakistan, and Sheikh Hasina and Khaleda Zia in Bangladesh. In Bangladesh, the two prime ministers whose parties have rotated through governments after the 1990 transition out of military rule—Sheikh Hasina for AL and Khaleda Zia leading the BNP—have both been women. In addition, women have held cabinet positions as ministers. At the same time, women's participation vanishes rapidly in South Asia when one looks beyond elites; the percentage of women in the parliament remains abysmal, and in the villages, women remain outside the realm of mainstream politics.[8] This holds true despite the existence of reserved seats for women in many South Asian countries—India, Pakistan, and Bangladesh. Rounaq Jahan writes of these two contradictory images—that of the powerful women leaders coexisting with "that of female masses, poor, illiterate, often veiled, huddled in groups in separate 'women only' polling booths or ration lines, or in labor lines seeking casual jobs."[9] Jahan attributes this contradiction to the family connections of South Asia's women leaders; they carried on dynastic politics that began with men. She writes that their careers were propelled by those of male relatives. Their family wealth and connections provided the "money, time, skill, experience, patronage, contacts and information"—resources that poor women do not have.[10]

In Bangladesh, formal rules have long recognized the need for women's representation in politics. But they have developed in increments. Following a legacy left by the Pakistani government, the constitution of Bangladesh reserved fifteen seats for women (4.8 percent) in the national Parliament, increased to thirty (9.7 percent) in 1979.[11] Between 1987 and 2005 the provision was scrapped and restored twice, until a final amendment increased the quota to forty-five seats.[12]

Women's representation in local government follows a similar trajectory. In 1976, the Local Government Ordinance established a three-tiered local government structure with two reserved seats for women at the union level. The 1983 Local Government (Union Parishad) Ordinance altered the structure of local government and increased the quota for women to three seats.[13] In all of these instances, the quotas were filled through nomination or indirect election. Thus, women relied on male MPs to choose them for these positions.[14] The 1997 act changed this; women have since then been chosen through direct elections to these reserved UP seats. Since its establishment, the number of women elected to the UP has jumped across the country; in 1992, 20 women won elections to become UP members, and by 2003 the number had grown to 12,684.[15] Following this move, the 2005 provision removed indirect elections for women's seats in the Parliament.

Gendered logics of appropriation dictate whether and how women are represented in governance. Women's representation—or lack thereof—is tied to their expected role in the community. Louise Chappell and Fiona Mackay write that gendered institutional logics do two things. They set appropriate masculine and feminine forms of behavior, coding "public authority, and political presence and agency as culturally masculine."[16] Gendered logics also influence political outcomes—"policies, legislation, and rulings"—that in turn set and reproduce broader gender expectations.[17] These logics tell us how "a particular social world works" and are "embodied in practices, sustained and reproduced by cultural assumptions and political struggles."[18] They limit certain behaviors and practices while allowing others.

Bangladeshis view politics as highly competitive and aggressive—unsuited for women's delicate nature and designated role as homemakers.[19] However, men are seen as strong enough to hold positions of power. Women could not run for direct elections precisely because it was assumed that they could not compete with men during elections.[20] Elora Shehabuddin finds that women's dependence on men and notions of appropriate social behavior prevented parliamentary candidates from campaigning effectively.[21] Candidates revealed that they relied on male household members for campaign financing. They could not compromise their self-respect—implying their reputation and honor—by frequenting businessmen's offices as they sought funding. Concerns about security and reputation limited campaigning options. Women could not visit public places or travel at night as freely as men.[22] Among other things, limited mobility, education, religious practices—in particular, the practice of purdah—and gender stereotypes that confine women to the household also limit women's ability to participate.[23] Thus, women's designated social roles and expected behaviors keep them out of governance.

When women take on leadership positions, such logics inhibit their active participation in decision making. This worldview dictates that women do not belong in government. When they do, men should take the lead. As Chappell and MacKay suggest, expectations shape political outcomes. Because women were historically nominated and not elected, they served under the influence of the male leaders who nominated them. At the UP, men neglect women officials and endanger their social and family lives—for example, by tarnishing their reputations.[24] Shehabuddin writes that according to journalists, male officials did not seek women's feedback even on women's issues. Male officials left women out of committees involving money, including development projects. They claimed that the government had provided no explicit instructions detailing women's duties, illustrating that they expected women to have responsibilities that differed from their own.[25] The assumed differentiation of duties subscribes to gendered logics of appropriation—the idea that men and women play different roles in governance despite belonging to the same office and the lack of any government directive indicating this to be the case.

At the same time, the dynamics of women's representation are changing. Sohela Nazneen and Sakiba Tasneem find that women in reserved seats feel that their voices have legitimacy since they are elected, particularly since they are elected by three wards in comparison to their male counterparts, elected by one.[26] They reach out to other actors, including women's organizations, for training and other assistance to increase their knowledge and skills.[27] This study questions the resilience of gendered institutional logics. It suggests that things are changing. Once elected, women do not want to play by gendered rules. Rather, they seek allies who can empower them to act in defiance. The next section explores PS's work in local elections.

LOCAL ELECTIONS

When it comes to elections, gendered logics are not the only worldview at play. Women's gender and socioeconomic status both obstruct their entry into local government. Together, these identities play into expectations regarding women's abilities to defeat establishment candidates and deliver on promises. A little over 11 percent of the groups formed before or during 2002 put up a candidate in the local election. This is not a particularly high number. But PS groups were fairly young at the time. CEP had started the program only five years before, and the average group was 3.4 years old at the time. Not surprisingly, over 78 percent of the PS mobilizing in the 2003 UP election were created during the initial setup phase of 1998–1999. Despite having the odds stacked heavily against them, half of the competing candidates won. Their efforts extended beyond designated seats; nearly a fourth took on establishment candidates from the rural elite, almost always men. Figure 8.1 breaks down the kinds of candidates PS groups chose to represent them. When it comes to NGO memberships, the vast majority belonged to BRAC. Only 19 percent of the candidates belonged to no NGO

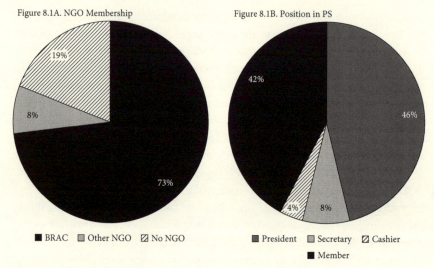

Figure 8.1A. NGO Membership   Figure 8.1B. Position in PS

Figure 8.1. Election Candidates

(figure 8.1). It is likely that PS members chose these candidates because of their embeddedness in the community and the leadership qualities they developed through NGO activity. Over 42 percent of the candidates were ordinary PS members; they did not hold elected positions (figure 8.1). This suggests that PS members were not choosing elite, vertically connected members to compete with establishment candidates (elected PS leaders were more educated and came from better-off families than ordinary PS members). Rather, they chose horizontally connected candidates who were deeply embedded in their communities.

The Candidates

Kaunia rests on the banks of the river Teesta. This northern subdistrict comprises mostly agricultural land. Its poor residents labor in the fields. The women here recalled having an animated discussion at their general meeting before the last UP election; they described their conversation as *kholamela* (open, honest, even unfiltered). They picked one of their own members as a candidate. Rani Begum was popular with the locals. She helped people when they were in trouble. "She can socialize with everyone," they added, "and has the skill to talk to everyone and pursue our demands. Most importantly she is well-off and does not have anything holding her back." The women felt that Rani Begum represented the poor. But she was not subject to the vulnerabilities that came with poverty—the lack of time, resources, or household help.

In the neighboring district of Dinjapur, another PS recalled that their PO asked them to consider running for UP elections. They said, "With the help of the *shongshod* [assembly] and the PO *bhai* we decided together that we will give one candidate from our Polli Shomaj." The group chose Dulali. She had attended school and could hold conversations. "Everyone knows her as good," they said, "so if she is elected, it will be good for society." A PS in Sirajganj's Ullapara chose Amena, who declined and suggested that Fatema would be a better option. She argued that Fatema was educated and knew how to "mix" with people. She could give speeches, and the village community knew her as a good person. The stories are similar across the country. In Rajbari's Pangsha, a PS picked a candidate who had passed eighth grade and could, in her leaders' opinion, talk to people. And another group from Manikganj Sadar picked a candidate who knew everyone, treated people well, and could speak eloquently.

In all of these instances, PS groups chose a particular kind of woman to represent them. Their candidates were not necessarily poor. But they were vertically and horizontally embedded—socially connected to both elite groups and the village community. They possessed certain skills—education, confidence, and eloquence—that PS members saw as essential for crafting a pathway into local government. Even though the women came from the village community, their socioeconomic status gave them the time, resources, education, and connections to carry out a campaign. In many ways, they possessed the attributes that Pranab Kumar Panday blames for the exclusion of ordinary women from Bangladeshi politics.[28] Thus, PS groups chose candidates strategically in order to push past the gendered institutional logics that disenfranchise them. But just as importantly, the chosen candidates were compassionate. PS members were confident that they would adequately represent the poor. They described these women as good people, using phrases like *bhalo manush* (good person), *shobai bhalo jane* (everyone knows them as good people), and *shahajyo kore* (helpful). They were also good communicators; they could talk to the poor village residents and truly understand their pain. Together, candidates' connections, compassion, and communication skills carried one big campaign message—that unlike the wealthy elite who subscribed to clientelist politics, PS candidates cared genuinely about the poor and would represent them well. A candidate who could connect with the constituency was an integral part of this promise.

The Campaign

PS groups embarked on extensive election campaigns. Their efforts shifted expectations regarding the nature of political leadership. They challenged the notion of local government being elite-dominated and exclusive of poor people's voices. Instead, they created an expectation that people's votes matter. PS groups did this in two ways. In addition to organizing rallies and putting up posters, the women went door to door mobilizing support for their candidate. They spoke to individual voters at length. Some accompanied elderly villagers to voting booths on Election Day. They felt that personalized attention made community members feel that their votes mattered. For one group from Ullapara, more than half of the members went canvassing for their candidate. They visited not just their own ward, but all neighboring wards. They asked both men and women for their votes. They fed the women *paan*. They sought out men as allies, engaging men from their households as well as the village youth to organize large rallies. The campaigners felt that villagers were very happy when approached by this very large group of women. "Ordinary voters told us, no one ever came to ask us for votes like this," they said. "[They told us] we may benefit or not benefit—but we will definitely vote for the PS candidate."

The women had one campaign message—that their candidate would stand up for the poor. Very often, their promise involved the distribution of resources. They assured voters that their candidate would get more government resources for the poor, which had an implicit assumption that they sought to shift clientelistic distributive practices. The PS group from Dinajpur's Chirir Bondor recalled embarking on their campaign with tremendous excitement. "Every member, alongside visiting their own relatives, visited every home in all twelve villages in the ward and spoke about Polli Shomaj, about Dulali, that Dulali will work for the poor," they said. "[That] poor people will get VGD VGF cards, will get justice in legal affairs, that poor people will be able to speak," they added. They claimed to have amassed massive support, "because most villagers are poor and in addition we asked all PS members to tell their family to vote for our candidate." The team felt that being women—and campaigning for a female candidate—was their biggest strength. They could understand the sentiments of the women whose homes they visited. "We said when we asked for votes, that Dulali is a good woman, an educated woman, she can speak well, does Union Shomaj." In addition to PS, Dulali belonged to Union Shomaj, a CEP program at the union level. Like most other candidates that PS groups put up for local elections, Dulali had demonstrated through her work that poor women, too, could participate in decision-making processes.

PS members sought to change the expectation that politicians do not care about the poor. In Khetlal, the voters resisted PS efforts at first. As they campaigned, many voters asked them, "What is the point of voting?" It is possible that there was a strong establishment candidate in the area who was trying to buy votes. Indeed, the group reported that other candidates' goons tried to stop them from campaigning. "We had to tolerate all this and keep working." The PS from Pangsha said that in the past, UP election candidates had made promises to the area's voters that they had not fulfilled. Thus, when PS made those promises villagers did not trust them. "They did not want to listen to us, they were annoyed." In addition, since vote buying was so common, PS members were often asked for material goods. In the vein of a typical electoral campaign, voters in Ullapara asked their PS for personal benefits. "When we went to campaign in ward three, we had to talk a lot," they reported. "And all the voters asked us, what will you give us? We had to explain."

Institutions often embody the power structures of the society that they exist within. Any efforts to shift them can create a backlash from those who seek to maintain the status quo. As PS groups sought to shift practices that excluded the poor, they faced sanctions. The rural elite threatened them for challenging establishment candidates. In Chirir Bondor, the interviewed group recalled that their first challenge came from the rural elite—the *goshthi prodhan* and *shomaj prodhan*—who pressured them to withdraw from the election. "We explained to them that we will not hurt anyone," they said. "[We told them] we are poor people, we are going to run in elections so that we can secure our demands and society benefits." They insisted in their conversations with the rural elite that they wanted to live well. If voters thought that their candidate Dulali was a good candidate, they would vote for her. "Then we came down to the field to work."

The groups also faced funding problems. Generally, the women raised their own funds. In Manikganj Sadar, members of the local PS went door to door to every house in their village, to campaign for their candidate, Rahima. They asked for votes on behalf of PS. They recalled telling voters, "Rahima is our neighbor. We will request her to fix the roads and bridges in the village, and get various government/NGO goods." The group collected a small donation—between Tk. 10 and Tk. 20—from every PS member, a total of Tk. 4,200. This was a significant amount of money for the women, most of whom lived in abject poverty. Their candidate did not have the means to pay for her own campaign. The group used these funds to submit her nomination form and make posters. They saw this as an investment. "Because if Rahima wins, she can help PS get government and NGO benefits, like VGF, VGD, old age allowance, and widow's allowance, and we worked for Rahima with that hope," they said. These efforts illustrate a shift in fundraising practices. Instead of relying on wealthy businessmen or the men in their own families—sources that would limit their ability to work independently—these women ran crowdsourced campaigns.

When it comes to local government, women's representation is thwarted by institutional logics that dictate who gets to make decisions. They face a highly competitive politics that is both male- and elite-dominated. Gail Omvedt writes that politics is a "lucrative source of income and power which men attempt to control."[29] The community's worldview encompassed two simultaneous expectations—that their typically greedy officials did not care about the poor, and that poor women could not take on these positions. PS members pushed back against the first expectation by demonstrating that poor people's voices mattered. They challenged the second by showcasing their own achievements in the area.

Some PS groups campaigned for other candidates from the community whom they believed to be strong advocates for the poor. One PS campaigned for Majed, an existing candidate. They went door to door, distributing flyers. They informed villagers that Majed was the most helpful and reliable candidate, and that he helped people during difficult times. They asserted that if Majed won, he would ensure that all poor community members would be able to exercise their rights. The above PS chose to support Majed, as they had faith in his leadership abilities and trusted him to stand by them in times of need. They carried the same message for him as other groups did for candidates from PS—that he would represent the poor.

COMMUNITY PROJECTS

As gendered institutional logics keep PS members out of formal governing spaces, they create new spaces of their own. They undertake development initiatives that would typically fall under the UP's purview. By doing what the state fails to do, they simultaneously fill in the gaps and change perceptions regarding women's role in governance. These initiatives involve both private and public goods, ranging from fundraising to ensuring that school-aged children were enrolled in school.

PS groups raise funds to finance weddings, burials, and health-related expenses for community members in crisis. Often, vulnerable community members have no family to support them. Storms had destroyed Jamila's home in the preceding year's monsoons. She lived in Pabna's Ishwardy. "Once her home broke down she was completely helpless," said her area's PS members. The women raised some money for her. "Villagers extended their arms to help her," they said, "because Jamila is extremely poor and everyone in our locality knows this." The women volunteered their labor to rebuild her home. They said that they had to help Jamila, since the home was her only asset. "She is extremely poor and did not have the capacity to rebuild her home." Jamila had lost her husband. Her two sons had married and lived on their own; they did not keep track of how she was doing. Jamila had no social insurance—financial or social support that she would ideally receive from her now estranged family. The state did not provide this kind of benefit. Families raise children expecting that the children will provide for them in their old age. Studies have yet to establish whether time has eroded children's support for their parents.[30] But Bangladesh's rapid structural transformations caused by globalization, urbanization, foreign and urban migration, and the rise of the nuclear family are likely to increase at least the physical distance between parents and their grown children. In keeping with these massive structural changes, the Bangladesh government passed the Parents' Maintenance Act in 2013. The act holds children responsible for their elderly parents' financial maintenance; they are required to provide food, shelter, medication, and clothing if they do not live together.[31] Jamila's children did not fix her home, and neither did the state.

When Mohsina's family did not respond to news of her death, her local PS in Rangpur Sadar stepped in to organize *janaza* (Muslim burial rites). Mohsina had moved to the area eight years ago, initially with her police officer husband. "The man came from Magura," PS members said, and was stationed in the area. He had met Mohsina during one of his job postings around the country. The women did not say where Mohsina was from, but they did know that she was Hindu at birth. In her past life, her name was Anjona. At one point, Mohsina's husband was transferred out of Rangpur. But soon he died in the line of duty. She moved back to the area soon after. During her last days, she lived alone, and when she died, no relative came forward to claim her body. PS member Laboni scrambled to the hospital when she heard of the death. She called the PS president from her cell phone. The president said, "I went there right away and asked to have a *chouki* [wooden bed frame] brought there from the market." She arranged to have Mohsina's body placed in the south of the village with a mosquito net around it. At first, they wanted to keep Mohsina's body next to their houses where they could bathe her with privacy, but the village folks said no. They were forced to keep her in a public place, next to the market. PS members guarded Mohsina's body all night. The women raised some funds from villagers. In the morning, they bathed Mohsina, put clothes on her, and buried her. They called villagers to attend. About a week later, they collected some rice from community members and used the funds from its sale to hold a prayer service. The women had Tk. 300 left. They asked the president of their market committee—a local committee governing the businesses in their village market—to locate Mohsina's friend, someone she considered as close as a sister. They made sure she received the remaining money.

Mohsina had no one to take care of her burial. PS members said, "After her death we realized that she has no relatives. In fact there was no one to bury her even. She had no sons." Burial rites and other arrangements were typically made by the men in the family—husbands, sons, brothers, and sometimes sons-in-law. Mohsina had a child from the time when she was Hindu. PS members had sent her child news of her death, but the child did not come. Here, PS members did more than just raise money—they fulfilled the physical and social responsibilities of the absent family. Mohsina's Hindu family had shunned her, and locals did not want to keep her body in the village, since she was once Hindu. The women of PS negotiated with the village folks to find an acceptable location—outside of the residential area, but still within village parameters.

PS groups dip into their horizontal networks when necessary. In particular, linkages with BRAC staff—the CEP PO, health workers, and legal aid staff—come in handy. PS member Halima needed a C-section when delivering her child in Faridpur's Sadarpur. But her husband, a day laborer, could not afford the fees. A fellow PS members contacted *shasthya shebika* (health worker) Shibra Rani. BRAC health workers educate rural Bangladeshi families on health issues, bring resources to their doors, and connect the sick to government or BRAC clinics. The

Sadarpur PS leaders brought Shibra Rani and their PO to the hospital. As they arranged for Halima's surgery, the PS president sought to speak to the doctor. He avoided her. The president then asked Shibra Rani to approach the doctor instead. Shibra Rani served as Halima's advocate. The PS president had possibly brought her along with the expectation that she could open doors that PS members could not—in this case, being able to obtain crucial information from the doctor.

PS members contribute funds and labor to provide public goods. In Nilfamari's Joldhaka, they paved a mud road that made travel difficult for villagers. The women met on a Friday—usually a day off—to repair the road. They claimed that it was only because of PS that the road was repaired. In Jamalpur's Dewangonj, another group bought mosquito nets for their local mosque. They sympathized with the village folk who gathered there at dawn to eat their early morning meal during Ramadan. "But it is at this time that the mosquitos are most torturous," they said. They raised the money themselves. They also dipped into their own funds.

One of the PS groups' most widespread efforts involves getting children into school. The women make lists of children who are not enrolled in classes. They speak to parents and dispel doubts about the benefits and costs of education. One PS in Pabna's Faridpur claimed to have made a list of all children over six who were not in school. They visited each household and spoke about the advantages of educating a child. They also discussed government stipends and free books. "Parents don't want to understand at first," they said. "They say we are poor, how will we bear the burden of education?" Some parents changed their minds upon learning that their children could attend school free of cost. "That is when they give us importance."

When PS members take on community initiatives, they do not face the same kind of resistance that they do while campaigning. Here, they serve the community without disrupting the status quo. Perhaps they make the UP's job easier by fulfilling community needs that would otherwise fall under the government's purview. And they do so without challenging existing logics of appropriateness directly—they are not competing with elite men. At the same time, as they provide services that cater to the community's needs, they shift people's worldviews—institutional logics as they exist in the locality—regarding both women as potential leaders and the kinds of services that poor people deserve.

LOCAL COMMITTEES

PS members engage in alternative governing spaces created by various NGOs, including BRAC. Elected local committees govern various aspects of rural Bangladeshi life, for example, schools, markets, mosques, and graveyards. But like the UP, government-created committees tend to be elite and male-dominated spaces. NGOs have created a parallel governing structure with committees of their own; these committees connect people with services. NGOs implement programs that draw on community members, often organized into small groups. As PS members dip into these spaces, they bring women's voices into decision-making spaces outside the UP's sphere of influence. Some PS members were elected to local committees on their own, and others were chosen based on their leadership role within the PS group.

PS member Eliza belonged to BRAC's Village Wash Committee. As part of BRAC's WASH (water, sanitation, and hygiene) program, this elected village-level committee creates yearly plans to ensure safe water for the village, identifies problems of access, mobilizes resources, and remains proactive in ensuring that every household has access to a sanitary latrine and safe water.[32] Eliza has never missed a meeting. She mentioned that the group discussed issues related to sanitation and hygiene, such as ways to procure safe water, and the importance of using sanitary latrines instead of defecating in open spaces. Eliza participated in these discussions. She raised issues specific to her village's needs and explored possible solutions to problems with the help of other group members. She mentioned feeling comfortable sharing her views in this space.

PS member Shumi joined an NGO school committee. She wanted to work with teachers and ensure that children kept up with their schoolwork. Although Bangladesh has achieved nearly universal primary enrollment rates, only a small percentage of children graduate to secondary school. Shumi asked teachers repeatedly to contact the parents when their children skipped classes. She met with the school administrators often. She insisted that the administration remove trash from school premises so that students could study in a healthy and sanitary environment. Another PS member joined the committee of a BRAC school that her child attended. The committee held monthly meetings with students' parents, where attendees discussed school attendance and education standards. Members notified the parents of children who missed school regularly.

As PS members engage with local committees created by BRAC and other NGOs, they engage in an alternative governing space that extends beyond the UP. At the same time, their endeavors are not completely removed from the state. Many development programs are developed and implemented through government-NGO partnerships. For example, BRAC WASH committees are implemented through consultation with village stakeholders, including UP officials; field staff maintain regular contact with government officials. Thus, PS members dip into decision-making spaces that exist outside of the government, and yet are not completely removed from it.

Conclusion

This chapter explores PS groups' efforts to engage in local governance in three arenas—in the UP, through community initiatives, and the alternative governing space of NGO committees. Their achievements illustrate that once the notion of governance is expanded beyond government to encompass parallel governing spheres—for example, in civil society or through NGO programs—new spaces crop up where women can influence decision making. Women find it easier to infiltrate governing spaces that exist outside of the state. When PS members campaigned for office, they faced threats from the rural elite who sought to preserve the status quo. Their campaigning efforts faced backlash, not just because they were women, but also because the rural elite engaged in fierce competition to protect their seats—the source of their power. But PS members faced these challenges, campaigning enthusiastically, and often winning elections. They shifted expectations, both regarding who gets to hold office and how officeholders govern. Independent community initiatives and NGO committees gave PS members the opportunity to engage in governance via alternative spaces. Thus, PS members—and indeed, women across Bangladesh—have found their way into governance by both "un-gendering" gendered political institutions and simultaneously creating new spaces where they can participate freely.

Conclusion

An out-of-Dhaka excursion took me to Tangail during a recent Bangladesh visit. Small-town family weddings promised good food, lively music, and all sorts of colorful fun. I longed to connect with the world beyond the city. I had missed this so much. The roads out of Dhaka still buzzed with traffic. My favorite highway-side stalls still served delicious tea. Small-town markets still bustled with delightful smells and shiny wares. As we drove past some of the smaller urban centers, I noticed sparkling signs for local AL offices plastered above freshly painted buildings. I could not stop thinking of them. Over a decade ago, I had taken my first field visit with RED to Dhamoirhaat, in the northwest *upazila* of Nogaon. I was to meet local PS members and understand the program well enough to start designing the PS study. While venturing around town on my first day, somewhat amazed that I was traveling in Bangladesh on my own, and even more bewildered by the vibrant commerce of a town so far removed from the world that it took forever to reach the night before, RED colleagues mentioned that Dhamoirhaat's proximity to India gave the locality this energy. Here, goods traveled across porous borders. They took people and culture with them. As I walked past busy markets, crowded tea stalls, and restaurants enlivened by loud teenagers, I came across a dilapidated shed. Above the rusty roof propped up on uneven wooden stilts, an old faded sign declared that this crumbling space was the local AL office.

Then and Now

Bangladesh looks very different now than it did in 2009. That was a time of immense hope. AL had won a landslide victory in the 2008 election following a three-year stint by an unelected army-backed caretaker government. Democracy had finally returned. The Bangladeshi people embraced it eagerly. The promise of a better modernity hung in the air. The new AL government had campaigned for these elections on their Vision 2021 strategy, pledging a technological revolution in addition to capital and labor investments. "Digital Bangladesh" was the AL slogan for the times. This was to be the era of economic development.

A decade has passed. Bangladesh's once unstable electoral authoritarian regime, frequently teetering between military rule and parliamentary democracy, has turned into a resilient one-party system. AL won re-election in 2014 and again in 2018. In 2014, BNP and the opposition boycotted the election after BNP leader Khaleda Zia was placed under house arrest, and many opposition members remained in hiding after arrests and police raids on their homes. Fewer than 40 percent of the population turned up at the polls.[1] Many AL leaders won uncontested seats. Their party controlled almost every seat in the parliament, creating a ruling party without opposition.[2] In 2018, the AL secured 288 out of 300 seats in parliament. BNP contested this time, even as many of its members were arrested. BNP leaders claimed that others were killed or disappeared. Now, the AL has been in office for over a decade. The crackdown on the opposition continues. Human rights organizations, including the UN Working Group on Enforced or Involuntary Disappearances, have urged the government to address a growing number of enforced disappearances.[3]

Local politics looks vastly different than it did in 2009. New democratic spaces have opened, while old ones have shrunk. In 2009, the government introduced the Local Government (Union Parishad) Act, which promotes social accountability via citizens' participation in local government. Specific initiatives include participatory budgeting and planning, better access to information and services, and mechanisms to include civil society organizations and NGOs in local planning.[4] The act sets up thirteen standing committees to take on specific issues in each UP; these committees include elected officials and local actors. At the same time, AL's hold has devolved into the villages. Elections for the position of chairman are now party-based. In the 2016 local election, the party's share of seats increased from 49 percent to 70 percent, whereas the BNP's decreased from 38 percent to 9 percent.[5]

On development, Bangladesh has moved up the ranks to an MHD country. With a Human Development Index score of 0.614, it ranks higher than some of its South Asian peers, including Sri Lanka and Pakistan.[6] On the Gender Development Index, which measures gender gap in development as the ratio of female to male human development, Bangladesh scores a remarkable 0.895, surpassing the average for South Asia (0.828) and even for MHD countries (0.845).[7] Women are more mobile than they have ever been, making up the vast majority of the ready-made garments industry's estimated 4.2 million workers. According to the Bureau of Manpower, Employment, and Training, they constituted 12.1 percent of Bangladesh's total foreign workforce in 2017.[8] Both sectors are fraught with human rights abuses.

Religious organizations have emerged with renewed vigor. In April 2013, thousands of men belonging to the Hefazat-e-Islam marched into Dhaka and gathered at Shapla Chottor for a rally, which their leaders began with reciting from the Qur'an.[9] Among other things, the group called for the death of the "atheist" bloggers who demanded the death penalty for JI leaders, on trial for war crimes during the 1971 Liberation War. The Hefazat emerged in the context of Bangladesh's War Crimes Trials, established by the AL government as part of another electoral promise. Earlier that year, the tribunal had given JI leader Kader Mollah a life sentence. In response, thousands of Bangladeshis gathered to protest at Shahbag. Protesters demanded the death penalty for Mollah. The Bangladesh Bloggers and Online Activist Network had initiated the Shahbag protest. These were the "atheist bloggers" that the Hefazat demanded the death penalty for. The Hefazat's demands extended into social relationships—for example, they asked to stop the "free mixing" of men and women. The Hefazat's members come from Bangladesh's villages, the same setting where NGOs continue to mobilize women. Its leaders and followers are groomed in *madrasas*, and its leader, ninety-three-year-old Ahmed Shafi, is chairman of the Bangladesh Qaumi madrasa education board. As organizations like Hefazat creep into public spaces and rural people's private lives, a more militant religious extremism has also emerged. In 2016, a group of young men stormed into Holey Artisan Bakery in Dhaka's affluent Gulshan area and killed twenty-two people; the attackers claimed allegiance to ISIS. In subsequent years, newspapers carried countless headlines of the Rapid Action Battalion, the police's elite anticrime and antiterrorist force, cracking down on militants across the country.

When one imagines the bustling restaurants of 2009 Dhamoirhaat, where young women and men ate breakfast and drank tea together in close proximity—it is because we are next to India, one of the locals explained—this creeping religious transformation seems worlds away. But these worlds collide in Bangladesh's villages. As I wrote in chapter 2, women's lives are dictated by multiple, overlapping factors—an aggressive aid-oriented neoliberal development strategy, the influx of NGOs into villages, NGO-ized women's movements, and the growing influence of Islamic groups. While the state pursued a strategy of increased privatization and growth, NGOs enhanced capitalist development by creating an army of skilled women who serve the ready-made garment factories in the cities, run small businesses in the villages, and sometimes travel to foreign countries for work. In the ten years since the PS study, many of these factors have intensified, leading to even greater contradictions than before. But along with expanding markets, increased agricultural outputs, intensifying NGO activity, and a growing female and nonagricultural labor force, there is now a one-party system whose reach extends into local politics.

Polli Shomaj

The PS program, too, has changed with the times. As of 2020, there were 12,487 PS groups operating in fifty-four districts. In the last decade, CEP strived to make the program sustainable. The goal is to thrust PS groups toward independent operations so that the program can put more effort into building new groups. To this end, CEP has initiated a path to graduation for PS groups so that they can run entirely on their own. As part of this move, the program has undertaken a drive to register PS groups with the government as nonprofits. As of September 2019, 261 groups were registered.[10] CEP has also changed its supervision strategy. Now, POs take a hands-off approach. They no longer oversee day-to-day affairs like organizing meetings and maintaining registers. Rather, they check in with their respective groups once every three months. Such relaxed oversight can resolve some of the power struggles between POs and PS leaders. At the same time, the program employs more POs. Now, POs provide technical and capacity-building support to PS leaders in multiple *upazilas* (sometimes a single *upazila*, sometimes more), which allows PS leaders to operate group activities on their own.

CEP has shifted its attention from program oversight to enhancing the leadership capacities of members. In 2009, we found it difficult to gauge the extent to which PS members received training or attended workshops arranged by BRAC. Most deliberative work began in discussions with the *poramorshodata*, local leaders from the community. These discussions are instrumental to PS work, and they still occur. But now, PS leaders attend an extensive three-day workshop on leadership, communication, and problem solving. Members rotate as they receive leadership training; the same person cannot receive training within a two-year period. CEP has also imposed term limits on leadership positions; the executive committee has to change every five years to allow for new leadership. This shift is motivated by the desire to build a broad leadership base— seven or eight leaders who can take charge during discussions and negotiations. It extends leadership beyond the typically elite women whom PS members elected year after year, as they possessed the leadership skills that others lacked. Indeed, PS members' achievements reflect their new leadership skills. According to the CEP website, 2,903 PS members have been elected into UP leadership positions since 2002.[11]

PS continues to operate in synergy with other BRAC programs. CEP has piloted a number of initiatives through PS groups. For example, some PS leaders provide community-based psychosocial support to survivors of violence. These women, whom CEP has labeled *monobondhu* (friend of the heart), are a first stop for survivors. They also link survivors to clinics for psychological support. Other initiatives include a women-led disaster management program and checking the eyesight of elderly community members.

On Programming

In writing a book about a development program, it is only fitting to offer some insights on policies and programming. Despite the temporal constraints—the book studies PS at a particular time in a particular context—there are a few lessons to consider. It is my hope that development practitioners and policymakers will draw on PS's experience and look at development in new ways.

Grassroots women's mobilization programs. Service delivery programs are not going away. Nor can one deny that they have made a remarkable difference in poor women's lives. But they cannot alone empower poor women. As a senior CEP official mentioned in one of our earliest meetings, "empowerment is a journey." It does not end with physical mobility, economic well-being, or access to health care. It is a path based on living, learning, and making choices unbound by institutional barriers. Grassroots mobilization programs can enhance women's agency. They provide women with the tools to confront everyday injustices. While the collective development model differs substantially from individualized neoliberal models, the two are not necessarily at odds with each other. Rather, they can be complementary. As the PS experience illustrates, a collective-based development model can fill in the gaps that neoliberal development leaves behind.

Women's leadership. The image of strong, independent women appears so often in development discourse that it has almost become a cliché. Across the world, NGOs provide women with skills and information as a means of empowerment. For example, training was one of BRAC's earliest initiatives. The idea is that well-informed women make better choices and lead better lives. But women's leadership can also bring social change. As the PS experience illustrates, strong, independent women can resist oppression and push for a more egalitarian society. One may expect that such women would incur society's displeasure for their lack of subservience. But we find that their communities support and celebrate them. Such leadership grows not just from education, but also from experience. PS members almost universally expressed the desire to be led by strong leaders. In the absence of external intervention, these would be elite women. But in case after case, PS members chose leaders with NGO leadership experience. These leaders negotiated relentlessly with power holders. Pushing back against informal institutions—especially considering the power relationships that they embody—requires confidence, knowledge, and resolve. NGO leadership provides women with these skills. Many PS leaders developed these qualities while holding leadership positions in BRAC's service delivery programs—especially health and microfinance. Indeed, Bangladesh's NGO density provides ample opportunities to let rural women lead.

Creating knowledge. Deliberation is an integral component of PS work. However, discourse cannot be created in a vacuum. Women may recognize injustices in their everyday lives. NGOs may inform them of their rights through awareness-raising trainings. But this knowledge does not translate to action when injustices are the rule-in-use—the prevalent norm. In Bangladesh, many NGOs embrace a discursive approach to training. This kind of deliberative knowledge can build consensus on injustices, allow for the realization of goals, and inspire communities to take action.

Relationships. PS emphasizes the importance of building cross-program linkages. In Bangladesh, intricate NGO networks have created a natural tapestry for such collaboration. For example, PS groups provide a platform for other BRAC programs to distribute services. Their work demonstrates that there is ample room for neoliberal and collective-based programs to work together. Such cross-cutting collaborations can embed development programs deeper in local communities. They can strengthen the vertical and horizontal connections that have contributed to PS groups' success.

Challenging Institutions

The Polli Shomaj story captures a particular world at a particular time. But macrostructural shifts do not necessarily eliminate possibilities for institutional change. They merely alter the playing field. To assume that the institutional shifts that PS groups achieved in 2009 would not be possible under party-based local elections would be unfruitful. Rather, one may ask how macro-structural shifts would impact negotiations between PS groups on the one hand, and state and society on the other.

Many will look upon this book with skepticism. Some informal institutions— like clientelism and child marriage—are so deeply entrenched in rural Bangladeshi society that one can hardly imagine a world without them. But institutions are simultaneously resilient and mutable. Even sociological institutionalists— who place the strongest institutional boundaries around actors and focus more on institutional resilience and influence than institutional change—expect that institutions will evolve. They see rules as "producing variation and deviation as well as conformity and standardization" as rules are both ambiguously interpreted and continuously adapted by actors.[12] As actors embrace rules, they understand and adapt them; in turn, rules influence how actors behave.[13] Indeed, new institutionalists emphasize such dynamic interactions between actors and institutions, as well as between institutions themselves.[14] This book identifies possibilities for institutional change, especially when new actors like PS enter an institutional setting. The PS story illustrates that institutional shifts happen when actors negotiate the rules-in-use, enact new rules, act as enforcers of these rules, and impose sanctions on community members who violate them. This holds true in all three areas of PS activity—distributive politics, rule of law, and local governance. PS's work shows that institutions that embody power can be disempowered.

But new institutionalists also warn that change happens in increments. Institutional shifts take time.

Institutional change can take us to unexpected places. As PS groups negotiate with state and society, most seek adherence to formal over informal institutions. But negotiations can bring messy results. Sometimes they end in adherence to formal institutions. Elsewhere, they lead to new informal institutions that may defy parchment rules, but are still acceptable to all actors. When it comes to service distribution, PS groups demand equitable and transparent allocation of safety nets. Sometimes they end up in the practice of transactionalism, paying money for services. Transactionalism is more encompassing than clientelism and yet far removed from formal rules. In other instances, formal rules may themselves be inequitable—for example, family laws pertaining to divorce and inheritance. Thus, negotiations may end in adherence to formal or informal institutions. Some outcomes are desirable by either or both parties, and others less so.

This book also begs for rethinking the idea of change, particularly in development discourse. During one of my first field visits, an RA said to me, "Nayma apa, most PS do not really do anything." Later that night, I met the group as they worked by candlelight during a power outage. They chatted among themselves, discussing the day's interviews and adding final touches to the questionnaires that they had filled out. I looked through the questionnaire for the PS group that we had discussed earlier. I could see why the RA would think that. The group had not stopped any child marriages. Nor had it acquired many cards. But looking over the narrative, I could see that the women had put up a tough fight. What many program evaluations get wrong is that empowerment cannot be measured by numbers alone. In the PS case, it is reflected in women's leadership— bringing the community together, deliberating on problems, and negotiating hard with those in power. Sometimes checking off program objectives can be an insufficient measure of change.

One must also consider how institutions change. Rules bind human action. But PS's work illustrates that rules can change with shifting expectations and enforced sanctions. The most remarkable part of this story is that it is not the rural elite who usher in these changes; it is poor rural women. Decades ago, WID advocates believed that women could uplift their communities as they helped themselves. This ended up putting the burden of development on women. I hesitate to suggest that we weigh women down with more responsibilities than they already bear. However, a one-time investment in large-scale grassroots organizations can engender structural changes to benefit women for years—perhaps generations. Women can usher in development. But real transformation can only occur if, instead of struggling to survive the institutions that hold them back, women overturn the institutions themselves.

Appendix

Methods

Data Collection

The Polli Shomaj evaluation began with a brief inception study undertaken in two phases. I visited two PS sites to understand the organization's activities and impact, one during my very first trip to Dhamoirhaat, Nogaon, and the second in Mymensingh Sadar. I observed meetings and met with PS leaders and BRAC staff to uncover the workings of the organization. My co-researchers and I then designed three questionnaires. The RAs attended a multiple-day workshop to familiarize themselves with the questionnaires. They tested the questionnaires on each other, and later, in the field. Revisions were made based on their feedback. Eventually, RAs collected data in 671 wards across forty of Bangladesh's poorest districts. RAs included political science, sociology and anthropology graduates, as well as individuals with previous experience in data collection. They collected data in five teams of eight to ten members. Once data collection ended in March 2010, a group of RAs stayed on for quantitative data entry. It was important that data entry was done by the same RAs who were in the field—in fact, many of them were team leaders—so that they could deliberate on possible reasons behind inconsistencies and missing data. Qualitative data was entered by an external firm. Data collection lasted from November 2009 to March 2010. A particular PS group could have been interviewed at any point within this timeframe. In the manuscript, I often refer to data reflecting a one- or two-year period preceding fieldwork. Depending on when a particular group was interviewed, this would be from 2007 (two years) or 2008 (one year) to 2009 for some groups, and from 2008 (two years) or 2009 (one year) to 2010 for other groups.

Experiments

The primary quantitative analysis strategy in this book is quasi-experimental research. Broadly, experimental research can help scholars understand the difference between possible outcomes in an instance where two outcomes cannot happen simultaneously. Here, experimental methods are used to explore whether PS members do things differently from the control group. They allow the comparison of PS members with a control group so that differences in outcomes between the two groups, the treatment effect, can be attributed to PS membership, all other things being the same. However, treatment effects can also be influenced by selection bias, a possible difference between the two groups caused by factors existing prior to the treatment. In true randomized experiments, also called randomized controlled trials, the researcher manipulates the environment and randomly assigns subjects to experimental and control groups. This randomization takes care of the selection bias. But my data does not come from a true experiment, which would require manipulation of the environment before the study. The absence of this manipulation gives me a quasi-experiment, and in particular, a natural experiment, where "the assignment of treatment is outside the researcher's control."[1] In fact, the decision regarding which wards received the treatment—in this case, wards with a PS group in it—had been made by the NGO much before the study took place; they were the poorest wards in their localities. Quasi-experiments do not have the high internal validity of randomized experiments; thus, I am not able to claim causality from my quantitative analysis in chapters 3 and 4. I rely on qualitative analysis to address this gap, strengthen internal validity, and show how PS changes institutions and practices.

Sampling

This book draws on two questionnaires from the PS study, incorporating two levels of analysis: the organization level and the individual level.

> *Questionnaire 1:* Choosing PS groups (organization level). Questionnaire
> 1 was designed for PS leaders who were interviewed as a group. This
> questionnaire captured PS organizational elements—institutional
> capacity, procedures, leadership quality, and activities. Approxi-
> mately 12,000 PS groups existed in 2009, of which over 9,125 were
> operating in Bangladesh's forty poorest districts (out of sixty-four
> total districts). The PS research team divided the selected districts into
> four geographical regions based on geographical and socioeconomic
> characteristics. Each RA team would start in one zone, and they
> would converge at the center. I aimed for a sample size of 650
> PS groups (7 percent of the total). Some oversampling in order to

accommodate failures or missing data resulted in a final sample size of 671 PS groups. Of these groups, 232 were from the north-central region of Bangladesh, 205 from the northwest, 60 from the east, and 143 from the south.

Questionnaire 2: Choosing the experimental and control groups (individual level). Questionnaire 2 was designed for individual PS members selected randomly from these groups and a comparable control group. The experimental group respondents were chosen from the 671 PS groups. RAs randomly selected two respondents from each group. In order to handle selection bias, I use a nonequivalent control group design, where I choose a control group that is comparable to the experimental group on as many demographic characteristics as possible. It is also important to consider levels of randomization. The treatment is administered at the ward level, since PS is a ward-level organization. We cannot just randomize at the individual level due to information spillover; comparing PS and non-PS members from the same ward may not show the treatment effect accurately, as non-PS members may have access to information from their proximity to PS. For the experimental group, we randomly chose two PS members from each of the 671 PS groups. For the control group, research assistants were asked to choose a neighboring ward with no PS presence and minimal NGO activity. Two control group respondents were chosen from this ward, to match the demographic characteristics of their corresponding experimental group counterparts. This way, the two groups differed on only two characteristics—involvement with NGOs in general and with PS in particular—that we expect will influence the treatment effects.

ANALYSIS

Matching Demographics

In order to account for some of the selection bias, I compare the experimental and control groups on demographic variables. Table A.1 compares the experimental and control groups on these demographic characteristics. The matching strategy was successful; the two groups resemble each other on thirteen out of sixteen demographic characteristics; differences are minimal and statistically insignificant. As we may expect, the two groups differ on PS membership and NGO activity; this was deliberate, as the control group was chosen from wards with minimal NGO activity. The two groups also differ minimally on profession; a slightly higher group of PS members work as *grihosthali*, household labor in other people's homes. This is a measure of vulnerability, and analyses will accommodate this difference.

TABLE A.1

DEMOGRAPHICS OF PS MEMBERS AND CONTROL GROUP (N = 2,684)

Respondent characteristics	PS	Control	Difference
Household income (mean in 1,000 Tk.)	57.459 (37.546)	55.673 (24.579)	1.786
Age (mean number of years)	31.788 (7.218)	31.707 (6.715)	0.080
Education (mean number of years)	2.925 (3.059)	2.940 (2.902)	−0.015
Household members in NGOs (mean)	0.719 (0.507)	0.636 (0.526)	0.083***
Household education (mean number of years)	2.707 (1.914)	2.752 (1.819)	−0.045
NGO membership (%)	77.273	64.009	13.264***
Bengali (%)	99.776	100.000	−0.224*
Muslim (%)	91.058	90.984	0.075
Female (%)	97.988	98.584	−0.596
Married (%)	97.243	97.168	0.075
Ever attended school (%)	57.601	60.432	−2.832
Occupation of grihosthali (%)	90.537	93.890	−3.353***
Ordinary villager (%)	99.553	99.553	0.000
Purdah (%)	63.629	61.300	2.329

Note: Standard deviations in parentheses.

*p<.1

***p<.01

Independent Variables

PS membership: Dummy variable measuring whether respondents belonged to a PS group (1 = PS; 0 = control).

Occupation: I use occupation to measure socioeconomic vulnerability. Household income is often a static and insufficient measure of vulnerability. This variable identifies whether the respondent works as grihosthali or daily contractual laborers. Grihosthali women are informal laborers who lack permanent employment. Typically, women from the poorest families take up this occupation (1 = grihosthali; 0 = other).

TABLE A.2

SERVICES RECEIVED BY PS MEMBERS AND CONTROL GROUP BY SERVICE
CATEGORY (N = 2,684)

	PS (% of respondents)	Control (% of respondents)	Difference	Chi-squared
Welfare (G)[1]	42.846	38.972	3.875	4.168*
Health (G)	59.687	59.687	0.000	0.000
Education (G)	14.382	13.562	0.820	.375
Other (G)	10.134	10.060	0.075	.004
Health (NGO)	17.511	14.456	3.055	4.664*
Education (NGO)	2.385	2.161	0.224	.151
Other (NGO)	0.969	0.671	0.298	.733

1. G and NGO refer to government and NGO-distributed services respectively.
*$p<.1$

Education: This variable measures respondents' years of formal
schooling. I expect that educated women would be more likely to
receive services by formal rules. In rural Bangladesh, education also
provides women with greater mobility, as they leave their household
to attend school. They would also develop conversational skills that
would be useful for bargaining.

Purdah: This dummy variable measures whether women practice
purdah—that is, the practice any form of covering or seclusion. This
could range from covering their faces and/or bodies within and
outside the household to restricting their engagement with men.
I include this variable to control for the notion of the vulnerable
Muslim woman, which would lead to an expectation that women
who practice purdah would be less likely to engage in extensive
bargaining, and consequently unlikely to obtain services by formal
rules (1 = purdah; 0 = no purdah).

Political affiliation: This dummy variable measures whether respondents are affiliated with any mainstream political party. I consider
this to be an indication of whether they are part of the "net." I ask
women about political affiliation instead of formal party membership, as they could be affiliated with a party but not a registered

Type of service	Group	Clientelism (%)	Transactionalism (%)	Formal rules (%)
Welfare (G)[1]	PS	50.082	9.720	40.198
(N = 1151)	Control	55.331	5.331	39.338
	Difference	−5.249	4.389	0.859
	Pearson chi-square	8.785*		
Health (G)	PS	6.518	7.204	86.278
(N = 2342)	Control	6.888	6.803	86.310
	Difference	−0.370	0.401	−0.032
	Pearson chi-square	0.254		
Education (G)	PS	5.584	0.000	94.416
(N = 382)	Control	3.243	1.622	95.135
	Difference	2.341	−1.622	−0.719
	Pearson chi-square	4.374		
Other (G)	PS	6.522	5.072	88.406
(N = 273)	Control	4.444	5.185	90.370
	Difference	2.077	−0.113	−1.965
	Pearson chi-square			
Health (NGO)	PS	6.320	54.275	39.405
(N = 486)	Control	3.226	73.733	23.041
	Difference	3.094	−19.458	16.364
	Pearson chi-square	19.570***		
Health (NGO)[2]	PS	9.790	28.671	61.538
(N = 239)	Control	7.527	47.312	45.161
	Difference	2.263	−18.640	16.377
	Pearson chi-square	8.505**		
Education (NGO)	PS	6.250	6.250	87.500
(N = 61)	Control	10.345	0.000	89.655
	Difference	−4.095	6.250	−2.155
	Pearson chi-square	2.132		

(continued)

TABLE A.3

TYPES OF EXCHANGE (PS VS. CONTROL) *(continued)*

Type of service	Group	Clientelism (%)	Transactionalism (%)	Formal rules (%)
Other (NGO) (N = 28)	PS			100.000
	Control			100.000
	Difference			0
	Pearson chi-square			

1. G and NGO refer to government and NGO-distributed services respectively.

2. Health statistics without birth control pills.

*p<.1

**p<.05

***p<.01

member. Thus, political affiliation would signify stronger political connections than party support, though it would fall short of formal party membership (1= political affiliation; 0 = no political affiliation).

Dependent Variables

Type of exchange: Whether exchange of services between service recipient and service provider was clientelistic (respondents received a service for kinship, labor, or votes), transactional (respondents received a service for money), or based on formal rules (1 = clientelistic; 2 = transactional; 3 = formal rules). In the field, respondents chose one of five responses that I categorized into these measures. Exchanges due to kinship, labor obligations, or votes were coded as clientelism, exchanges for money were coded as transactionalism, and services received free of cost were coded as formal rules.

Multilevel Logistic Regression

I test the effects of PS membership on service distribution using multilevel logistic regression. In particular, I use the Generalized Linear Mixed Models (GLMM) function of SPSS, with randomly varying intercept. The data is cross-sectional at a single time point. GLMM allows for analysis of multilevel data where observations may not be independent. It also allows for non-normal distributions. Using multilevel regression allows for accommodation of difference across the various levels, where traditional regression could lead to overstating statistical significance. First, I created a null model with a randomly varying intercept. This model was statistically significant, suggesting sufficient variation across groups to

WHO GIVES WHAT? PS VS. CONTROL

Type of service		NGO	Acquaint-ance	Elite	Female UP	H&E provider
Welfare (G)	PS	3.789	3.954	78.089	11.697	2.471
(N = 1151)[1]	Control	0.184	2.941	88.787	6.250	1.838
	Difference	3.605	1.013	−10.698	5.447	0.633
	Pearson chi-square	32.539***				
Health (G)	PS	1.887	6.861	9.434	1.201	80.617
(N = 2342)	Control	0.595	7.738	9.949	0.680	81.037
	Difference	1.292	−0.877	−0.515	0.520	−0.420
	Pearson chi-square	10.365*				
Education (G)	PS	0.508	1.015	7.614	2.030	88.832
(N = 382)	Control	0	0.541	7.027	0	92.432
	Difference	0.508	0.475	0.587	2.030	−3.600
	Pearson chi-square	5.151				
Other (G)	PS	0	2.899	7.246	0	89.855
(N = 273)	Control	0	1.481	7.407	0	91.111
	Difference	0	1.417	−0.161	0	−1.256
	Pearson chi-square	.638				
Health (NGO)	PS	24.535	49.442	1.859	0.743	23.420
(N = 486)	Control	15.668	67.281	1.843	0	15.207
	Difference	8.867	−17.839	0.015	0.743	8.213
	Pearson chi-square	16.962**				
Education (NGO)	PS	9.375	6.250	0	0	84.375
(N = 61)	Control	6.897	10.345	0	0	82.759
	Difference	2.478	−4.095	0	0	1.616
	Pearson chi-square	.430				
Other (NGO)	PS	16.667	72.222	5.556	0	5.556
(N = 28)	Control	30.000	40.000	30.000	0	0
	Difference	−13.333	32.222	−24.444	0	5.556
	Pearson chi-square	4.877				

1. G and NGO refer to government and NGO-distributed services respectively.

*p<.1

**p<.05

***p<.01

require a multilevel model. The multilevel model has three levels: the ward (level 1, the level of randomization), individual (level 2, the level of interview), and incidents (level 3, the level of analysis). The GLMM function relates the dependent variable to the independent variables through a specified link function, which in this case is a multinomial logit function. The model holds all the control variables as fixed. I include random effects at each level (ward and individual) as well as the intercept. The data have been tested for multicollinearity.

PS Program Details

Formation

In 1998, BRAC's CEP, then known as the Social Development Programme, first formed PS as a poor women's civil society organization at the ward level. Initially a federation of VOs—a village-level group of women belonging to BRAC's microfinance program—the program later expanded its membership beyond BRAC microfinance clients to include poor women from the community.[2] In 2009, the program had 12,000 groups across Bangladesh, covering approximately 30 percent of all rural wards in the country. As of 2020, there were 12,487 PS groups in fifty-four *upazilas*.

Staff

PS groups are supervised by BRAC field staff called CEP POs, field workers who report to district managers in regional offices. In 2009, POs helped plan and supervise meetings, oversaw activities, and connected PS members to the larger community. But POs no longer help PS members arrange meetings. Now, they check in with each group once every three months. They provide technical support to PS leaders for building their capacity through meetings of the Union Coordination Forum, a forum at the union level. PS groups take on the rest of their efforts on their own—they arrange bimonthly meetings, keep records, and coordinate with local government and service providers to pursue their activities. They continue to raise awareness on social issues in their communities.

Record-Keeping

PS groups are required to keep records in a register; they write down group decisions as resolutions. As many PS members are illiterate, some groups invite teenage members of BRAC's Adolescent Development Program (ADP) called *kishori netris* (youth leaders) to write in the register during meetings.

Program Objectives

The program has four areas of activity, which I organized into three broad goals. In 2009, these activities were organized differently, into three program objectives. The activities remain the same.

1. Distributive politics: assisting the rural poor, especially the most marginalized, in accessing government and nongovernment services and resources, such as safety nets, social protection schemes, education stipends, tube wells, and latrines (activity 1).
2. Local governance: participating in the local power structure through competing for membership in local governing bodies, including the UP, school committees, market committees, etc. (activity 2), and engaging in local development activities, such as social forestry, rural infrastructure development, birth registration, etc. (activity 3).
3. Rule of Law: preventing and protesting social injustices and violence, particularly against women, such as dowry, child marriage, domestic violence, acid attacks, and rape (activity 4). In addition, members track human rights abuses in the community and work with local field staff to connect survivors with medical and legal help.

Leadership

The executive committee includes the president, secretary, cashier, and eight other members who belong to various subcommittees. In 2009 there were six subcommittees; now there are four. They work on preventing social injustices, family and community development, local affairs, and acquiring services. Groups hold executive committee and general meetings in alternate months.

Acknowledgments

I would often marvel at the long list of acknowledgments accompanying my favorite books. I never imagined that one day, my own list would be just as long. I am so grateful for the overwhelming generosity of friends, acquaintances, and sometimes complete strangers. You offered your time, mentorship, feedback, and advice graciously and without complaint. The excellent work of many Bangladeshi scholars—especially women—made this book possible. I stand on your shoulders.

My adviser Vincent Boudreau gave me the methodological guidance to tackle an incredibly complex project. My undergraduate adviser and mentor, Michael Johnston, inspired me to study political science; two decades later, he read my full manuscript in the middle of a global pandemic. I am deeply indebted to Philip Oldenburg, Dina Siddiqi, Elora Shehabuddin, Ali Riaz, Naeem Mohaiemen, Nadine Murshid, Sajeda Amin, and Cyril Ghosh for their advice, friendship, and mentorship, on the book and beyond. You have helped me navigate the world in a way that I could never have on my own. I am thankful to Anthony Delli Paoli, Kyoko Mona, Mehrab Ali, and Wameq Raza for brainstorming methods with me. To Manhattanville College's writing night crew—Carleigh Brower, John Proctor, Liz Faber, and Mike Castaldo—thank you for those very long, snack-filled evenings that we spent both commiserating and writing. My friends from the Graduate Center—Humayun Kabir, Yekaterina Oziashvili, Nazmul Sultan, Ahmed Shamim, and Flannery Amdahl—thank you for your compassion, friendship, and support. To the many conference panel chairs and discussants who have read and commented on my work—I owe you. To my anonymous reviewers—your feedback has made this book so much better. To my editor Kim Guinta—thank you for believing in this project. And to my friends Caralyn Bialo, Elizabeth Cherry, Julie Siddique, Meghan Freeman, David Gutman, Anna Cheung, and Jorge Cardenas—I am so very grateful for you.

In 2009, I packed up my things and moved to Bangladesh for dissertation fieldwork. My friend Iffat Ahmed graciously offered to keep my things in her parents' garage. They thought I was leaving behind clothes. But even after giving away an entire car trunk full of books, what I left behind were only more books. I was starting with nothing but an abstract idea of what I wanted to do. And I took nothing with me. I had not lived in Bangladesh for a decade and a half. Frequent visits were not enough. This time, I wanted to know my country and its people intimately. By the time I left in 2011, I knew that I had truly come home. I cherish the time I spent with my grandparents, Nawajesh Ali Khan and Asia Khan. Your stories unlocked a deeper window to history than any book could have. My brilliant cousin Shahab Enam Khan pushed my intellectual horizons—thank you for the many inspiring conversations and opening new doors. My friends Zareen Alam, Sarah Shehabuddin, Zareen Hosein, Tisa Muhaddes, and Rubaiyath Sarwar—you made those two years extra beautiful. Ali Mama and Amola—you took such good care of me.

To my colleagues at BRAC—your groundbreaking work continues to amaze me. How lucky am I to have worked with and learned from you! This book is based on data from the Polli Shomaj study. I am deeply indebted to Ashrafuzzaman Khan, Rehnuma Rahman, and the entire Polli Shomaj team—you dedicated yourself to a project that seemed impossibly difficult at times. Without your skills, the dataset—and this book—would not exist. Ziauddin Hyder, you gave a young graduate student the opportunity of a lifetime when you asked me to lead the Polli Shomaj study. The sociologists and anthropologists in RED's Social Development research team—Dr. Mohammad Rafi, Ashrafuzzaman Khan, Mrinmoy Samadder—you have turned me into a true interdisciplinary scholar and taught me field methods in a way that I could have never learned on my own. You befriended me, and supported me through my first awkward encounters and anxious fumbling with Bangla. My colleagues at RED—Narayan Das, Swapan Deb Roy, and so many others—you have helped every step of the way. I am thankful to Anna Minj and Imran Matin for supporting this project. And last but not least, my wonderful colleagues at CEP—I am deeply grateful for the work that you do and for having the chance to study it. Palash Kumar Ghosh and Kazi N. Fattah—you have been so very generous with my many demands on your time. Md. Emamul Hoque, Fokhrul Alam, Md. Masudur Rahman, and Rita Roselin Costa—thank you for reading the manuscript closely and offering many insightful comments.

This book's path crosses a decade. The last mile felt impossibly difficult at times. As the COVID-19 pandemic upended our lives with tragedies, delays, separation from loved ones, and complete disruption of daily life, two things kept me going. I could not forget the interminable optimism of PS members in the field. You inspired me to push this project past the finish line. My newly unearthed love of writing did the rest. I owe a big thank-you to Lori Soderlind for teaching me the craft, to Elizabeth Cherry for being my partner in crime, and to Laura Portwood-Stacer for her invaluable advice at many stages of the project.

It is only fitting to save the most important people for the ending. I struggle to find words that reflect the depth of my gratitude to my family. My brother Shahryar Qayum has always supported me; this includes getting me out of tricky situations both at home and while out in the world. Our puppy Sparky put up with my forced cuddles—I hope you have an unending supply of vanilla ice cream on the rainbow bridge. And to my parents M. A. Qayum and Salma Qayum for their countless sacrifices and limitless patience. This book is for you.

Glossary of Terms

apa. sister

bhai. brother

bhalo chele. good boy/good potential groom

bhalo manush. good person

bichar. justice

birangona. war heroine

biye bhanga. canceled wedding

chharachhari. separation or divorce

denmohor. payment made to a bride's family from a groom's family during marriage as part of Islamic marital contract

dukkho koshto. troubles or pain

ganja. weed

gono adalot. citizens' court

gosthi/gusti. kinship group

gosthi prodhan. leader of kinship group

gram adalot. Union Parishad–administered village court

gram sarkar. village government

grihosthali. household laborer

hadith. written records of the sunnah

janaza. Muslim burial rites

joutuk. dowry

kharap kotha. gossip or negative comments

khas . government-owned agricultural land allocated to landless families

kholamela. open

khota. censorious remark

kishori netri. youth leader

loker mukhe. word of mouth

madrasa. Islamic school

matobbor. informal village leader

meye dekha. practice of seeing a potential bride before forming a wedding alliance

mile mishe thaka. to live in harmony

muktijoddha. freedom fighter

niyom. rule

noshto. spoiled

panchayat. traditional village council

poramorshodata. adviser

poribesh. environment

pouroshova. municipal corporation

purdah. seclusion

reeti. tradition

shahajyo kora. to help

shajiye dawa. to adorn

shalish. village court

shalishkar. decision maker in village court

shasthyo apa. health worker

shobai bhalo jane. to have a good reputation

shomaj/samaj. community or society

shomaj/samaj prodhan. leader of a community or society

shongshar. domestic life

shongshar kora. to live a domestic life

shongshari. one perceived as having the mindset and skills to live a domestic life

sunnah. practices and sayings of the Prophet Muhammad

talaaq. divorce

thana. police station

upazila. subdistrict

upobritti. education stipend

Notes

1. All names have been changed to protect respondents' identities.

2. *Apa* translates literally to sister, signifying the close relationship that health workers shared with their communities.

3. For media reports on BRAC as a global NGO, see "The List"; "BRAC in Business"; "BRAC Ranked Top Global NGO for 3rd Consecutive Year." On BRAC's global expansion, see N. Hossain and Sengupta, "Thinking Big, Going Global."

4. Smillie, *Freedom from Want*, 154.

5. "The Other Government in Bangladesh"; Kelly, "Growing Discontent"; Wood, "States without Citizens"; Karim, *Microfinance and Its Discontents*.

6. BRAC, *2018 Annual Report*.

7. Bangladesh is geographically divided into districts. Each district is further divided into subdistricts or *upazilas*, unions, wards, and villages. The UP is the lowest level of local government. It is run by elected officials, including one chairman, nine members (one member from each ward), and three women members in reserved seats. Generally, each elected UP member is designated to a particular ward within their union. Other officials include a block supervisor from the Directorate of Agriculture, health assistant, family planning assistant, family welfare worker, Ansar-VDP (a paramilitary force), representatives from the freedom fighters and cooperative groups, and other field staff. Unlike elected members, these individuals do not have voting rights. Government of Bangladesh, "Local Government Structure."

8. Community Empowerment Programme, "Community Institution Building: Polli Shomaj and Union Shomaj." The PS program has undergone numerous changes since the PS study took place in 2009–2010. It has four objectives now, though at the time it had three. The activities remain the same. I have organized the four program objectives into three broad goals: distributive politics: assisting the rural poor, including the most marginalized, in accessing government and nongovernment services and resources, such as safety nets, social protection schemes, education stipends, tube wells, and latrines (activity 1); local governance: participating in the local power structure through competing for membership in local governing bodies, including the UP, school committees,

market committees, etc. (activity 2), and engaging in local development activities, such as social forestry, rural infrastructure development, etc. (activity 3); rule of law: preventing and protesting social injustices and violence, particularly against women, such as dowry, child marriage, domestic violence, acid attacks, and rape (activity 4). PS members also track human rights abuses in the community, and work with local field staff to connect survivors with medical and legal help. See the conclusion and the appendix section on PS program details.

9. Community Empowerment Programme, "Background Information on Polli Shomaj."

CHAPTER 1 — INSTITUTIONS

1. World Bank, "Decline of Global Extreme Poverty Continues but Has Slowed."

2. United Nations Development Programme, "Beyond Income, beyond Averages, beyond Today," 148.

3. Goetz and Sengupta, "Who Takes the Credit?"; Karim, *Microfinance and Its Discontents*.

4. D. Lewis and Hossain, "A Tale of Three Villages"; N. Hossain, "The Politics of What Works."

5. E. Chowdhury, *Transnationalism Reversed*, 2.

6. Abu-Lughod, *Do Muslim Women Need Saving?*

7. Shehabuddin, *Reshaping the Holy.*

8. Auyero, *Poor People's Politics*; Shehabuddin, *Reshaping the Holy*; Singerman, *Avenues of Participation.*

9. Rhodes, *Understanding Governance*; Lowndes, "Institutionalism," 55.

10. Lowndes, "Varieties of New Institutionalism"; Lowndes, "Institutionalism."

11. Goodin, "Institutions and Their Design."

12. Putnam, Leonardi, and Nanetti, *Making Democracy Work*, 8.

13. March and Olsen, "The New Institutionalism," 738.

14. Lowndes, "Institutionalism," 62.

15. Koelble, "The New Institutionalism in Political Science and Sociology," 232. See also North, "Economic Performance through Time"; North, *Institutions, Institutional Change, and Economic Performance*; Ostrom, *Governing the Commons*; Ostrom, Gardner, and Walker, *Rules, Games, and Common-Pool Resources*; Popkin, *The Rational Peasant*; Aldrich, "Rational Choice and Turnout"; Przeworski, *Democracy and the Market.*

16. North, "Institutions"; Koelble, "The New Institutionalism in Political Science and Sociology."

17. Lowndes and Roberts, *Why Institutions Matter*, 31.

18. Hall, *Governing the Economy*, 19.

19. W. Powell and DiMaggio, *The New Institutionalism in Organizational Analysis*, 10.

20. Koelble, "The New Institutionalism in Political Science and Sociology," 235.

21. March and Olsen, *Rediscovering Institutions*, 17.

22. March and Olsen, ch. 2.

23. Some scholars identify further categories of institutionalism, such as normative institutionalism, discursive institutionalism, and feminist institutionalism.

24. Mackay, "Conclusion," 181.

25. Goodin, "Institutions and Their Design," 1–2.

26. Mahoney and Thelen, *Explaining Institutional Change*, 4.

27. North, "Economic Performance through Time," 361.

28. Lowndes, "Institutionalism," 64–65.

29. O'Donnell, "On Informal Institutions, Once Again," 285.

30. Brinks, "The Rule of (Non) Law," 224.

31. Chappell and Mackay, "What's in a Name?," 25.

32. Waylen, "Analysing Gender in Informal Institutions." Scholarship in this category includes North, *Institutions, Institutional Change, and Economic Performance*; March and Olsen, *Rediscovering Institutions*; and Huntington, *Political Order in Changing Societies*.

33. Helmke and Levitsky, "Informal Institutions and Comparative Politics," 729.

34. Helmke and Levitsky, 729.

35. Helmke and Levitsky, 729.

36. Ostrom, "Institutional Rational Choice"; Lowndes, Pratchett, and Stoker, "Local Political Participation," 542.

37. Mackay, Kenny, and Chappell, "New Institutionalism through a Gender Lens," 580.

38. Lowndes proposes Peter Hall's idea of standard operating procedures as a solution, referring to "the specific rules of behavior that are agreed upon and (in general) followed by agents, whether explicitly or tacitly agreed." Lowndes and Roberts, *Why Institutions Matter*, 47; Peter Hall, *Governing the Economy*. But Rothstein argues that this, being a public administration concept, provides little room for cultural norms. Rothstein, "Political Institutions," 146.

39. Helmke and Levitsky, introduction to *Informal Institutions and Democracy*.

40. Brinks, "The Rule of (Non) Law."

41. Brinks, "Informal Institutions and the Rule of Law"; Brinks, "The Rule of (Non) Law."

42. Chappell and Mackay, "What's in a Name?," 27.

43. Helmke and Levitsky, introduction to *Informal Institutions and Democracy*, 26.

44. March and Olsen, "The Logic of Appropriateness," 478.

45. March and Olsen, "The Logic of Appropriateness," 478.

46. Chappell and Mackay, "What's in a Name?"; Brinks, "The Rule of (Non) Law"; Helmke and Levitsky, "Informal Institutions and Comparative Politics."

47. Helmke and Levitsky, introduction to *Informal Institutions and Democracy*, 26.

48. Qayum, Khan, and Rahman, "Rural Organizations and Active Citizenship in Bangladesh."

49. In 2018, RED was merged with three different institutes at BRAC University.

50. The PS study includes four sets of interviews. We interviewed 671 PS groups using a semi-structured questionnaire. PS leaders answered questions about PS as an organization, such as its membership, leadership, operational procedures, and activities. We then interviewed individual PS members and a comparable control group using a semi-structured questionnaire, with a total sample size of 2,684. These interviews capture individuals' demographic characteristics, political activities, and interactions with both society and decision makers. We then surveyed every household in four selected wards. Additional questionnaires were developed for interviews with BRAC staff and UP members.

51. Gerring and Seawright, "Case Selection Techniques in Case Study Research."

52. Tsai, *Accountability without Democracy*, 8.

53. Brinks, "The Rule of (Non) Law."

CHAPTER 2 — A GENDERED STORY

1. Jahan, "Bangladesh in 1972," p. 199.

2. Asadullah, Savoia, and Mahmud, "Paths to Development."

3. "Leaving the LDCs Category."

4. Ahmad, "Hunger Halved Well before MDG Time."

5. Bengal, one of the wealthier regions of the British subcontinent, saw dramatic impoverishment and landlessness over the course of British rule; this was sped up by the famine of 1943–1944, which caused between 1.5 million and 3 million deaths. N. Hossain, *The Aid Lab*, 23; Sen, "Starvation and Exchange Entitlements."

6. S. Ali, *Understanding Bangladesh*, 32.

7. S. Ali, 32-33.

8. Toor, "Containing East Bengal."

9. United Nations, *Report of the High Level Consultants Mission to Bangladesh March–April 1972*, 4. Also see World Bank, *Bangladesh - Reconstructing the Economy*.

10. Government of Bangladesh, The Constitution of the People's Republic of Bangladesh.

11. Rounaq Jahan, "Bangladesh in 1973," 134.

12. The causes of the famine are much debated (particularly, how Bangladesh was able to avert a food crisis in 1972 in the immediate aftermath of the war but not in 1974). For more on this, see Sen, "Starvation and Exchange Entitlements"; Sen, "The Economics of Life and Death"; N. Hossain, *The Aid Lab*; Dowlah, "The Politics and Economics of Food and Famine in Bangladesh in the Early 1970s">; Sobhan, "Politics of Food and Famine in Bangladesh."

13. Huque, "Local Leadership," 229; Mannan, "Who Rules Whom?," 76; Blair, "Participation, Public Policy, Political Economy and Development in Rural Bangladesh, 1958–85," 1236.

14. S. Islam, "The Role of the State in the Economic Development of Bangladesh during the Mujib Regime (1972–1975)."

15. N. Hossain, *The Aid Lab*, 125.

16. S. Ali, *Understanding Bangladesh*, 151.

17. S. Ali, 151.

18. S. Ali, 140.

19. Karim, "Democratizing Bangladesh State, NGOs, and Militant Islam," 295.

20. Earlier in 1972, the government had passed a law to try all collaborators in a tribunal and took some of them into custody. Bangladesh passed the International Crimes Tribunal Act in 1973, which demanded the trial of both Bangladeshis and members of the Pakistan Army. The same year, the government revoked the citizenship of known war criminal and JI leader Gholam Azam, along with that of thirty-eight others. The exiled leaders sought refuge in Pakistan. However, in November 1973, the AL government declared amnesty for the arrested, with the exception of collaborators who had already been charged with a crime. The amnesty came in the aftermath of the Simla Pact between India and Pakistan, which called for the release of arrested Pakistanis in Bangladesh, in exchange for Indian and Bangladeshi prisoners of war in Pakistan.

21. N. Hossain, *The Aid Lab*, 134; Blair, "Participation, Public Policy, Political Economy and Development in Rural Bangladesh, 1958–85," 1237.

22. Huque, "The Problem of Local Government Reform in Rural Bangladesh"; Nasrin, "Reforms in Local Government"; Siddiquee, "Politics and Administration in Local Councils."

23. M. Rahman, "Bangladesh in 1982."

24. S. Ali, *Understanding Bangladesh*, 175.

25. Kukreja, *Civil-Military Relations in South Asia*, 165.

26. S. Ali, *Understanding Bangladesh*, 178; Crook and Manor, *Democracy and Decentralisation in South Asia and West Africa*, 90.

27. Schroeder, "Decentralization in Rural Bangladesh," 1146.

28. Crook and Manor, *Democracy and Decentralisation in South Asia and West Africa*, 85.

29. Campbell and Pedersen, introduction to *The Rise of Neoliberalism and Institutional Analysis*, 1.

30. Monbiot, "Neoliberalism."

31. Although Williamson has since written that conflating the Washington Consensus with neoliberalism or the primacy of the market is a wide misuse of his term, it signifies broad agreements among key Washington institutions that the state should step back from the economy. Williamson, "What Washington Means by Policy Reform"; Williamson, "What Should the World Bank Think about the Washington Consensus?"

32. Ferguson, *The Anti-Politics Machine*, 15.

33. Lipset, "Some Social Requisites of Democracy"; Przeworski et al., "What Makes Democracies Endure?"; Przeworski and Limongi, "Modernization"; Rostow, "The Stages of Economic Growth."

34. Ferguson, *The Anti-Politics Machine*, 15.

35. Escobar, *Encountering Development*, 5.

36. Evans and Sewell, "Neoliberalism," 36.

37. N. Hossain, *The Aid Lab*, 80; Mookherjee, "Gendered Embodiments"; Saikia, *Women, War, and the Making of Bangladesh*, 44.

38. Saikia, 186.

39. Saikia, 186.

40. Mookherjee, *The Spectral Wound*.

41. Saikia, *Women, War, and the Making of Bangladesh*, 56–57; Hossain, *The Aid Lab*, 81.

42. D'Costa and Hossain, "Redress for Sexual Violence before the International Crimes Tribunal in Bangladesh," 341–342.

43. D'Costa and Hossain, 341.

44. D'Costa and Hossain, 341–342.

45. Mookherjee, "'Remembering to Forget.'"

46. N. Hossain, *The Aid Lab*.

47. N. Hossain, 81–83.

48. D'Costa and Hossain, "Redress for Sexual Violence before the International Crimes Tribunal in Bangladesh," 332; N. Hossain, *The Aid Lab*, 81; Mookherjee, *The Spectral Wound*.

49. Mookherjee, "Gendered Embodiments," 45.

50. Mookherjee, 40.

51. Saikia, *Women, War, and the Making of Bangladesh*, 57.

52. Saikia, 57.

53. Saikia, 57.

54. Mookherjee, "'Remembering to Forget.'"

55. N. Hossain, *The Aid Lab*, 132.

56. Maniruzzaman, "Bangladesh in 1974," 119–120.

57. Maniruzzaman, 119–120.

58. N. Hossain, *The Aid Lab*, 108.

59. M. Islam, "The Politics of the Public Food Distribution System in Bangladesh," 708; N. Hossain, *The Aid Lab*, 108; Sobhan, "Politics of Food and Famine in Bangladesh."

60. N. Hossain, *The Aid Lab*, 106; Alamgir, *Famine in South Asia*.

61. N. Hossain, *The Aid Lab*, 107.

62. N. Hossain, 6.

63. Roushan Jahan, "Men in Seclusion, Women in Public"; Qayum and Samadder, "Eradicating Extreme Poverty in Bangladesh."

64. S. Ali, *Understanding Bangladesh*, 139.

65. Franda, *Bangladesh, the First Decade*, 358.

66. N. Hossain, "The Politics of What Works," 6.

67. N. Hossain, 6.

68. Jamil et al., "The Immunization Programme in Bangladesh."

69. Howes and Islam, "Community-Led Total Sanitation and Its Successors in Bangladesh, Case 2."

70. Government of Bangladesh, "The Fourth Five-Year Plan, 1990–1995"; Government of Bangladesh, "The Fifth Five Year Plan"; Qayum and Samadder, "Eradicating Extreme Poverty in Bangladesh."

71. Sobhan, *Challenging the Injustice of Poverty*, 13.

72. Qayum and Samadder, "Eradicating Extreme Poverty in Bangladesh."

73. Government of Bangladesh, "Unlocking the Potential," 149–150.

74. Qayum, "Women, NGOs, and the Bangladesh Miracle."

75. Khandker, Pitt, and Fuwa, "Subsidy to Promote Girls' Secondary Education"; Ahmed and Sharmeen, "Assessing the Performance of Conditional Cash Transfer Programs for Girls and Boys"; N. Hossain, "The Politics of What Works"; N. Hossain, Hassan, et al., "The Problem with Teachers."

76. Qayum, "Women, NGOs, and the Bangladesh Miracle."

77. I draw on Edwards and Hulme's definition of NGOs as "intermediary organizations engaged in funding or offering other forms of support to communities and other organisations that seek to promote development." Hulme and Edwards, *NGOs, State and Donors*, 21, quoted in White, "NGOs, Civil Society, and the State in Bangladesh," 307.

78. D. Lewis, "Non-Governmental Organizations and Civil Society," 34.

79. T. Ali, "Technologies of Peasant Production and Reproduction."

80. Shehabuddin, "Feminism and Nationalism in Cold War East Pakistan."

81. Shehabuddin.

82. N. Hossain, *The Aid Lab*.

83. T. Ali, "Technologies of Peasant Production and Reproduction," 436.

84. T. Ali, 446.

85. N. Hossain, *The Aid Lab*, 134.

86. N. Hossain, 134.

87. S. Rahman, "Development, Democracy and the NGO Sector," 454.

88. Smillie, *Freedom from Want*, 29–30.

89. Grameen Bank, "Founder."

90. N. Fernando and Meyer, "ASA—the Ford Motor Model of Microfinance."

91. Karim, *Microfinance and Its Discontents*, 160. Other prominent NGOs of the time include Nijera Kori, Gonoshastha Kendro, and Gono Shahajya Shangstha.

92. Karim, *Microfinance and Its Discontents*, 14.

93. Fruttero and Gauri, "The Strategic Choices of NGOS"; S. Rahman, "Development, Democracy and the NGO Sector."

94. Zohir, "NGOs in Development," 30.

95. Feldman, "NGOs and Civil Society"; D. J. Lewis, "NGOs, Donors, and the State in Bangladesh"; S. Rahman, "Development, Democracy and the NGO Sector."

96. Fruttero and Gauri, "The Strategic Choices of NGOS."

97. Kabeer, "Making Rights Work for the Poor," 2.

98. S. Rahman, "Development, Democracy and the NGO Sector"; D. Lewis, "Non-Governmental Organizations and Civil Society"; Qayum, "Women, NGOs, and the Bangladesh Miracle."

99. Netherlands Ministry of Foreign Affairs, "Evaluation of the Netherlands Development Programme with Bangladesh, 1972–1996," quoted in Kabeer, "Making Rights Work for the Poor."

100. Fruttero and Gauri, "The Strategic Choices of NGOS."

101. White, "NGOs, Civil Society, and the State in Bangladesh," 308.

102. Centre for the Study of Developing Societies, *The State of Democracy in South Asia*.

103. S. Rahman, "Development, Democracy and the NGO Sector"; Karim, *Microfinance and Its Discontents*; Wood, "States without Citizens."

104. D. J. Lewis, "NGOs, Donors, and the State in Bangladesh," 37.

105. White, "NGOs, Civil Society, and the State in Bangladesh," 308–309.

106. Mahmud, "Informal Women's Groups in Rural Bangladesh," 209.

107. Mahmud, 216.

108. Feldman, "NGOs and Civil Society," 53.

109. Higgitt, "Women's Leadership Building as a Poverty Reduction Strategy."

110. Kabeer, "Growing Citizenship from the Grassroots."

111. Kabeer, "Making Rights Work for the Poor."

112. Kabeer.

113. Azim, Menon, and Siddiqi, "Negotiating New Terrains," 1.

114. Jayawardena, *Feminism and Nationalism in the Third World*, 73.

115. Nazneen, "The Women's Movement in Bangladesh."

116. Roushan Jahan, "Men in Seclusion, Women in Public.

117. Jayawardena, *Feminism and Nationalism in the Third World*, 87–88.

118. Roushan Jahan, "Men in Seclusion, Women in Public"; Nazneen, "The Women's Movement in Bangladesh," 5.

119. Jayawardena, *Feminism and Nationalism in the Third World*, 93.

120. Jayawardena, 93.

121. Jayawardena, 94.

122. Jayawardena, 99.

123. Shehabuddin, "Feminism and Nationalism in Cold War East Pakistan," 53.

124. Shehabuddin, 53.

125. Roushan Jahan, "Men in Seclusion, Women in Public."

126. *Begum's* objective was promoting the welfare and development of Bengali women. The magazine was founded in Calcutta in 1947 and moved to Dhaka in 1952. Shehabuddin, "Feminism and Nationalism in Cold War East Pakistan," 50–51.

127. Roushan Jahan, "Men in Seclusion, Women in Public."

128. Roushan Jahan.

129. Roushan Jahan.

130. Begum and Huq, *Ami Nari*; Shehabuddin, *Feminism and Nationalism in Cold War East Pakistan.*

131. Mookherjee, "Gendered Embodiments."

132. Roushan Jahan, "Men in Seclusion, Women in Public"; Prashad, *The Darker Nations.*

133. Nazneen and Sultan, "Struggling for Survival and Autonomy," 193.

134. Nazneen and Sultan, 195–196.

135. Nazneen and Sultan, 195–196.

136. E. Chowdhury, "'Transnationalism Reversed.'"

137. E. Chowdhury, 415.

138. E. Chowdhury, 419.

139. N. Hossain, Nazneen, and Sultan, "National Discourses on Women's Empowerment in Bangladesh," 14–15.

140. Nazneen and Sultan, "Struggling for Survival and Autonomy," 197.

141. "Bangladesh Police and Garment Workers Clash over Wage Rise."

142. Safi and Rushe, "Rana Plaza, Five Years On"; Manik and Yardley, "Bangladesh Finds Gross Negligence in Factory Fire."

143. Safi and Rushe, "Rana Plaza, Five Years On."

144. Students, too, have taken to the streets, organizing around issues such as reserved quotas and traffic safety. In 2018, schoolchildren blocked traffic in Dhaka after two teenagers were killed by a speeding bus; they took over from the traffic police, directing traffic and demonstrating what traffic safety could look like. The same year, university students across the country organized to demand the removal of quotas in the government's recruitment policies; quotas covered 56 percent of civil service positions.

145. Wood, "Clashing Values in Bangladesh."

146. D'Costa, "Faith, NGOs and the Politics of Development in Bangladesh."

147. Wood, "Clashing Values in Bangladesh."

148. Wood.

149. Karim, "Democratizing Bangladesh State, NGOs, and Militant Islam," 297.

150. Karim, 298.

151. Wood, "Clashing Values in Bangladesh."

152. Riaz, *God Willing*, 125–127.

153. Karim, "Democratizing Bangladesh State, NGOs, and Militant Islam."

154. Rafi and Chowdhury, "Human Rights and Religious Backlash," 20.

155. Karim, "Democratizing Bangladesh State, NGOs, and Militant Islam."

156. Shehabuddin, *Reshaping the Holy*, 13–14.

157. Shehabuddin, 13–14.

158. Riaz, *The Politics of Islamization in Bangladesh*, 55.

159. Shehabuddin, "Bangladesh in 1998."

CHAPTER 3 — POOR WOMEN'S POLITICS

1. According to the World Food Programme, the VGD program provides poor women with complementary services over 24 months to "improve their nutrition and enhance their livelihoods and self-reliance." Services may include fortified grains, savings programs, microcredit, and training in health, nutrition, civil and legal rights, and other areas. World Food Programme, "Vulnerable Group Development (VGD)," 1.

2. In 2005, 56 million Bangladeshis lived in poverty. World Bank, "Bangladesh—Poverty Assessment for Bangladesh," 2; World Food Programme, "Vulnerable Group Development (VGD)," 1.

3. Research and Evaluation Division, *The Net*; Research and Evaluation Division, *Who Gets What and Why*.

4. Deshwara, "Many Denied VGF Cards, Nepotism Alleged."

5. Parts of this section appear in Qayum, "Women, NGOs, and the Bangladesh Miracle."

6. See J. Fernando, "Nongovernmental Organizations, Micro-Credit, and Empowerment of Women"; Feldman, "NGOs and Civil Society"; Karim, *Microfinance and Its Discontents*; Leve, "Failed Development and Rural Revolution in Nepal."

7. Kabeer, *Reversed Realities*, 5–8; Tinker, *Persistent Inequalities*, 3–4.

8. Tinker, 39.

9. Campbell and Pedersen, introduction to *The Rise of Neoliberalism and Institutional Analysis*, 5.

10. Mackay, Kenny, and Chappell, "New Institutionalism through a Gender Lens," 580.

11. Kabeer, *Reversed Realities*, 26–29; Baneria and Feldman, *Unequal Burden*; Sen, "Gender and Cooperative Conflicts"; Sen, "Gender Inequality and Theories of Justice."

12. Yunus, "How Social Business can Create a World without Poverty."

13. R. Rahman, "Impact of Grameen Bank on the Situation of Poor Rural Women"; Khandker, "Microfinance and Poverty"; Pitt and Khandker, "The Impact of Group-Based Credit Programs on Poor Households in Bangladesh"; Schuler and Hashemi, "Credit Programs, Women's Empowerment, and Contraceptive Use in Rural Bangladesh"; Hashemi, Schuler, and Riley, "Rural Credit Programs and Women's Empowerment in Bangladesh"; Littlefield et al., "Is Microfinance an Effective Strategy to Reach the Millennium Development Goals?"

14. Hulme and Mosley, *Finance against Poverty*, vols. 1 and 2; Mosley and Hulme, "Microenterprise Finance"; Mayoux, "Tackling the Down Side"; Karim, *Microfinance and Its Discontents*; Goetz and Sengupta, "Who Takes the Credit?"; Kabeer, "Conflicts over Credit."

15. Montgomery et al., "Credit for the Poor in Bangladesh"; Kabeer, "Conflicts over Credit"; Goetz and Sengupta, "Who Takes the Credit?"; Ackerly, "Testing the Tools of Development"; Karim, *Microfinance and Its Discontents*; Montgomery, "Disciplining or Protecting the Poor?"; Hulme and Maitrot, "Has Microfinance Lost Its Moral Compass?"; Karim, "Demystifying Micro-Credit."

16. Karim, *Microfinance and Its Discontents*, xvi.

17. Schuster, *Social Collateral*; Karim, *Microfinance and Its Discontents*.

18. Karim, *Microfinance and Its Discontents*; Goetz and Sengupta, "Who Takes the Credit?"; Kabeer, "Conflicts over Credit."

19. Karim, "Demystifying Micro-Credit," 10.

20. Shahabuddin et al., "Exploring Maternal Health Care-Seeking Behavior of Married Adolescent Girls in Bangladesh."

21. Campbell and Pedersen, introduction to *The Rise of Neoliberalism and Institutional Analysis*, 5.

22. Sen, *Development as Freedom*.

23. Evans, "Collective Capabilities, Culture, and Amartya Sen's *Development as Freedom*," 56.

24. Evans, 56.

25. These objectives are (1) assisting the rural poor in accessing government safety nets and NGO resources; (2) participating in the local power structure; (3) undertaking local development activities; and (4) preventing and reacting to social injustices and violence, particularly against women. See the prologue and the appendix for more details.

26. Interviews took place between 2009 and 2010. Numbers recorded data for the year preceding the exact interview date. For groups interviewed in 2009, the data would capture events from 2008 to 2009, and for groups interviewed in 2010, the data would capture events from 2009 to 2010. See Appendix section on Data Collection

27. Fattah and Kabir, "No Place Is Safe."

28. The EC includes a president, a secretary, a cashier, and eight subcommittee members split up into five subcommittees. These subcommittees are responsible for specific activities. However, subcommittees were fairly new during my fieldwork; they had only existed for six months. Therefore, I do not include them in the analysis. Currently, PS groups operate with four subcommittees as well as an advisory committee drawn from locally influential people. Community Empowerment Programme, "Operational Guidebook for Management of Polli Shomaj."

29. At the time, members contributed Tk. 5 per year. The amount is higher now.

30. Community Empowerment Programme, "Operational Guidebook for Management of Polli Shomaj." This guidebook was created after the study was conducted. I use it for my analysis because the messaging provided by BRAC, both in writing and verbally, remains the same.

31. Leve, "Failed Development and Rural Revolution in Nepal"; Sharma, "The State and Women's Empowerment in India"; Freire, *Pedagogy of the Oppressed*.

32. Freire.

33. Freire, 72, 80.

34. Sharma, "The State and Women's Empowerment in India," 94.

35. Leve, "Failed Development and Rural Revolution in Nepal," 58; Freire, *Pedagogy of the Oppressed*.

36. Kabeer, "Making Rights Work for the Poor."

37. Evans, *Embedded Autonomy*, 12.

38. Evans, 29.

39. Polanyi, *The Great Transformation*, 48.

40. Koelble, "The New Institutionalism in Political Science and Sociology," 232, 235.

41. Evans, *Embedded Autonomy*. See also Gerschenkron, *Economic Backwardness in Historical Perspective*; Weber, *Economy and Society*; Polanyi, *The Great Transformation*; Hirschman, *The Strategy of Economic Development*.

42. Putnam, Leonardi, and Nanetti, *Making Democracy Work*, 67; Sellers, "State-Society Relations."

43. Krishna, *Active Social Capital*; Krishna, "Enhancing Political Participation in Democracies."

44. Tsai, "Solidary Groups, Informal Accountability, and Local Public Goods Provision in Rural China," 356.

45. Rashid and Alim, "A Study on BRAC's Palli Shamaj."

46. The program has since set term limits for elected leaders.

47. Sharma, "The State and Women's Empowerment in India."

48. Now, the PS program deliberately seeks to "graduate" PS groups so that they become independent. See the conclusion.

49. Registers were expected to include the following: meeting proceedings; attendance; resolutions (referring to decisions taken) and their implementation; lists of ultra-poor members, disabled persons, and service recipients; names of subcommittees, committee members, and their assignments; and records of joint funds. Community Empowerment Programme, "Grameen Shongothon Toiri o Khomotayon."

CHAPTER 4 — CLIENTS, RULES, AND TRANSACTIONS

1. Jahanara Parvez was elected to the UP in a seat reserved for women. Since 1997, the Bangladesh government has reserved three out of twelve seats in the local government for women. These women are locally referred to as *mohila* (female) members.

2. Interviews were conducted between November 2009 and March 2010. The data capture a two-year period preceding the interview. For some individuals this is from 2007 to 2009, and for others, it is from 2008 to 2010. See Appendix section on Data Collection.

3. Scott, "Patron-Client Politics and Political Change in Southeast Asia," 92.

4. Stokes, "Political Clientelism," 650.

5. Research and Evaluation Division, *The Net*, 2.

6. Research and Evaluation Division, *The Net*, 66.

7. Research and Evaluation Division, *Who Gets What and Why*, 15.

8. Bratton, "Civil Society and Political Transitions in Africa," 8.

9. Research and Evaluation Division, *Who Gets What and Why*, 31.

10. Research and Evaluation Division, *Ashram Village*.

11. Research and Evaluation Division, *Who Gets What and Why*, 165.

12. Kinship groups typically trace their origins to common ancestors. The groups consist of blood relatives are demarcated by clear lines, maintain social norms, and have their own leaders. Research and Evaluation Division, *Who Gets What and Why*, 14.

13. Research and Evaluation Division, *Who Gets What and Why*, 31.

14. J. Powell, "Peasant Society and Clientelist Politics"; Scott, "Patron-Client Politics and Political Change in Southeast Asia." Also see discussion in Mohmand, *Crafty Oligarchs, Savvy Voters*, 19–21.

15. N. Hossain and Matin, "Engaging Elite Support for the Poorest?," 381.

16. D. Lewis and Hossain, "A Tale of Three Villages" 37. Lewis and Hossain describe *samaj* as a religious community that provides structure to the village. However, the term often refers to the larger community.

17. Adnan, *Annotation of Villages Studies in Bangladesh and West Bengal*; H. Rahman, "Crisis and Insecurity"; Toufique and Turton, *Hands Not Land*.

18. Research and Evaluation Division, *Ashram Village*.

19. Research and Evaluation Division, *Who Gets What and Why*, 46–47.

20. N. Hossain and Matin, "Engaging Elite Support for the Poorest?"

21. Matin, "Targeted Development Programmes for the Extreme Poor," 15.

22. Stokes, "Political Clientelism"; Kitschelt and Wilkinson, "Citizen-Politician Linkages"; Mohmand, *Crafty Oligarchs, Savvy Voters*.

23. Stokes identifies vote-buying and patronage—the exchange of goods or resources (especially employment) respectively for votes, or the promise of votes—as subtypes of clientelism, which is a larger phenomenon embodying control over goods that can extend beyond a particular election. But the exchange is still tied to electoral support for the provider. Stokes, "Political Clientelism," 650–651.

24. Kitschelt and Wilkinson, "Citizen-Politician Linkages," 2.

25. Mohmand, *Crafty Oligarchs, Savvy Voters*, 23.

26. Bussell, *Clients and Constituents*, 9.

27. Della Porta and Vannucci, *Corrupt Exchanges*, 20.

28. Michael Johnston defines corruption as "the abuse of public roles and resources for private benefit." Public officials engaged in this practice deviate and gain personal advantage from their official roles. Johnston, "The Political Consequences of Corruption," 460.

29. Government of Bangladesh, "National Social Security Strategy (NSSS) of Bangladesh."

30. David, Matin, and Hulme, "Programs for the Poorest"; Ahmed et al., "Food Aid Distribution in Bangladesh"; Matin, "Targeted Development Programmes for the Extreme Poor."

31. Different points of contact include NGOs; acquaintances (friends, neighbors, or relatives); male UP officials or members of the rural elite, including chairmen, UP members, other government officials, or village/community chiefs; female UP members; and health and education professionals, including teachers, doctors, and nurses. I consider female UP officials as a distinct category. It became clear in the field that there was a gender differentiation when it comes to whom women prefer to approach for services. The data do not permit this differentiation for all categories of providers.

32. Generally, a higher percentage of PS members receive these services. The difference could indicate that more poor people receive services in PS areas. The difference is statistically significant. See appendix table A.3.

33. The seven types of service include government (G) and non-government (NGO) resources. They are: (1) Welfare (G): VGD, VGF, widow allowance, disability allowance, freedom fighter's allowance, food for work, and all other government safety net cards; (2) Health (G): birth control pills, immunization, latrines, and tube wells; (3) Education (G): tuition, books, and education stipends; (4) Other (G): access to *khas* land, use of water bodies, disaster relief, and winter clothes (5): Health (NGO): tube wells, latrines, and birth control; (6) Education (NGO): education stipends and books; and (7) Other (NGO): disaster recovery goods such as tin to repair roofs; in-kind assistance for livelihoods, such as animals, vans, and trees; and winter clothes.

34. Appendix table A.3.

35. See appendix for details on GLMM and measures of control variables.

36. NGO health services also demonstrate a pronounced difference. However, when we remove birth control pills, the sample size is too low to run reliable regression analysis.

37. This includes the ward level (Level 1, the level of randomization); the individual level (Level 2, which includes most of the control variables); and the level of exchange or

incident (Level 3, which is the level of analysis). See appendix for details on randomization, sampling, and other details.

CHAPTER 5 — RULE OF LAW

1. Saikia, *Women, War, and the Making of Bangladesh*, 53.

2. The government also established its own village courts (*gram adalot*) under the Village Court Act 2006. In this chapter, I am focused solely on the informal village courts that have traditionally existed in Bangladesh.

3. Golub, "Non-State Justice Systems in Bangladesh and the Philippines," 3.

4. For more on *shalish*, see Golub, "The Political Economy of Improving Traditional Justice Systems"; Berger, "Global Village Courts"; Siddiqi, "Scandals of Seduction and the Seductions of Scandal"; Islam, "Towards a Brief History of Alternate Dispute Resolution in Rural Bangladesh"; Alim and Rafi, "Shalish and Role of BRAC Federation"; Rasul and Islam, "Performance and Effectiveness of Village Court in Bangladesh"; Kolisetty, "Examining the Effectiveness of Legal Empowerment as a Pathway out of Poverty"; Alim and Ali, "NGO-Shalish and Justice-Seeking Behaviour in Rural Bangladesh."

5. S. Hossain, "Public Interest Litigation on Violence against Women in Bangladesh"; Government of Bangladesh, The Penal Code, 1860.

6. Brinks, "The Rule of (Non) Law."

7. Most cases coming to *shalish* fell into one of these four categories.

8. Rules-in-use refer to the dos and don'ts as they exist on the ground. Ostrom, "Institutional Rational Choice"; Lowndes, Pratchett, and Stoker, "Local Political Participation."

9. Rahnuma Ahmed defines dowry as "property or valuable security" which the bride's family gives or agrees to give to the groom's family "as the condition of (or consideration for) marriage." R. Ahmed, "Changing Marriage Transactions and Rise of Demand System in Bangladesh," WS 24.

10. N. Ahmed and Kashem, "Exploring the Socio-cultural Context of Dowry Practice in Bangladesh"; Naved and Persson, "Dowry and Spousal Physical Violence against Women in Bangladesh"; Naved and Persson, "Factors Associated with Spousal Physical Violence against Women in Bangladesh"; Amin and Cain, "The Rise of Dowry in Bangladesh"; Young and Hassan, "An Assessment of the Prevalence, Perceived Significance, and Response to Dowry Solicitation."

11. Shehabuddin, *Reshaping the Holy*.

12. Shehabuddin.

13. World Bank, "Bangladesh Can Prosper with More and Better Jobs for Women, Report Says."

14. Bradley and Pallikadavath, "Dowry and Women's Lives in Kerala"; Bradley, "Dowry, Activism and Globalisation."

15. R. Ahmed, "Changing Marriage Transactions and Rise of Demand System in Bangladesh."

16. Shehabuddin, *Reshaping the Holy*.

17. Rozario, "Dowry in Rural Bangladesh"; Qayum, Samadder, and Rahman, "Group Norms and the BRAC Village Organization"; White, "Patriarchal Investments."

18. F. Chowdhury, "Dowry, Women, and Law in Bangladesh."

19. Shehabuddin, *Reshaping the Holy*; R. Ahmed, "Changing Marriage Transactions and Rise of Demand System in Bangladesh."

20. International doctrines protect children from child marriage. The Convention on the Consent to Marriage, Minimum Age for Marriage and Registration of Marriages, entered into force in 1964, stipulates that no marriage can be entered into without "free and full" consent, which, according to the Universal Declaration of Human Rights, renders such consent invalid when one of the parties is not old enough to make an informed decision. The United Nations General Assembly has passed multiple resolutions to end child, early, and forced marriage. United Nations Children's Fund, "Child Marriage"; United Nations General Assembly, *Convention on Consent to Marriage, Minimum Age for Marriage and Registration of Marriages*; United Nations General Assembly, *Child, Early and Forced Marriage*.

21. Shehabuddin, *Reshaping the Holy*. In 2017, the Child Marriage Restraint Bill was passed, allowing parents to get special permission to allow their children's marriage if this is in their "best interest." Arora and Westcott, "Human Rights Groups Condemn New Bangladesh Child Marriage Law."

22. Kamal et al., "Child Marriage in Bangladesh."

23. Nguyen and Wodon, "Global and Regional Trends in Child Marriage."

24. Kamal, "Decline in Child Marriage and Changes in Its Effect on Reproductive Outcomes in Bangladesh."

25. United Nations Children's Fund, "Plan of Action Launched to Eliminate Child Marriage in Bangladesh."

26. United Nations Children's Fund, "Ending Child Marriage."

27. Kamal, "Decline in Child Marriage and Changes in Its Effect on Reproductive Outcomes in Bangladesh"; Mahmud and Amin, "Girls' Schooling and Marriage in Rural Bangladesh."

28. Amin, Ahmed, et al., "Delaying Child Marriage through Community-Based Skills-Development Programs for Girls."

29. Amin, Asadullah, et al., "Can Conditional Transfers Eradicate Child Marriage?"

30. Chappell and Mackay, "What's in a Name?," 28.

31. I would like to thank Ayesha Ray, Nadine Murshid, Chaumtoli Huq, and Asif Dowla for the Twitter conversation around this conceptualization.

32. White, "Patriarchal Investments."

33. The terms *chele* and *meye* translate to "boy" and "girl," respectively, but they can also refer to groom and bride, respectively, in the context of marriage.

34. F. Chowdhury, "The Socio-cultural Context of Child Marriage in a Bangladeshi Village."

35. Dalmia and Lawrence, "The Institution of Dowry in India."

36. White, "Patriarchal Investments."

37. Aziz and Maloney, "Life Stages Gender and Fertility in Bangladesh."

38. F. Chowdhury, "The Socio-cultural Context of Child Marriage in a Bangladeshi Village."

39. United Nations Children's Fund, "Baseline Survey Report on Rural Adolescents in Bangladesh"; Blanchet, *Lost Innocence, Stolen Childhoods*.

40. Huda, "Dowry in Bangladesh," 255.

41. I draw on the definition of violence as adopted in the 1993 Declaration on the Elimination of Violence against Women as "any act of gender-based violence that results in, or is likely to result in, physical, sexual or psychological harm or suffering to women,

including threats of such acts, coercion or arbitrary deprivation of liberty, whether occurring in public or in private life." Incidents tracked include domestic violence, harassment,
and sexual assault of women and girls, and are by no means comprehensive. I am particularly wary of the difficulties in measuring psychological harm, which the data do not capture outside of physical violence. I also recognize that dowry and child marriage constitute
forms of violence. Sustainable Development Goals Fund, "Case Study"; United Nations
General Assembly, Declaration on the Elimination of Violence against Women.

42. These laws include The Cruelty to Women (Deterrent Punishment) Ordinance of
1983, its 1988 amendment, the Women and Children (Special Provision) Act of 1995, and
the Women and Children Repression Prevention Bill of 2000. Shehabuddin, *Reshaping
the Holy*, 100.

43. Sustainable Development Goals Fund, "Case Study."

44. Naved et al., "Physical Violence by Husbands." The study was part of the World
Health Organization multicountry study on domestic violence against women.

45. Naved et al.

46. Shehabuddin, *Reshaping the Holy*.

47. BBC, "Bangladesh Says Prostitution Legal."

48. Adnan, "Land Grabs and Primitive Accumulation in Deltaic Bangladesh"; Feldman and Geisler, "Land Expropriation and Displacement in Bangladesh"; Chakma,
"The Post-Colonial State and Minorities."

49. Shehabuddin, *Reshaping the Holy*, 88.

50. The Muslim Marriage Dissolution act includes nine stipulations for a woman initi-
ating divorce; for example, if the woman's husband has been missing for over four years, if
he has not supported her for over two years, and if he has taken another wife illegally. A
woman may also initiate divorce if her husband gives her the right in their marriage
registration form, or by giving up her *denmohor*. Shehabuddin, 88.

51. Respondents were asked if human rights violations occurred in their families and
communities, and about the responses to and outcomes for those incidents. These are
cases that may or may not have gone to *shalish*. Respondents were also asked about *shalish* in their area, but the analysis of incident outcomes (whether they adhere to formal
or informal institutions) does not include these data. This is because *shalish* outcomes
cannot be clearly identified as adhering to formal or informal rules. Respondents do not
always report enough detail for such classification, and the wide variety of resolutions, formal, informal, and overlapping, makes it impossible to classify outcomes.
Thus, for this particular analysis, I limit my analysis to human rights violations taking
place in the family, which leaves the analysis with a very small N. Finally, respondents
were also asked about human rights violations in the community, which has a much
larger N. But these data could not be included when looking at whether incidents were
resolved. This is because respondents in the same locality often mentioned the same incident. While these data capture respondents' reactions to incidents, they do not illustrate whether incidents were resolved, and consequently, whether formal or informal
rules were followed, due to overlapping data points. I use these community-level incidents later in the chapter, holding them as a baseline for measuring individual action.
Finally, the data encapsulate reported incidents. Because many incidents go unreported,
one will never know the number of incidents that actually occurred. This remains the
case across datasets on human rights violations.

52. Nawaz, "An Analysis of the Role of Community Empowerment Program (CEP) in Combatting Domestic Violence against Women."

53. Nawaz.

CHAPTER 6 — CHANGING DISTRIBUTIVE POLITICS

1. PESP was implemented in 2002. Earlier iterations of this program included the Food for Education (FFE) and Primary Education Stipend (PES) programs. The two were later combined into PESP. Government of Bangladesh, United Nations Children's Fund, and Power and Participation Research Center, "Bangladesh Primary Education Stipends," 1.

2. Government of Bangladesh, United Nations Children's Fund, and Power and Participation Research Center, 3.

3. Coleman, "Social Capital in the Creation of Human Capital," S104.

4. Coleman, S104.

5. Granovetter, "The Strength of Weak Ties" (1983); Granovetter, "The Strength of Weak Ties" (1973).

6. Collier, "Social Capital and Poverty."

7. Katungi, Edmeades, and Smale, "Gender, Social Capital and Information Exchange in Rural Uganda."

8. Evans, *Embedded Autonomy*, 12. While Evans identifies society primarily as industrial capital, he extends it to encompass labor in an analysis of the Indian state of Kerala. In Kerala, peasant movements and associations led by members of the Congress Party eventually morphed into the Communist Party, which maintains connections with actors mobilizing on the ground. At the same time, the state remains independent due to its financial reliance on the national government.

9. Evans, 235–236.

10. Singerman, *Avenues of Participation*, 10, 133.

11. Bayat, *Life as Politics*.

12. Community Empowerment Programme, "Operational Guidebook for Management of Polli Shomaj."

13. Helmke and Levitsky, introduction to *Informal Institutions and Democracy*," 26.

14. Brinks, "The Rule of (Non) Law."

15. March and Olsen, "The Logic of Appropriateness," 479.

16. Helmke and Levitsky, introduction to *Informal Institutions and Democracy*, 24-25.

17. Community Empowerment Programme, "Operational Guidebook for Management of Polli Shomaj."

18. Community Empowerment Programme.

19. Conning and Kevane, "Community-Based Targeting Mechanisms for Social Safety Nets."

20. Zaman et al., "Stories of Targeting."

21. McAdam and Scott, "Organizations and Movements," 15; Chappell, "Comparing Political Institutions," 225.

22. For example, BRAC's Challenging the Frontiers of Poverty Reduction—Targeting the Ultra Poor (CFPR-TUP) program provides the poorest 15 percent of the population with productive physical assets such as poultry and livestock, to help them build a long-lasting asset base.

23. Kitschelt and Wilkinson, "Citizen-Politician Linkages," 2.

24. Tsai, *Accountability without Democracy*, 88–89.

25. Tsai, 89–90.

26. N. Hossain and Matin, "Engaging Elite Support for the Poorest?"

27. In the remainder of this section, I shift levels of analysis to the individual level. I draw on individual interviews of both PS members and the control group to illustrate rural Bangladeshis' preference for leaders who are, in Tsai's words, morally good.

28. Answers are captured as multiple responses. Other answers include voting to exercise one's right as a citizen (30.9 percent), everyone in the household votes (7.1 percent), everyone in the village votes (6.8 percent), and liked the candidate (5.4 percent).

29. Pierce, *Moral Economies of Corruption*, 5–6.

30. Pierce, 5–6.

31. Lowndes, "Institutionalism," 62–63.

32. March and Olsen, *Rediscovering Institutions*; Streeck and Thelen, "Institutional Change in Advanced Political Economies"; Mahoney and Thelen, "A Theory of Gradual Institutional Change"; Lowndes, "Institutionalism."

33. N. Hossain and Matin, "Engaging Elite Support for the Poorest?"

CHAPTER 7 — NEGOTIATING JUSTICE

1. Taslim, "Governance, Policies and Economic Growth in Bangladesh."

2. O'Donnell, "The Quality of Democracy," 33.

3. I adapt O'Donnell's criteria to the Bangladesh context for this list. O'Donnell, 33.

4. Siddiqi, "Paving the Way to Justice," 4.

5. Alim and Ali, "NGO-Shalish and Justice-Seeking Behaviour in Rural Bangladesh," 2.

6. Shehabuddin, *Reshaping the Holy*.

7. Siddiqi, "Paving the Way to Justice," 10.

8. Siddiqi, "Scandals of Seduction and the Seductions of Scandal," 513.

9. O'Donnell, "The Quality of Democracy," 41.

10. O'Donnell, 41.

11. Pereira, *The Fractured Scales*, 1.

12. Pereira, 1.

13. Shehabuddin, *Reshaping the Holy*, 107.

14. Shehabuddin.

15. Berger, "Global Village Courts," 2.

16. Siddiqi, "Scandals of Seduction and the Seductions of Scandal," 513.

17. Siddiqi, "Paving the Way to Justice."

18. Van Cott, "Dispensing Justice at the Margins of Formality," 250.

19. Siddiqi, "Paving the Way to Justice," 8.

20. Golub, "Non-State Justice Systems in Bangladesh and the Philippines"; Siddiqi, "Paving the Way to Justice"; Alim and Ali, "NGO-Shalish and Justice-Seeking Behaviour in Rural Bangladesh."

21. Alim and Ali.

22. Alim and Ali, 8.

23. Siddiqi, "Paving the Way to Justice."

24. World Bank, "Whispers to Voices," 12.

25. Siddiqi, "Paving the Way to Justice," 11.

26. Sanctions indicate the presence of an informal institution. Brinks, "The Rule of (Non) Law."

27. Shehabuddin, *Reshaping the Holy.*

28. Rozario, "Dowry in Rural Bangladesh"; White, "Patriarchal Investments"; Qayum, Samadder, and Rahman, "Group Norms and the BRAC Village Organization."

29. R. Ahmed, "Changing Marriage Transactions and Rise of Demand System in Bangladesh."

30. A. Ahmed and Sharmeen, "Assessing the Performance of Conditional Cash Transfer Programs for Girls and Boys."

31. Karim, *Microfinance and Its Discontents.*

32. Asadullah and Chaudhury, "Reverse Gender Gap in Schooling in Bangladesh"; A.M.R. Chowdhury, Nath, and Choudhury, "Enrolment at Primary Level"; A.M.R. Chowdhury, Nath, and Choudhury, "Equity Gains in Bangladesh Primary Education."

33. Mahmud and Amin, "Girls' Schooling and Marriage in Rural Bangladesh."

34. Asadullah, "Returns to Education in Bangladesh."

35. Mahmud and Amin, "Girls' Schooling and Marriage in Rural Bangladesh," 4.

36. Mahmud and Amin, "Girls' Schooling and Marriage in Rural Bangladesh."

37. Parts of this section are from Qayum, "Women, NGOs, and the Bangladesh Miracle."

38. F. Chowdhury, "Dowry, Women, and Law in Bangladesh."

39. Mackay, Kenny, and Chappell, "New Institutionalism through a Gender Lens."

40. As with all such incidents, we only know of *shalish* events as reported by PS; this may not include all *shalish* held in their areas. Since the number of *shalish* held does not exist on record, we have no way of knowing this number.

41. Siddiqi, "Paving the Way to Justice," 5.

CHAPTER 8 — GOVERNING LOCALLY

1. Although we do not know how many members the group had in 2003, the women recalled that it grew from twenty-two members during its inception to eighty-five members when they were interviewed.

2. I build on Mark Bevir's conceptualization of governance, which refers to "all processes of governing, whether undertaken by a government, market, or network, whether over a family, tribe, formal or informal organization, or territory, and whether through laws, norms, power or language. Governance differs from government in that it focuses less on the state and its institutions and more on social practices and activities." Bevir, *Governance*, 4.

3. In the Calcutta municipal elections of 1923 women first received the right to vote. The Government of India Act of 1935 gave special provisions to women that were first implemented in the 1946 elections. Voting rights were limited to women who were urban-based, owned a certain amount of property, paid taxes, were above twenty-one, and were literate. Universal adult franchise was implemented in 1956. F. Chowdhury, "Women and Election."

4. Centre for the Study of Developing Societies, *The State of Democracy in South Asia*, 265.

5. Numbers average PS members and the control group, since the two groups do not differ much.

6. Rounaq Jahan, "Women in South Asian Politics," 857.

7. Omvedt, "Women in Governance in South Asia"; Rounaq Jahan, "Women in South Asian Politics."

8. Omvedt, "Women in Governance in South Asia," 4746.

9. Rounaq Jahan, "Women in South Asian Politics," 848.

10. Rounaq Jahan, 848.

11. Panday, "Representation without Participation," 491.

12. Panday, 491–492.

13. Panday, 491–492.

14. Panday, 491–492.

15. Khan and Ara, "Women, Participation and Empowerment in Local Government." These are imperfect figures—they are numbers, not percentages. But they are the best available data.

16. Chappell and Mackay, "What's in a Name?," 29.

17. Chappell and Mackay, 30.

18. Thornton and Ocasio, *Institutional Logics*, 101.

19. F. Chowdhury, "Problems of Women's Participation in Bangladesh Politics."

20. N. Chowdhury, "Bangladesh," 98.

21. Shehabuddin, *Reshaping the Holy*, 163.

22. Shehabuddin, 163.

23. Panday, "Representation without Participation."

24. Panday.

25. Shehabuddin, *Reshaping the Holy*, 164–165.

26. Nazneen and Tasneem, "A Silver Lining," 37.

27. Nazneen and Tasneem, 37.

28. Panday, "Representation without Participation."

29. Omvedt, "Women in Governance in South Asia," 4747.

30. Amin, "Family Structure and Change in Rural Bangladesh"; Kabir, Szebehely, and Tishelman, "Support in Old Age in the Changing Society of Bangladesh."

31. Government of Bangladesh, Bangladesh Parents' Maintenance Act 2013.

32. Fisher et al., "Knowledge, Attitudes, Practices and Implications of Safe Water Management."

CONCLUSION

1. Qayum, "Bangladesh."

2. Riaz, "Bangladesh's Failed Election."

3. Office of the High Commissioner for Human Rights, "UN Expert Group Urges Bangladesh to Stop Enforced Disappearances"; Human Rights Watch, "Bangladesh: End Crackdown on Opposition Supporters."

4. D. Lewis and Hossain, "Local Political Consolidation in Bangladesh," 5.

5. D. Lewis and Hossain, 5.

6. United Nations Development Programme, "Briefing Note for Countries on the 2019 Human Development Report: Bangladesh."

7. United Nations Development Programme.

8. Bari, "Overseas Migration of Female Workers on the Rise despite Reports of Abuse."

9. Qayum, "Taking Sides."

10. Community Empowerment Programme, *CEP at a Glance as of September 2019*.

11. Community Empowerment Programme, "Community Empowerment."

12. Lowndes, "Institutionalism," 69.

13. Lowndes, 69.

14. Lowndes, 64.

APPENDIX

1. De La O and Wantchekon, "Experimental Research on Democracy and Development," 387.

2. Each ward is composed of a number of villages.

Bibliography

Abu-Lughod, Lila. *Do Muslim Women Need Saving?* Cambridge, MA: Harvard University Press, 2013.

Ackerly, Brooke A. "Testing the Tools of Development: Credit Programmes, Loan Involvement, and Women's Empowerment." *IDS Bulletin* 26, no. 3. Brighton, UK: Institute of Development Studies, University of Sussex, 1995.

Adnan, Shapan. *Annotation of Village Studies in Bangladesh and West Bengal: A Review of Socio-economic Trends over 1942–1988.* Comilla, Bangladesh: Bangladesh Academy for Rural Development, 1990.

———. "Land Grabs and Primitive Accumulation in Deltaic Bangladesh: Interactions between Neoliberal Globalization, State Interventions, Power Relations and Peasant Resistance." *Journal of Peasant Studies* 40, no. 1 (January 2013): 87–128.

Ahmad, Reaz. "Hunger Halved Well before MDG Time." *Daily Star* (Dhaka). June 14, 2013. https://www.thedailystar.net/news/hunger-halved-well-before-mdg-time.

Ahmed, Akhter U., Shahidur Rashid, Manohar Sharma, and Sajjad Zohir. "Food Aid Distribution in Bangladesh: Leakage and Operational Performance." FCND Discussion Paper No. 173. Washington, DC: Food Consumption and Nutrition Division, International Food Policy Research Institute, 2004.

Ahmed, Akhter U., and Taniya Sharmeen. "Assessing the Performance of Conditional Cash Transfer Programs for Girls and Boys in Primary and Secondary Schools in Bangladesh." Washington, DC: International Food Policy Research Institute, 2004.

Ahmed, Neaz, and Abul Kashem. "Exploring the Socio-cultural Context of Dowry Practice in Bangladesh." *Sociology and Anthropology* 3, no. 3 (2015): 171–178.

Ahmed, Rahnuma. "Changing Marriage Transactions and Rise of Demand System in Bangladesh." *Economic and Political Weekly* 22, no. 171 (1987): WS22–WS26.

Alamgir, Mohiuddin. *Famine in South Asia: Political Economy of Mass Starvation.* Cambridge, MA: Oelgeschlager, Gunn and Hain, 1980.

Aldrich, John H. "Rational Choice and Turnout." *American Journal of Political Science* 37, no. 1 (1993): 246–278.

Ali, S. Mahmud. *Understanding Bangladesh.* New York: Columbia University Press, 2010.

Ali, Tariq Omar. "Technologies of Peasant Production and Reproduction: The Post-Colonial State and Cold War Empire in Comilla, East Pakistan, 1960–70." *South Asia: Journal of South Asia Studies* 42, no. 3 (May 4, 2019): 435–451.

Alim, Md. Abdul, and Tariq Omar Ali. "NGO-Shalish and Justice-Seeking Behaviour in Rural Bangladesh." BRAC Research Report. Dhaka: Research and Evaluation Division, BRAC, 2007.

Alim, Md. Abdul, and Mohammad Rafi. "Shalish and Role of BRAC Federation." Social Studies Research Report, vol. 30. Dhaka: Research and Evaluation Division, BRAC, 2003.

Amin, Sajeda. "Family Structure and Change in Rural Bangladesh." *Population Studies* 52, no. 2 (July 1, 1998): 201–213.

Amin, Sajeda, Johana Ahmed, Jyotirmoy Saha, Md. Irfan Hossain, and Eashita Farzana Haque. "Delaying Child Marriage through Community-Based Skills-Development Programs for Girls: Results from a Randomized Controlled Study in Rural Bangladesh." New York: Population Council, 2016. https://knowledgecommons.popcouncil.org/departments_sbsr-pgy/557/.

Amin, Sajeda, Niaz Asadullah, Sara Hossain, and Zaki Wahhaj. "Can Conditional Transfers Eradicate Child Marriage?" IZA Policy Paper 118. Bonn: IZA Institute of Labor Economics, 2016.

Amin, Sajeda, and Mead Cain. "The Rise of Dowry in Bangladesh." In *The Continuing Demographic Transition*, edited by G. W. Jones. Oxford: Clarendon Press, 1998.

Arora, Medhavi, and Ben Westcott. "Human Rights Groups Condemn New Bangladesh Child Marriage Law." CNN, March 3, 2017. https://www.cnn.com/2017/03/02/asia/bangladesh-child-marriage-law/index.html.

Asadullah, Mohammad Niaz. "Returns to Education in Bangladesh." *Education Economics* 14, no. 4 (December 2006): 453–468.

Asadullah, Mohammad Niaz, and Nazmul Chaudhury. "Reverse Gender Gap in Schooling in Bangladesh: Insights from Urban and Rural Households." *Journal of Development Studies* 45, no. 8 (September 2009): 1360–1380.

Asadullah, Mohammad Niaz, Antonio Savoia, and Wahiduddin Mahmud. "Paths to Development: Is There a Bangladesh Surprise?" *World Development* 62 (2014): 138–154.

Auyero, Javier. *Poor People's Politics: Peronist Survival Networks and the Legacy of Evita.* Durham, NC: Duke University Press, 2001.

Azim, Firdous, Nivedita Menon, and Dina M. Siddiqi. "Negotiating New Terrains: South Asian Feminisms." *Feminist Review* 91, no. 1 (February 6, 2009): 1–8.

Aziz, K., M. Ashraful, and Clarence Maloney. "Life Stages, Gender and Fertility in Bangladesh." Working Paper 3. Dhaka: International Centre for Diarrhoeal Disease Research, 1985. http://dspace.icddrb.org/jspui/bitstream/123456789/2564/1/Life%20stages%20gender%20and%20fertility%20in%20bangladesh%2C%20Monograph%20No%203.pdf.

Baneria, Lourdes, and Shelley Feldman. *Unequal Burden: Economic Crises, Persistent Poverty, and Women's Work.* Boulder, CO: Westview Press, 1992.

"Bangladesh Police and Garment Workers Clash over Wage Rise." Al Jazeera, January 13, 2009. https://www.aljazeera.com/news/2019/01/bangladesh-police-garment-workers-clash-wage-hike-190113150811791.html.

Bari, Labiba Faiaz. "Overseas Migration of Female Workers on the Rise despite Reports of Abuse." *Dhaka Tribune* (Dhaka). March 28, 2018. https://www.dhakatribune.com

/bangladesh/2018/03/28/overseas-migration-female-workers-rise-despite-reports
-abuse/.

Bayat, Asef. *Life as Politics: How Ordinary People Change the Middle East.* Stanford, CA: Stanford University Press, 2009.

BBC. "Bangladesh Says Prostitution Legal." BBC, March 14, 2000. http://news.bbc.co .uk/2/hi/south_asia/677280.stm.

Begum, Maleka, and Shed Azizul Huq. *Ami Nari: Tinsho Bocchorer (18–20 Shatak) Bangali Narir Itihash [I Am Woman: 300 Years (18th to 20th c.) of Bengali Women's History].* Dhaka: University Press, 2001.

Berger, Tobias. "Global Village Courts: International Organizations and the Bureaucratization of Rural Justice Systems in the Global South." In *Palaces of Hope—The Anthropology of Global Organizations,* edited by Ronald Niezen and Maria Sapignolli, 198–218. New York: Cambridge University Press, 2017.

Bevir, Mark. *Governance: A Very Short Introduction.* Oxford: Oxford University Press, 2012.

Blair, Harry. "Participation, Public Policy, Political Economy and Development in Rural Bangladesh, 1958–85." *World Development* 13, no. 12 (1985): 1231–1247.

Blanchet, Therese. *Lost Innocence, Stolen Childhoods.* Dhaka: University Press, 1996.

BRAC. *2018 Annual Report.* Dhaka: BRAC, 2019. http://www.brac.net/publications /annual-report/2018/.

"BRAC in Business." *Economist.* February 18, 2010. https://www.economist.com/node /15546464.

"BRAC Ranked Top Global NGO for 3rd Consecutive Year." *Daily Star* (Dhaka). March 26, 2018. https://www.thedailystar.net/country/brac-ranked-top-global-non -government-organisation-ngo-3rd-year-in-row-2018-bangladesh-bd-1553701.

BRAC Research and Evaluation Division. *See* Research and Evaluation Division

Bradley, Tamsin. "Dowry, Activism and Globalisation." In *Interrogating Harmful Cultural Practices: Gender, Culture and Coercion,* edited by Tamsin Bradley and Chia Longman. New York: Routledge, 2015.

Bradley, Tamsin, and Saseendran Pallikadavath. "Dowry and Women's Lives in Kerala: What Has Changed in a Decade?" *Contemporary South Asia* 21, no. 4 (December 2013): 444–461.

Bratton, Michael. "Civil Society and Political Transition in Africa." IDR Reports, 11, No. 6. Boston: Institute for Development Research, 1994.

Brinks, Daniel M. "Informal Institutions and the Rule of Law: The Judicial Response to State Killings in Buenos Aires and São Paulo in the 1990s." *Comparative Politics* 36, no. 1 (2003): 1–9.

———. "The Rule of (Non) Law: Prosecuting Police Killings in Brazil and Argentina." In *Informal Institutions and Democracy: Lessons from Latin America,* edited by Gretchen Helmke and Steven Levitsky. Baltimore: Johns Hopkins University Press, 2006.

Bussell, Jennifer. *Clients and Constituents: Political Responsiveness in Patronage Democracies.* New York: Oxford University Press, 2019.

Campbell, John L., and Ove K. Pedersen. Introduction to *The Rise of Neoliberalism and Institutional Analysis,* edited by John L. Campbell and Ove K. Pedersen. Princeton, NJ: Princeton University Press, 2001.

Centre for the Study of Developing Societies. *The State of Democracy in South Asia.* New Delhi: Oxford University Press, 2008.

Chakma, Bhumitra. "The Post-Colonial State and Minorities: Ethnocide in the Chittagong Hill Tracts, Bangladesh." *Commonwealth and Comparative Politics* 48, no. 3 (July 2010): 281–300.

Chappell, Louise. "Comparing Political Institutions: Revealing the Gendered 'Logic of Appropriateness.'" *Politics and Gender* 2, no. 2 (2006): 223–235.

Chappell, Louise, and Fiona Mackay. "What's in a Name? Mapping the Terrain of Informal Institutions and Gender Politics." In *Gender and Informal Institutions*, edited by Georgina Waylen. London: Rowman and Littlefield, 2017.

Chowdhury, A. Mushtaque R., Samir R. Nath, and Rasheda K. Choudhury. "Enrolment at Primary Level: Gender Difference Disappears in Bangladesh." *International Journal of Educational Development* 22, no. 2 (2002): 191–203.

———. "Equity Gains in Bangladesh Primary Education." *International Review of Education* 49, no. 6 (November 2003): 601–619.

Chowdhury, Elora Halim. "'Transnationalism Reversed': Engaging Religion, Development and Women's Organizing in Bangladesh." *Women's Studies International Forum* 32, no. 6 (2009): 414–423.

———. *Transnationalism Reversed: Women Organizing against Gendered Violence in Bangladesh.* Albany: State University of New York Press, 2011.

Chowdhury, Farah Deeba. "Dowry, Women, and Law in Bangladesh." *International Journal of Law, Policy, and the Family* 24, no. 2 (2010): 198–221.

———. "Problems of Women's Participation in Bangladesh Politics." *Round Table* 98, no. 404 (October 2009): 555–567.

———. "The Socio-cultural Context of Child Marriage in a Bangladeshi Village." *International Journal of Social Welfare* 13, no. 3 (July 2004): 244–253.

———. "Women and Election: Issues in Bangladesh." *Pakistan Journal of History and Culture* 20, no. 1 (1999): 93–107.

Chowdhury, Najma. "Bangladesh: Gender Issues and Politics in a Patriarchy." In *Women and Politics Worldwide*, edited by Barbara J. Nelson and Najma Chowdhury. New Haven, CT: Yale University Press, 1994.

Coleman, James S. "Social Capital in the Creation of Human Capital." *American Journal of Sociology* 94, no. 1 (1988): S95–120.

Collier, Paul. "Social Capital and Poverty." Social Capital Initiative Working Paper No. 4. Washington, DC: Social Development Department, World Bank, 1998.

Community Empowerment Programme. "Background Information on Polli Shomaj." Dhaka: Community Empowerment Programme, BRAC, n.d.

———. "CEP at a Glance as of September 2019." Dhaka: BRAC Community Empowerment Programme, BRAC, 2019.

———. "Community Empowerment." https://www.brac.net/program/community-empowerment/. Accessed May 15, 2021.

———. "Community Institution Building: Polli Shomaj and Union Shomaj." Dhaka: Community Empowerment Programme, BRAC, n.d.

———. "Grameen Shongothon Toiri o Khomotayon, Polli Shomaj & Union Shomaj, Kormoshuchi Bastobayon Nirdeshika." Dhaka: Community Empowerment Programme, BRAC, n.d.

———. "Operational Guidebook for Management of Polli Shomaj—A Community-Based Organization Initiated and Supported by BRAC." Dhaka: Community Empowerment

Programme, BRAC, 2015. http://www.brac.net/sites/default/files/portals/Polli Shomaj operational guidebook.pdf.

Conning, Jonathan, and Michael Kevane. "Community-Based Targeting Mechanisms for Social Safety Nets: A Critical Review." *World Development* 30, no. 3 (2002): 375–394.

Crook, Richard C., and James Manor. *Democracy and Decentralisation in South Asia and West Africa: Participation, Accountability, and Performance.* Cambridge: Cambridge University Press, 1998.

Dalmia, Sonia, and Pareena G. Lawrence. "The Institution of Dowry in India: Why It Continues to Prevail." *Journal of Developing Areas* 38, no. 2 (2005): 71–93.

David, M., Imran Matin, and David Hulme. "Programs for the Poorest: Learning from the IGVGD Program in Bangladesh." *World Development* 31, no. 3 (2003): 647–664.

D'Costa, Bina. "Faith, NGOs and the Politics of Development in Bangladesh." In *Civil Society, Religion and Global Governance: Paradigms of Power and Persuasion*, edited by Helen James, 219–237. London: Routledge, 2007.

D'Costa, Bina, and Sara Hossain. "Redress for Sexual Violence before the International Crimes Tribunal in Bangladesh: Lessons from History, and Hopes for the Future." *Criminal Law Forum* 21, no. 2 (July 14, 2010): 331–359.

De La O, Ana L., and Leonard Wantchekon. "Experimental Research on Democracy and Development." In *Cambridge Handbook of Experimental Political Science*, edited by James N. Druckman, Donald P. Green, James H. Kuklinski, and Arthur Lupia. New York: Cambridge University Press, 2011.

Della Porta, Donatella, and Alberto Vannucci. *Corrupt Exchanges: Actors, Resources, and Mechanisms of Political Corruption.* Abingdon, UK: Routledge, 2017.

Deshwara, Mintu. "Many Denied VGF Cards, Nepotism Alleged." *Daily Star* (Dhaka). May 21, 2017. http://www.thedailystar.net/country/many-denied-vgf-cards-nepotism -alleged-1408450.

Dowlah, Caf. "The Politics and Economics of Food and Famine in Bangladesh in the Early 1970s—With Special Reference to Amartya Sen's Interpretation of the 1974 Famine." *International Journal of Social Welfare* 15, no. 4 (October 2006): 344–356.

Escobar, Arturo. *Encountering Development: The Making and Unmaking of the Third World.* Princeton, NJ: Princeton University Press, 1995.

Evans, Peter B. "Collective Capabilities, Culture, and Amartya Sen's Development as Freedom." *Studies in Comparative International Development* 37, no. 2 (June 2002): 54–60.

———. *Embedded Autonomy: States and Industrial Transformation.* Princeton, NJ: Princeton University Press, 2012.

Evans, Peter B., and William H. Sewell Jr. "Neoliberalism: Policy Regimes, International Regimes, and Social Effects." In *Social Resilience in the Neoliberal Era*, edited by Peter A. Hall and Michele Lamont. New York: Cambridge University Press, 2013.

Fattah, Kazi Nazrul, and Zarina Nahar Kabir. "No Place Is Safe: Sexual Abuse of Children in Rural Bangladesh." *Journal of Child Sexual Abuse* 22, no. 8 (November 1, 2013): 901–914.

Feldman, Shelley. "NGOs and Civil Society: (Un)Stated Contradictions." *Annals of the American Academy of Political and Social Science* 554, no. 1 (November 21, 1997): 46–65.

Feldman, Shelley, and Charles Geisler. "Land Expropriation and Displacement in Bangladesh." *Journal of Peasant Studies* 39, no. 3–4 (July 2012): 971–993.

Ferguson, James. *The Anti-Politics Machine: "Development," Depoliticization, and Bureaucratic Power in Lesotho.* Minneapolis: University of Minnesota Press, 1994.

Fernando, Jude L. "Nongovernmental Organizations, Micro-Credit, and Empowerment of Women." *Annals of the American Academy of Political and Social Science* 554, no. 1 (November 21, 1997): 150–177.

Fernando, Nimal, and Richard Meyer. "ASA—the Ford Motor Model of Microfinance." *ADB Finance for the Poor* 3, issue 2. Manila: Asian Development Bank, 2002.

Fisher, Stephanie, Babar Kabir, Edward Lahiff, and Malcolm MacLachlan. "Knowledge, Attitudes, Practices and Implications of Safe Water Management and Good Hygiene in Rural Bangladesh: Assessing the Impact and Scope of the BRAC WASH Programme." *Journal of Water and Health* 9, no. 1 (2011): 80–93.

Franda, Marcus. *Bangladesh, the First Decade.* New Delhi: South Asian Publishers; Hanover, NH: Universities Field Staff International, 1982.

Freire, Paulo. *Pedagogy of the Oppressed.* New York: Continuum, 1970.

Fruttero, Anna, and Varun Gauri. "The Strategic Choices of NGOS: Location Decisions in Rural Bangladesh." *Journal of Development Studies* 41, no. 5 (July 2005): 759–787.

Gerring, John, and Jason Seawright. "Case Selection Techniques in Case Study Research: A Menu of Qualitative and Quantitative Options." *Political Research Quarterly* 61, no. 2 (2008): 294–308.

Gerschenkron, Alexander. *Economic Backwardness in Historical Perspective: A Book of Essays.* Cambridge, MA: Belknap Press of Harvard University Press, 1962.

Goetz, Anne Marie, and Rina Sengupta. "Who Takes the Credit? Gender, Power and Control over Loan Use in Rural Credit Programs in Bangladesh." *World Development* 24, no. 1 (1996): 45–63.

Golub, Stephen. "Non-State Justice Systems in Bangladesh and the Philippines." Paper prepared for the United Kingdom Department for International Development, 2013.

———. "The Political Economy of Improving Traditional Justice Systems: A Case Study of NGO Engagement with Shalish in Bangladesh." *World Bank Legal Review*, December 11, 2012, 67–88.

Goodin, Robert E. "Institutions and Their Design." In *The Theory of Institutional Design.* New York: Cambridge University Press, 1996.

Government of Bangladesh. The Constitution of the People's Republic of Bangladesh (1972). http://bdlaws.minlaw.gov.bd/act-367.html.

———. "The Fifth Five Year Plan." Dhaka: Planning Commission, Ministry of Planning, Government of the Republic of Bangladesh, 1997.

———. "The Fourth Five-Year Plan, 1990–1995." Dhaka: Planning Commission, Ministry of Planning, Government of the Republic of Bangladesh, 1995.

———. "Local Government Structure." Dhaka: Local Government Division (LGD), Ministry of LGRD and Co-operatives, Government of the People's Republic of Bangladesh, n.d.

———. "National Social Security Strategy (NSSS) of Bangladesh." Dhaka: General Economics Division (GED), Planning Commission, Government of the People's Republic of Bangladesh, 2015.

———. The Parents' Maintenance Act 2013 (*Pita-Matar Bhoron Poshon Ain* 2013). http://bdlaws.minlaw.gov.bd/act-1132.html.

———. The Penal Code, 1860. Act No. XLV. Chapter XVI. Of Offenses Affecting the Human Body. Accessed August 1, 2020. http://bdlaws.minlaw.gov.bd/act-11/section-3232.html.

———. "Unlocking the Potential: National Strategy for Accelerated Poverty Reduction." Dhaka: General Economic Division, Planning Commission, Government of the People's Republic of Bangladesh, 2005.

Government of Bangladesh, United Nations Children's Fund, and Power and Participation Research Center. "Bangladesh Primary Education Stipends: A Qualitative Assessment." Dhaka: Directorate of Primary Education, Government of the People's Republic of Bangladesh, UNICEF, and PPRC, 2013.

Grameen Bank. "Founder." Grameen Bank: Bank for the Poor. Accessed January 1, 2018. http://www.grameen.com/founder-2/.

Granovetter, Mark. "The Strength of Weak Ties." *American Journal of Sociology* 78, no. 6 (1973): 1360–1389.

———. "The Strength of Weak Ties: A Network Theory Revisited." *Sociological Theory* 1 (1983): 201–233.

Hall, Peter A. *Governing the Economy: The Politics of State Intervention in Britain and France*. New York: Oxford University Press, 1986.

Hashemi, Syed M., Sidney Ruth Schuler, and Ann P. Riley. "Rural Credit Programs and Women's Empowerment in Bangladesh." *World Development* 24, no. 4 (1996): 635–653.

Helmke, Gretchen, and Steven Levitsky. "Informal Institutions and Comparative Politics: A Research Agenda." *Perspectives on Politics* 2, no. 4 (2004): 725–740.

———. Introduction to *Informal Institutions and Democracy: Lessons from Latin America*, edited by Gretchen Helmke and Steven Levitsky. Baltimore: Johns Hopkins University Press, 2006.

Higgitt, Ryan. "Women's Leadership Building as a Poverty Reduction Strategy: Lessons from Bangladesh." *Journal of South Asian Development* 6, no. 1 (April 2011): 93–119.

Hirschman, Albert. *The Strategy of Economic Development*. New Haven, CT: Yale University Press, 1958.

Hossain, Akhtar. "Anatomy of Hartal Politics in Bangladesh." *Asian Survey* 40, no. 3 (2000): 508–529.

Hossain, Naomi. *The Aid Lab: Understanding Bangladesh's Unexpected Success*. New York: Oxford University Press, 2017.

———. "The Politics of What Works: The Case of the Vulnerable Group Development Programme in Bangladesh." CPRC Working Paper 92. Manchester, UK: Chronic Poverty Research Centre, 2007.

Hossain, Naomi, Mirza Hassan, Md. Ashikur Rahman, Khondokar Ali, and M. Islam. "The Problem with Teachers: The Political Settlement and Education Quality Reforms in Bangladesh." ESID Working Paper 86. Manchester, UK: Effective States and Inclusive Development Research Centre, University of Manchester, 2017.

Hossain, Naomi, and Imran Matin. "Engaging Elite Support for the Poorest? BRAC's Targeted Ultra Poor Programme for Rural Women in Bangladesh." *Development in Practice* 17, no. 3 (2007): 380–392.

Hossain, Naomi, Sohela Nazneen, and Maheen Sultan. "National Discourses on Women's Empowerment in Bangladesh: Continuities and Change." IDS Working Paper 368. London: Institute of Development Studies, University of Sussex, 2011.

Hossain, Naomi, and Anasuya Sengupta. "Thinking Big, Going Global: The Challenge of BRAC's Global Expansion." IDS Working Paper 339. Brighton, UK: Institute of Development Studies, University of Sussex, 2009.

Hossain, Sara. "Public Interest Litigation on Violence against Women in Bangladesh: Possibilities and Limits." In *Gender, Violence and the State in Asia*, edited by Amy Barrow and Joi L. Chia. New York: Routledge, 2016.

Howes, Mick, and Md. Akramul Islam. "Community-Led Total Sanitation and Its Successors in Bangladesh, Case 2: Dishari." Manchester, UK: Institute of Development Studies, University of Sussex, n.d.

Huda, Shahnaz. "Dowry in Bangladesh: Compromizing [*sic*] Women's Rights." *South Asia Research* 26, no. 3 (2006): 249–268.

Hulme, David, and Michael Edwards. *NGOs, States and Donors: Too Close for Comfort?* London: Macmillan, 1997.

Hulme, David, and Mathilde Maitrot. "Has Microfinance Lost Its Moral Compass?" *Economic and Political Weekly* 49, no. 48 (2014): 77–85.

Hulme, David, and Paul Mosley. *Finance against Poverty.* Vols. 1 and 2. London: Routledge, 1996.

Human Rights Watch. "Bangladesh: End Crackdown on Opposition Supporters," February 8, 2018. https://www.hrw.org/news/2018/02/08/bangladesh-end-crackdown -opposition-supporters.

Huntington, Samuel P. *Political Order in Changing Societies.* New Haven, CT: Yale University Press, 1968.

Huque, Ahmed Shafiqul. "Local Leadership: Development, Problems and Potential in Bangladesh." *Asia Pacific Journal of Public Administration* 29, no. 2 (2007): 223–239.

———. "The Problem of Local Government Reform in Rural Bangladesh: The Failure of Swanirvar Gram Sarkar." PhD thesis, Department of Political Science, University of British Columbia, 1984. https://open.library.ubc.ca/collections/ubctheses/831/items/1 .0096411.

Islam, Farmanul. "Towards a Brief History of Alternate Dispute Resolution in Rural Bangladesh." *Bangladesh Journal of Law* 4, nos. 1 and 2 (2000): 99–114.

Islam, Mohammad Mozahidul. "The Politics of the Public Food Distribution System in Bangladesh: Regime Survival or Promoting Food Security?" *Journal of Asian and African Studies* 50, no. 6 (December 16, 2015): 702–715.

Islam, Syed Sirajul. "The Role of the State in the Economic Development of Bangladesh during the Mujib Regime (1972–1975)." *Journal of Developing Areas* 19, no. 2 (1985): 185–208.

Jahan, Rounaq. "Bangladesh in 1972: Nation Building in a New State." *Asian Survey* 13, no. 2 (1973): 199-210.

———. "Bangladesh in 1973: Management of Factional Politics." *Asian Survey* 14, no. 2 (1974): 125–135.

———. "Women in South Asian Politics." *Third World Quarterly* 9, no. 3 (July 1, 1987): 848–870.

Jahan, Roushan. "Men in Seclusion, Women in Public: Rokeya's Dream and Women's Struggles in Bangladesh." In *The Challenge of Local Feminisms*, 87–109. New York: Routledge, 2019.

Jamil, Kanta, Abbas Bhuiya, Kim Streatfield, and Nitai Chakrabarti. "The Immunization Programme in Bangladesh: Impressive Gains in Coverage, but Gaps Remain." *Health Policy and Planning* 14, no. 1 (1999): 49–58.

Jayawardena, Kumari. *Feminism and Nationalism in the Third World*. Reprint ed. New York: Verso Books, 2016.

Johnston, Michael. "The Political Consequences of Corruption: A Reassessment." *Comparative Politics* 18, no. 4 (1986): 459–477.

Kabeer, Naila. "Conflicts over Credit: Re-evaluating the Empowerment Potential of Loans to Women in Rural Bangladesh." *World Development* 29, no. 1 (2001): 63–84.

——. "Growing Citizenship from the Grassroots: Nijera Kori and Social Mobilization in Bangladesh." *Bangladesh Development Studies* 29, nos. 3 & 4, 2003: 1–20.

——. "Making Rights Work for the Poor: Nijera Kori and the Construction of 'Collective Capabilities' in Rural Bangladesh." IDS Working Paper 200. Institute of Development Studies, University of Sussex, 2003.

——. *Reversed Realities: Gender Hierarchies in Development Thought*. London: Verso Books, 1994.

Kabir, Zarina Nahar, Marta Szebehely, and Carol Tishelman. "Support in Old Age in the Changing Society of Bangladesh." *Ageing and Society* 22, no. 5 (2002): 615–636.

Kamal, S. M. Mostafa. "Decline in Child Marriage and Changes in Its Effect on Reproductive Outcomes in Bangladesh." *Journal of Health, Population and Nutrition* 30, no. 3 (2012): 317–330.

Kamal, S. M. Mostafa, Che Hashim Hassan, Gazi Mahabubul Alam, and Yan Ying. "Child Marriage in Bangladesh: Trends and Determinants." *Journal of Biosocial Science* 47, no. 1 (2015): 120–139.

Karim, Lamia. "Democratizing Bangladesh State, NGOs, and Militant Islam." *Cultural Dynamics* 16, no. 2–3 (2004): 291–318. http://cdy.sagepub.com/content/16/2-3/291.short.

——. "Demystifying Micro-Credit: The Grameen Bank, NGOs, and Neoliberalism in Bangladesh." *Cultural Dynamics* 20, no. 1 (2008): 5–29.

——. *Microfinance and Its Discontents: Women in Debt in Bangladesh*. Minneapolis: University of Minnesota Press, 2011.

Katungi, Enid, Svetlana Edmeades, and Melinda Smale. "Gender, Social Capital and Information Exchange in Rural Uganda." *Journal of International Development* 20, no. 1 (January 2008): 35–52.

Kelly, Annie. "Growing Discontent." *Guardian*, February 19, 2008. https://www.theguardian.com/society/2008/feb/20/internationalaidanddevelopment.bangladesh.

Khan, Mostafizur Rahman, and Fardaus Ara. "Women, Participation and Empowerment in Local Government: Bangladesh Union Parishad Perspective." *Asian Affairs* 29, no. 1 (2006): 73–92.

Khandker, Shahidur R. "Microfinance and Poverty: Evidence Using Panel Data from Bangladesh." *World Bank Economic Review* 19, no. 2 (2005): 263–286.

Khandker, Shahidur R., Mark Pitt, and Nobuhiko Fuwa. "Subsidy to Promote Girls' Secondary Education: The Female Stipend Program in Bangladesh." MPRA Paper

No. 23688. Munich: Munich Personal RePEc Archive, University Library of Munich, 2003. https://mpra.ub.uni-muenchen.de/23688/1/MPRA_paper_23688.pdf.

Kitschelt, Herbert, and Steven I. Wilkinson. "Citizen-Politician Linkages: An Introduction." In *Patrons, Clients, and Policies: Patterns of Democratic Accountability and Political Competition*, edited by Herbert Kitschelt and Steven I. Wilkinson, 1–49. Cambridge, UK: Cambridge University Press, 2007.

Koelble, Thomas A. "The New Institutionalism in Political Science and Sociology." *Comparative Politics* 27, no. 2 (1995): 231–243.

Kolisetty, Akhila. "Examining the Effectiveness of Legal Empowerment as a Pathway out of Poverty: A Case Study of BRAC." Justice and Development Working Paper Series 26. Washington, DC: World Bank, 2014.

Krishna, Anirudh. *Active Social Capital: Tracing the Roots of Development and Democracy*. New York: Columbia University Press, 2002.

———. "Enhancing Political Participation in Democracies: What Is the Role of Social Capital?" *Comparative Political Studies* 35, no. 4 (2002): 437–460.

Kukreja, Veena. *Civil-Military Relations in South Asia: Pakistan, Bangladesh and India*. New Delhi: Sage Publications, 1992.

"Leaving the LDCs Category: Booming Bangladesh Prepares to Graduate." *United Nations Department of Economic and Social Affairs*. March 13, 2019. https://www.un .org/development/desa/en/news/policy/leaving-the-ldcs-category-booming -bangladesh-prepares-to-graduate.html.

Leve, Lauren. "Failed Development and Rural Revolution in Nepal: Rethinking Subaltern Consciousness and Women's Empowerment." In *Theorizing NGOs: States, Feminisms, and Neoliberalism*, edited by Victoria Bernal and Inderpal Grewal. Durham, NC: Duke University Press, 2014.

Lewis, David. "NGOs, Donors, and the State in Bangladesh." *Annals of the American Academy of Political and Social Science* 554 (November 1997): 33–42.

———. "Non-Governmental Organizations and Civil Society." In *Routledge Handbook of Contemporary Bangladesh*, edited by Ali Riaz and Mohammad Sajjadur Rahman. London: Routledge, 2015.

Lewis, David, and Abul Hossain. "Local Political Consolidation in Bangladesh: Power, Informality and Patronage." *Development and Change*, 2019. https://onlinelibrary .wiley.com/doi/full/10.1111/dech.12534.

———. "A Tale of Three Villages: Power, Difference and Locality in Rural Bangladesh." *Journal of South Asian Development* 3, no. 1 (June 1, 2008): 33–51.

Lipset, Seymour Martin. "Some Social Requisites of Democracy: Economic Development and Political Legitimacy." *American Political Science Review* 53, no. 1 (1959): 69–105.

"The List: The World's Most Powerful Development NGOs." *Foreign Policy*, July 1, 2008. http://foreignpolicy.com/2008/07/01/the-list-the-worlds-most-powerful-development -ngos/.

Littlefield, Elizabeth, Jonathan Morduch, and Syed M. Hashemi. "Is Microfinance an Effective Strategy to Reach the Millennium Development Goals?" *CGAP Focus Note* 24. Washington, DC: CGAP, 2003.

Lowndes, Vivien. "Institutionalism." In *Theory and Methods in Political Science*, edited by Vivian Lowndes, David Marsh, and Gerry Stoker. 4th ed. London: Palgrave, 2018.

———. "Varieties of New Institutionalism: A Critical Appraisal." *Public Administration* 74, no. 2 (June 1996): 181–197.

Lowndes, Vivien, Lawrence Pratchett, and Gerry Stoker. "Local Political Participation: The Impact of Rules-in-Use." *Public Administration* 84, no. 3 (August 2006): 539–561.

Mackay, Fiona. "Conclusion: Towards a Feminist Institutionalism." In *Gender, Politics and Institutions: Towards a Feminist Institutionalism*. Edited by Mona Lena Crook and Fiona Mackay. London: Palgrave Macmillan, 2011.

Mackay, Fiona, Meryl Kenny, and Louise Chappell. "New Institutionalism through a Gender Lens: Towards a Feminist Institutionalism?" *International Political Science Review* 31, no. 5 (November 2010): 573–588.

Mahmud, Simeen. "Informal Women's Groups in Rural Bangladesh: Operation and Outcomes." In *Group Behaviour and Development: Is the Market Destroying Cooperation?*, edited by Judith Heyer, Frances Stewart, and Rosemary Thorp. New York: Oxford University Press, n.d.

Mahmud, Simeen, and Sajeda Amin. "Girls' Schooling and Marriage in Rural Bangladesh." In *Children's Lives and Schooling across Societies*, 15:71–99. Bingley, UK: Emerald Group Publishing, 2006.

Mahoney, James, and Kathleen Thelen. *Explaining Institutional Change: Ambiguity, Agency, and Power*. New York: Cambridge University Press, 2009.

———. "A Theory of Gradual Institutional Change." In *Explaining Institutional Change: Ambiguity, Agency, and Power*. New York: Cambridge University Press, 2009.

Manik, Julfikar Ali, and Jim Yardley. "Bangladesh Finds Gross Negligence in Factory Fire." *New York Times*. December 17, 2012. https://www.nytimes.com/2012/12/18/world/asia/bangladesh-factory-fire-caused-by-gross-negligence.html.

Maniruzzaman, Talukder. "Bangladesh in 1974: Economic Crisis and Political Polarization." *Asian Survey* 15, no. 2 (1975): 117–128.

Mannan, Manzurul. "Who Rules Whom? Structural Instability and Governance Patterns in Bangladesh." *Nepalese Journal of Public Policy and Governance* 28, no. 1 (2011): 69–80.

March, James G., and Johan P. Olsen. "Institutional Perspectives on Political Institutions." *Governance* 9, no. 3 (July 1996): 247–264.

———. "The Logic of Appropriateness." In *The Oxford Handbook of Political Science*, edited by Robert E. Goodin. New York: Oxford University Press, 2011.

———. "The New Institutionalism: Organizational Factors in Political Life." *American Political Science Review* 78, no. 3 (1984): 734–749.

———. *Rediscovering Institutions*. New York: Free Press, 1989.

Matin, Imran. "Targeted Development Programmes for the Extreme Poor: Experiences from BRAC Experiments." CPRC Working Paper No. 20, PRCPB Working Paper No. 2. Manchester: Chronic Poverty Research Centre (CPRC), 2002. https://assets.publishing.service.gov.uk/media/57a08d21e5274a31e0001678/20Matin.pdf.

Mayoux, Linda. "Tackling the Down Side: Social Capital, Women's Empowerment and Micro-Finance in Cameroon." *Development and Change* 32 (2001): 435–464.

McAdam, Doug, and W. Richard Scott. "Organizations and Movements." In *Social Movements and Organization Theory*, edited by Gerald F. Davis, Doug McAdam, W. Richard Scott, and Mayer N. Zald. New York: Cambridge University Press, 2002.

Mohmand, Shandana Khan. *Crafty Oligarchs, Savvy Voters: Democracy under Inequality in Rural Pakistan*. Cambridge, UK: Cambridge University Press, 2019.

Monbiot, George. "Neoliberalism—the Ideology at the Root of All Our Problems." *Guardian*. April 15, 2016. https://www.theguardian.com/books/2016/apr/15/neoliberalism -ideology-problem-george-monbiot.

Montgomery, Richard. "Disciplining or Protecting the Poor? Avoiding the Social Costs of Peer Pressure in Micro-Credit Schemes." *Journal of International Development* 8, no. 2 (1996): 289–305.

Montgomery, Richard, Debapriya Bhattacharya, David Hulme, and Paul Mosley. "Credit for the Poor in Bangladesh: The BRAC Rural Development Programme and the Government Thana Resource Development and Employment Programme." In *Finance against Poverty*, vol. 2, edited by David Hulme and Paul Mosley, 94–176. London: Routledge, 1996.

Mookherjee, Nayanika. "Gendered Embodiments: Mapping the Body-Politic of the Raped Woman and the Nation in Bangladesh." *Feminist Review* 88, no. 1 (April 7, 2008): 36–53.

———. "'Remembering to Forget': Public Secrecy and Memory of Sexual Violence in the Bangladesh War of 1971." *Journal of the Royal Anthropological Institute* 12, no. 2 (June 1, 2006): 433–450.

———. *The Spectral Wound: Sexual Violence, Public Memories, and the Bangladesh War.* Durham, NC: Duke University Press, 2015.

Mosley, Paul, and David Hulme. "Microenterprise Finance: Is There a Conflict between Growth and Poverty Alleviation?" *World Development* 26, no. 5 (1998): 783–790.

Nasrin, Farzana. "Reforms in Local Government: Experiences from Bangladesh." *Journal of Asia Pacific Studies* 3, no. 1 (2013): 37–56.

Naved, Ruchira Tabassum, Safia Azim, Abbas Bhuyia, and Lars Åke Persson. "Physical Violence by Husbands: Magnitude, Disclosure and Help-Seeking Behavior of Women in Bangladesh." *Social Science and Medicine* 62, no. 12 (2006): 2917–2929.

Naved, Ruchira Tabassum, and Lars Åke Persson. "Dowry and Spousal Physical Violence against Women in Bangladesh." *Journal of Family Issues* 31, no. 6 (June 2010): 830–856.

———. "Factors Associated with Spousal Physical Violence against Women in Bangladesh." *Studies in Family Planning* 36, no. 4 (2005): 289–300.

Nawaz, Farah. "An Analysis of the Role of Community Empowerment Program (CEP) in Combatting Domestic Violence against Women: A Case Study of Bangladesh." *Social Sciences and the Humanities* 26, no. 4 (2018): 2841–2856.

Nazneen, Sohela. "The Women's Movement in Bangladesh: A Short History and Current Debates." Country Study. Dhaka: Friedrich-Ebert-Stiftung (FES Bangladesh), 2017.

Nazneen, Sohela, and Maheen Sultan. "Struggling for Survival and Autonomy: Impact of NGO-ization on Women's Organizations in Bangladesh." *Development* 52, no. 2 (2009): 193–199.

Nazneen, Sohela, and Sakiba Tasneem. "A Silver Lining: Women in Reserved Seats in Local Government in Bangladesh." *IDS Bulletin* 41, no. 5. Manchester, UK: Institute of Development Studies, University of Sussex, and Blackwell Publishing, 2010.

Netherlands Ministry of Foreign Affairs. "Evaluation of the Netherlands Development Programme with Bangladesh, 1972–1996: Sub-Report 10." *Evaluation of Netherlands-Funded NGOs 1972–1996.* Dhaka: Policy and Operations Evaluation Department, Ministry of Foreign Affairs, n.d.

Nguyen, Minh Cong, and Quentin Wodon. "Global and Regional Trends in Child Marriage." *Review of Faith and International Affairs* 13, no. 3 (July 3, 2015): 6–11.

North, Douglass C. "Economic Performance through Time." *American Economic Review* 84, no. 3 (1994): 359–368.

———. "Institutions." *Journal of Economic Perspectives* 5, no. 1 (1991): 97–112.

———. *Institutions, Institutional Change, and Economic Performance.* New York: Cambridge University Press, 1990.

O'Donnell, Guillermo. "On Informal Institutions, Once Again." In *Informal Institutions and Democracy: Lessons from Latin America,* edited by Gretchen Helmke and Steven Levitsky. Baltimore: Johns Hopkins University Press, 2006.

———. "The Quality of Democracy: Why the Rule of Law Matters." *Journal of Democracy* 15, no. 4 (2004): 32–46.

Office of the High Commissioner for Human Rights. "UN Expert Group Urges Bangladesh to Stop Enforced Disappearances." News and Events, 2017. https://www.ohchr .org/EN/NewsEvents/Pages/DisplayNews.aspx?NewsID=21220&LangID=E.

Omvedt, Gail. "Women in Governance in South Asia." *Economic and Political Weekly* 40, no. 44/45 (2005): 4746–4752.

Ostrom, Elinor. *Governing the Commons: The Evolution of Institutions for Collective Action.* New York: Cambridge University Press, 1990.

———. "Institutional Rational Choice: An Assessment of the Institutional Analysis and Development Framework." In *Theories of the Policy Process,* edited by Paul A. Sabatier. Boulder, CO: Westview Press, 2007.

Ostrom, Elinor, Roy Gardner, and James Walker. *Rules, Games, and Common-Pool Resources.* Ann Arbor: University of Michigan Press, 1994.

"The Other Government in Bangladesh." *Economist.* July 23, 1998. https://www.economist .com/node/169223.

Panday, Pranab Kumar. "Representation without Participation: Quotas for Women in Bangladesh." *International Political Science Review* 29, no. 4 (September 2008): 489–512.

Pereira, Faustina. *The Fractured Scales: The Search for a Uniform Personal Code.* Calcutta: STREE, 2002.

Pierce, Steven. *Moral Economies of Corruption: State Formation and Political Culture in Nigeria.* Durham, NC: Duke University Press, 2016.

Pitt, Mark M., and Shahidur R. Khandker. "The Impact of Group-Based Credit Programs on Poor Households in Bangladesh: Does the Gender of Participants Matter?" *Journal of Political Economy* 106, no. 5 (1998): 958–996.

Polanyi, Karl. *The Great Transformation: The Political and Economic Origins of Our Time.* Boston: Beacon Press, 2001.

Popkin, Samuel L. *The Rational Peasant: The Political Economy of Rural Society in Vietnam.* Berkeley: University of California Press, 1979.

Powell, John Duncan. "Peasant Society and Clientelist Politics." *American Political Science Review* 64, no. 2 (1970): 411–425.

Powell, Walter W., and Paul J. DiMaggio. *The New Institutionalism in Organizational Analysis.* Chicago: University of Chicago Press, 2012.

Prashad, Vijay. *The Darker Nations: A People's History of the Third World.* New York: New Press, 2008.

Przeworski, Adam. *Democracy and the Market: Political and Economic Reforms in Eastern Europe and Latin America.* Cambridge: Cambridge University Press, 1991.

Przeworski, Adam, Michael Alvarez, Jose Antonio Cheibub, and Fernando Limongi. "What Makes Democracies Endure?" *Journal of Democracy* 7, no. 1 (1996): 39–55.

Przeworski, Adam, and Fernando Limongi. "Modernization: Theories and Facts." *World Politics* 49, no. 2 (1997): 155–183.

Putnam, Robert D., Robert Leonardi, and Raffaella Y. Nanetti. *Making Democracy Work: Civic Traditions in Modern Italy.* Princeton, NJ: Princeton University Press, 2002.

Qayum, Nayma. "Bangladesh: A Long Road Ahead." *Al Jazeera*, January 18, 2014. https://www.aljazeera.com/indepth/opinion/2014/01/bangladesh-long-road-ahead -20141136164361993.html.

——. "Taking Sides." *The Revealer: A Review of Religion and Media*, January 15, 2014. https://therevealer.org/bangladesh-taking-sides/.

——. "Women, NGOs, and the Bangladesh Miracle." In *Voices from South Asia: Interdisciplinary Perspectives on Women's Status, Challenges and Futures*, edited by Emma J. Flatt, Vani Swarupa Murali, and Silvia Tieri. Singapore: World Scientific, 2020.

Qayum, Nayma, Ashrafuzzaman Khan, and Rehnuma Rahman. "Rural Organizations and Active Citizenship in Bangladesh: Evaluation of BRAC's Polli Shomaj." Research Monograph Series No. 55. Dhaka: Research and Evaluation Division, BRAC, 2012.

Qayum, Nayma, and Mrinmoy Samadder. "Eradicating Extreme Poverty in Bangladesh: National Strategies and Activities." Research Monograph Series No. 56. Dhaka: Research and Evaluation Division, BRAC, 2013.

Qayum, Nayma, Mrinmoy Samadder, and Rehnuma Rahman. "Group Norms and the BRAC Village Organization: Enhancing Social Capital Baseline." Dhaka: Research and Evaluation Division, BRAC, 2012.

Rafi, Mohammad, and A.M.R. Chowdhury. "Human Rights and Religious Backlash: The Experience of a Bangladeshi NGO." *Development in Practice* 10, no. 1 (2000): 19–30.

Rahman, Hussain Zillur. "Crisis and Insecurity: The 'Other' Face of Poverty." In *Rethinking Rural Poverty: Bangladesh as a Case Study*, edited by Hussain Zillur Rahman and Mahabub Hossain, 113–131. New Delhi: Sage Publications, 1995.

Rahman, M. Ataur. "Bangladesh in 1982: Beginnings of the Second Decade." *Asian Survey* 23, no. 2 (1983): 149–157.

Rahman, Rushidan Islam. "Impact of Grameen Bank on the Situation of Poor Rural Women." Vol. 1. Grameen Bank Evaluation Project Working Paper. Dhaka: Bangladesh Institute of Development Studies, Agriculture and Rural Development Division, 1986.

Rahman, Sabeel. "Development, Democracy and the NGO Sector: Theory and Evidence from Bangladesh." *Journal of Developing Societies* 22, no. 4 (December 1, 2006): 451–473.

Rashid, Ahmed Tareq, and Md. Abdul Alim. "A Study on BRAC's Palli Shamaj." BRAC Research Report. Dhaka: Research and Evaluation Division, BRAC, 2005.

Rasul, Md. Golam, and Md. Taufiqul Islam. "Performance and Effectiveness of Village Court in Bangladesh: A Comparative Study in Two Unions between Project and Non-Project Area." *Journal of South Asian Studies* 5, no. 1 (2017): 27–37.

Research and Evaluation Division. *Ashram Village: An Analysis of Resource Flows.* Dhaka: Research and Evaluation Division, BRAC, 1980.

——. *The Net: Power Structure in Ten Villages.* Dhaka: Research and Evaluation Division, BRAC, 1980.

———. *Who Gets What and Why: Resource Allocation in a Bangladesh Village*. Dhaka: Research and Evaluation Division, BRAC, 1983.

Rhodes, R.A.W. *Understanding Governance: Policy Networks, Governance, Reflexivity and Accountability*. London: Open University Press, 1997.

Riaz, Ali. "Bangladesh's Failed Election." *Journal of Democracy* 25, no. 2 (2014): 119–130.

———. *God Willing: The Politics of Islamism in Bangladesh*. Lanham, MD: Rowman and Littlefield, 2004.

———. *The Politics of Islamization in Bangladesh*. Edited by A. Riaz. London: Routledge, 2010.

Rostow, Walt W. "The Stages of Economic Growth." *Economic History Review* 12, no. 1 (1959): 1–16.

Rothstein, Bo. "Political Institutions: An Overview." In *Oxford Handbook of Political Science*, edited by Robert E. Goodin. Oxford: Oxford University Press, 2011.

Rozario, Santi. "Dowry in Rural Bangladesh: An Intractable Problem?" In *Dowry: Bridging the Gap between Theory and Practice*. London: Zed Books, 2009.

Safi, Michael, and Dominic Rushe. "Rana Plaza, Five Years on: Safety of Workers Hangs in Balance in Bangladesh." *Guardian*. April 24, 2018. https://www.theguardian.com /global-development/2018/apr/24/bangladeshi-police-target-garment-workers-union -rana-plaza-five-years-on.

Saikia, Yasmin. *Women, War, and the Making of Bangladesh: Remembering 1971*. Durham, NC: Duke University Press, 2011.

Schroeder, Larry. "Decentralization in Rural Bangladesh." *Asian Survey* 25, no. 11 (1985): 1134–1147.

Schuler, Sidney Ruth, and Syed M. Hashemi. "Credit Programs, Women's Empowerment, and Contraceptive Use in Rural Bangladesh." *Studies in Family Planning* 25, no. 2 (1994): 65–76.

Schuster, Caroline E. *Social Collateral: Women and Microfinance in Paraguay's Smuggling Economy*. Oakland: University of California Press, 2015.

Scott, James C. "Patron-Client Politics and Political Change in Southeast Asia." *American Political Science Review* 66, no. 1 (1972): 91–113.

Sellers, Jefferey M. "State-Society Relations." In *The Sage Handbook of Governance*, edited by Mark Bevir. London: Sage Publications, 2011.

Sen, Amartya. *Development as Freedom*. New York: Anchor Books, 1999.

———. "The Economics of Life and Death." *Scientific American* 268, no. 5 (1993): 40–47.

———. "Gender and Cooperative Conflicts." WIDER Working Papers, World Institute of Development Economics Research. Helsinki, Finland, 1987.

———. "Gender Inequality and Theories of Justice." In *Women, Culture, and Development: A Study of Human Capabilities*, edited by Martha Nussbaum and Jonathan Glover, 259–273. New York: Oxford University Press, 1995.

———. "Starvation and Exchange Entitlements: A General Approach and Its Application to the Great Bengal Famine." *Cambridge Journal of Economics* 1, no. 1 (1977): 33–59.

Shahabuddin, A., Christiana Nöstlinger, Thérèse Delvaux, Malabika Sarker, Alexandre Delamou, Azucena Bardají, Jacqueline E. W. Broerse, and Vincent De Brouwere. "Exploring Maternal Health Care-Seeking Behavior of Married Adolescent Girls in Bangladesh: A Social-Ecological Approach." *PLOS ONE* 12, no. 1 (2017): e0169109.

Sharma, Aradhana. "The State and Women's Empowerment in India: Paradoxes and Politics." In *Theorizing NGOs: States, Feminisms, and Neoliberalism*. Durham, NC: Duke University Press, 2014.

Shehabuddin, Elora. "Bangladesh in 1998: Democracy on the Ground." *Asian Survey* 39, no. 1 (1999): 148–154.

———. "Feminism and Nationalism in Cold War East Pakistan." *South Asia Chronicle* 4 (2014): 49–68.

———. *Reshaping the Holy: Democracy, Development, and Muslim Women in Bangladesh*. New York: Columbia University Press, 2008.

Siddiqi, Dina. "Paving the Way to Justice: The Experience of Nagorik Uddyog, Bangladesh." London: One World Action, 2003.

———. "Scandals of Seduction and the Seductions of Scandal." *Comparative Studies of South Asia, Africa and the Middle East* 35, no. 3 (2015): 508–524.

Siddiquee, Noore Alam. "Politics and Administration in Local Councils: Problems of People's Participation in Rural Bangladesh." *Social Action* 48 (1998): 58–82.

Singerman, Diane. *Avenues of Participation: Family, Politics, and Networks in Urban Quarters of Cairo*. Princeton, NJ: Princeton University Press, 1995.

Smillie, Ian. *Freedom from Want: The Remarkable Success Story of BRAC, the Global Grassroots Organization That's Winning the Fight against Poverty*. Dhaka: University Press, 2009.

Sobhan, Rehman. *Challenging the Injustice of Poverty*. New Delhi: Sage India, 2010.

———. "Politics of Food and Famine in Bangladesh." *Economic and Political Weekly* 14, no. 8 (1979): 1973–1980.

Stokes, Susan C. "Political Clientelism." In *The Oxford Handbook of Comparative Politics*, edited by Charles Boix and Susan C. Stokes. Oxford: Oxford University Press, 2007.

Streeck, Wolfgang, and Kathleen Thelen. "Institutional Change in Advanced Political Economies." In *Debating Varieties of Capitalism: A Reader*, edited by Bob Hancké. New York: Oxford University Press, 2009.

Sustainable Development Goals Fund. "Case Study: Addressing Violence against Women in Bangladesh." Dhaka: Sustainable Development Goals Fund, 2017. https://www.sdgfund.org/case-study/addressing-violence-against-women-bangladesh.

Taslim, M. A. "Governance, Policies and Economic Growth in Bangladesh." In *Ship Adrift: Governance and Development in Bangladesh*, edited by Nurul Islam and M. Asaduzzaman. Dhaka: Bangladesh Institute of Development Studies, 2008.

Thornton, Patricia H., and William Ocasio. "Institutional Logics." In *The Sage Handbook of Organizational Institutionalism*, edited by Royston Greenwood, Christine Oliver, Roy Suddaby, and Kerstin Sahlin-Andersson. London: Sage Publications, 2008.

Tinker, Irene. *Persistent Inequalities: Women and World Development*. New York: Oxford University Press, 1990.

Toor, Saadia. "Containing East Bengal: Language, Nation, and State Formation in Pakistan, 1947–1952." *Cultural Dynamics* 21, no. 2 (July 2009): 185–210.

Toufique, K. A., and C. Turton. *Hands Not Land: How Livelihoods Are Changing in Rural Bangladesh*. Dhaka: Bangladesh Institute of Development Studies, 2002.

Tsai, Lily. *Accountability without Democracy: Solidary Groups and Public Goods Provision in Rural China*. New York: Cambridge University Press, 2007.

———. "Solidary Groups, Informal Accountability, and Local Public Goods Provision in Rural China." *American Political Science Review* 101, no. 2 (2007): 355–372.

United Nations. *Report of the High Level Consultants Mission to Bangladesh March, April 1972.* S-0900-0001-03-00001, 1972. https://search.archives.un.org/report-of-the-high-level-consultants-mission-to-bangladesh-march-april-1972.

United Nations Children's Fund. "Baseline Survey Report on Rural Adolescents in Bangladesh: Kishori Abhijan Project." Dhaka, 2002.

———. "Child Marriage." UNICEF Data: Monitoring the Situation of Children and Women, 2019. https://data.unicef.org/topic/child-protection/child-marriage/.

———. "Ending Child Marriage: Towards Evolution of Social Behavior." Communication for Development, 2019. https://www.unicef.org/bangladesh/en/ending-child-marriage.

———. "Plan of Action Launched to Eliminate Child Marriage in Bangladesh." Press release, August 14, 2018. https://www.unicef.org/bangladesh/en/press-releases/plan-action-launched-eliminate-child-marriage-bangladesh.

United Nations Development Programme. "Beyond Income, beyond Averages, beyond Today: Inequalities in Human Development in the 21st Century." Human Development Report 2019. New York: United Nations Development Program, 2019. http://hdr.undp.org/sites/default/files/hdr2019.pdf.

———. "Briefing Note for Countries on the 2019 Human Development Report: Bangladesh." Human Development Report 2019. New York: United Nations Development Program, 2019. http://hdr.undp.org/sites/all/themes/hdr_theme/country-notes/BGD.pdf.

United Nations General Assembly. *Child, Early and Forced Marriage.* A/C.3/73/L.22/Rev.1. New York, 2018. https://undocs.org/A/C.3/73/L.22/Rev.1.

———. *Convention on Consent to Marriage, Minimum Age for Marriage and Registration of Marriages.* New York, 1962. https://www.ohchr.org/EN/ProfessionalInterest/Pages/MinimumAgeForMarriage.aspx.

———. *Declaration on the Elimination of Violence against Women.* A/RES/48/104. New York, 1993. https://www.refworld.org/docid/3b00f25d2c.html.

Van Cott, Donna Lee. "Dispensing Justice at the Margins of Formality: The Informal Rule of Law in Latin America." In *Informal Institutions and Democracy: Lessons from Latin America,* edited by Gretchen Helmke and Steven Levitsky. Baltimore: Johns Hopkins University Press, 2006.

Waylen, G. "Analysing Gender in Informal Institutions: An Introduction." In *Gender and Informal Institutions,* 1–22. Lanham, MD: Rowman and Littlefield, 2017.

Weber, Max. *Economy and Society: An Outline of Interpretive Sociology.* Berkeley: University of California Press, 1978.

White, Sarah C. *Arguing with the Crocodile: Gender and Class in Bangladesh.* London: Zed Books, 1992.

———. "NGOs, Civil Society, and the State in Bangladesh: The Politics of Representing the Poor." *Development and Change* 30, no. 2 (1999): 307–326.

———. "Patriarchal Investments: Marriage, Dowry and Economic Change in Rural Bangladesh." Center for Development Studies Working Paper 19. Bath, UK: Center for Development Studies, University of Bath, 2013. www.bath.ac.uk/cds/.

Williamson, John. "What Should the World Bank Think about the Washington Consensus?" *World Bank Research Observer* 15, no. 12 (2000): 251–264.

————. "What Washington Means by Policy Reform." In *Latin American Adjustment: How Much Has Happened?*, edited by John Williamson. Washington, DC: Institute for International Economics, 1990.

Wood, Geoffrey D. "Clashing Values in Bangladesh: NGOs, Secularism and the Umma." In *Recreating the Commons: NGOs in Bangladesh*, edited by Farida Chowdhury Khan, Ahrar Ahmad, and Munir Quddus. Dhaka: University Press, 2009.

————. "States without Citizens: The Problem of the Franchise State." In *NGOs, States and Donors: Too Close for Comfort*, edited by David Hulme and M. Edwards. London: Macmillan, 1997.

World Bank. "Bangladesh Can Prosper with More and Better Jobs for Women, Report Says." Press release, April 28, 2019. www.worldbank.org/en/news/press-release/2019/04/28/bangladesh-more-and-betters-jobs-for-women-needed-for-faster-growth.

————. "Bangladesh—Poverty Assessment for Bangladesh: Creating Opportunities and Bridging the East-West Divide." Bangladesh Development Series Paper No. 26. Dhaka: World Bank, 2008.

————. *Bangladesh—Reconstructing the Economy: Main Report (English).* South Asia Series No. SA 35. Washington, DC: World Bank Group, 1972. http://documents.worldbank.org/curated/en/240201468013773779/Main-report. http://documents.worldbank.org/curated/en/240201468013773779/pdf/multiopage.pdf.

————. "Decline of Global Extreme Poverty Continues but Has Slowed: World Bank." Press release, September 19, 2018. https://www.worldbank.org/en/news/press-release/2018/09/19/decline-of-global-extreme-poverty-continues-but-has-slowed-world-bank.

————. "Whispers to Voices: Gender and Social Transformation in Bangladesh." Bangladesh Development Series No. 22. Dhaka: World Bank, 2008. https://openknowledge.worldbank.org/bitstream/handle/10986/26334/430450NWPoBDgender0Box032734 4B01PUBLIC1.pdf?sequence=1&isAllowed=y.

————. "World Development Indicators." Washington, DC: World Bank, 2011. Accessed April 20, 2011. https://data.worldbank.org/.

World Food Programme. "Vulnerable Group Development (VGD): Making a Difference to the Extreme Poor Women in Bangladesh through a Social Safety Net Programme." Programme Outcome Report on Vulnerable Group Development Activity. *World Food Programme.* Dhaka: World Food Programme, 2007.

Young, Kim A., and Shahidul Hassan. "An Assessment of the Prevalence, Perceived Significance, and Response to Dowry Solicitation and Domestic Violence in Bangladesh." *Journal of Interpersonal Violence* 33, no. 19 (2018): 2968–3000.

Yunus, Muhammad. "How Social Business can Create a World without Poverty." *Christian Science Monitor*, February 15, 2008. http://www.csmonitor.com/2008/0215/p09s01-coop.html.

Zaman, Shahaduz, Imran Matin, Hasanur Rahman, Tariq Ali, Marufia Noor, Mamun-ur- Rashid, and Rezvina Parveen. "Stories of Targeting: Process Documentation of Selecting the Ultra Poor for CFPR/TUP Programme." CFPR-TUP Working Paper Series No. 1. Dhaka: BRAC Research and Evaluation Division, Aga Khan Foundation, 2004. http://dspace.bracu.ac.bd/xmlui/handle/10361/13177.

Zohir, Sajjad. "NGOs in Development: An Overview of the 'NGO Sector' in Bangladesh." In *Recreating the Commons? NGOs in Bangladesh*, edited by Farida Chowdhury Khan, Ahrar Ahmad, and Munir Quddus. Dhaka: Bangladesh Development Initiative and University Press, 2009.

Index

About the Author

Nayma Qayum is an associate professor at Manhattanville College. Her scholarship exists at the nexus of participation and institutions—the norms, rules, and practices that guide behavior and shape people's interactions with state and society—with a focus on gender. Dr. Qayum received her PhD in political science from the Graduate Center, City University of New York. Her work has appeared in *New Political Science*, *Migration Information Source*, Reset: Dialogues on Civilizations, *Al Jazeera*, *Washington Post*, *The Revealer*, *World Policy Blogs*, and *Foreign Policy Blogs*.